Data Structure in Python

From Basics to Expert Proficiency

Contents

Introduction

In the ever-evolving domain of computer science, data structures and algorithms form the bedrock upon which software applications are built. A profound understanding of these concepts is indispensable for any aspiring software engineer or computer scientist. This book, *Data Structure in Python: From Basics to Expert Proficiency*, is meticulously crafted to impart a comprehensive understanding of data structures and algorithms using the Python programming language.

Data structures are integral components that facilitate the organization, management, and storage of data for efficient access and modification. From the rudimentary arrays and linked lists to the more sophisticated trees and graphs, each data structure is designed to address specific computational problems. An adept knowledge of these structures not only aids in problem-solving but also enhances the performance and scalability of software solutions.

Algorithms, on the other hand, are systematic procedures that provide step-by-step instructions to accomplish a particular task or solve a specific problem. The symbiotic relationship between data structures and algorithms provides a powerful toolkit for tackling complex programming challenges. Understanding the intricacies of algorithmic design and analysis is pivotal in selecting the most appropriate data structure for a given problem, thereby optimizing the computational efficiency.

Python, known for its readability and simplicity, serves as an ideal language for learning and implementing data structures and algorithms. Its extensive standard library and dynamic typing capability further make it a versatile tool for both educational purposes and real-world applications. As such, this book leverages Python to elucidate the fundamental concepts of data structures and algorithms, making it accessible to learners with varying degrees of prior programming experience.

The structure of this book is meticulously designed to introduce concepts in a logical progression. It begins with an introductory overview that lays the foundation, followed by details on Python programming basics. As we delve deeper into the chapters, we explore specific data structures, starting from basic arrays to complex trees and graphs. Each chapter encompasses both theoretical explanations and practical implementations, ensuring a well-rounded understanding.

Moreover, the book emphasizes the importance of algorithm analysis and the Big O notation—a framework for evaluating the efficiency of algorithms. As we navigate through the various sorting and searching algorithms, readers will gain insight into how different approaches affect performance and resource usage. The advanced data structures chapter encapsulates cutting-edge structures that are pivotal in solving modern computational problems.

This book aspires to equip readers with a robust understanding of data structures and algorithms, empowering them to conceive and implement efficient solutions. Whether you are a novice programmer seeking to build a foundational understanding or an experienced developer aiming to refine your skills, this book serves as a comprehensive guide in your pursuit of excellence in the field of data structures and algorithms.

Welcome to the journey of mastering data structures and algorithms with Python. Let us embark on this intellectual endeavor with rigor, precision, and a commitment to excellence.

Chapter 1

Introduction to Data Structures and Algorithms

Data structures and algorithms are fundamental components of computer science, essential for organizing, managing, and manipulating data efficiently. This chapter introduces key concepts and classifications of data structures, defines what an algorithm is, and explains the importance of algorithms in solving computational problems. Additionally, it covers basic terminology, algorithm analysis, Big O notation, and time and space complexity, providing a comprehensive foundation for selecting the appropriate data structure for specific tasks.

1.1 What are Data Structures?

Data structures are a systematic way of organizing and managing data to enable efficient access and modification. They are the foundational constructs upon which software systems are built, facilitating the storage, retrieval, and processing of data. In computer science, data structures provide the means to solve complex computational problems by laying the groundwork for efficient algorithm design and implementation.

At the core, data structures represent a collection of data values, the relationships among them, and the functions or operations that can be applied to the data. These structures dictate the organization, manipulation, and storage of data in a computer's memory or any other storage device, improving both the efficiency and quality of software applications.

There are two primary classifications of data structures: primitive and non-primitive. Primitive data structures are the most basic types of data, inherent to the language being used, such as integers, floats, characters, and booleans. Non-primitive data structures, on the other hand, build upon these basic types to construct more sophisticated forms, which can be further divided into linear and non-linear structures. Understanding these categories is crucial for selecting the appropriate data structure based on the requirements and constraints of a given problem.

Linear data structures include arrays, linked lists, stacks, and queues. These structures arrange data in a sequential manner, meaning each element has a unique predecessor and successor. Key characteristics of linear data structures include:

- **Arrays**: A collection of elements identified by index or key, stored in contiguous memory locations. Arrays allow for constant-time access to elements but may require shifting during insertion or deletion, leading to inefficient operations.

```
# Example of an array in Python
array = [1, 2, 3, 4, 5]
print(array[2]) # Outputs: 3
```

```
Output:
3
```

- **Linked Lists**: Consists of nodes where each node contains a data element and a reference (or link) to the next node in the sequence. Linked lists support efficient insertion and deletion operations but require sequential access to retrieve an element by index.

```
# Example of a simple linked list in Python
class Node:
    def __init__(self, data):
        self.data = data
        self.next = None

class LinkedList:
```

```
    def __init__(self):
        self.head = None

    def append(self, data):
        new_node = Node(data)
        if self.head is None:
            self.head = new_node
        else:
            current = self.head
            while current.next:
                current = current.next
            current.next = new_node

linked_list = LinkedList()
linked_list.append(1)
linked_list.append(2)
linked_list.append(3)
```

- **Stacks**: A linear data structure that follows the Last-In-First-Out (LIFO) principle, wherein the last element inserted is the first one to be removed. Operations include push (insertion), pop (removal), and peek (accessing the top element without removal).

```
# Example of a stack in Python using a list
stack = []
stack.append(1) # Push
stack.append(2) # Push
stack.append(3) # Push
print(stack.pop()) # Pop, Outputs: 3
print(stack) # [1, 2]
```

```
Output:
3
[1, 2]
```

- **Queues**: A linear data structure adhering to the First-In-First-Out (FIFO) protocol, where the first element added is the first one to be removed. Common operations include enqueue (insertion) and dequeue (removal).

```
# Example of a queue in Python using a list
from collections import deque
queue = deque()
queue.append(1) # Enqueue
queue.append(2) # Enqueue
queue.append(3) # Enqueue
print(queue.popleft()) # Dequeue, Outputs: 1
print(queue) # deque([2, 3])
```

```
Output:
1
deque([2, 3])
```

Non-linear data structures include trees and graphs. These structures represent data elements that are hierarchically or interconnected, allowing for more complex relationships between data elements:

- **Trees**: A hierarchical data structure with a root element and sub-elements or children, forming an acyclic graph. Trees are utilized in scenarios such as expression parsing, hierarchical data representation, and in binary search trees for efficient searching and sorting.

```
# Example of a simple binary tree in Python
class TreeNode:
    def __init__(self, key):
        self.left = None
        self.right = None
        self.val = key

root = TreeNode(1)
root.left = TreeNode(2)
root.right = TreeNode(3)
root.left.left = TreeNode(4)
root.left.right = TreeNode(5)
```

- **Graphs**: A generalization of trees where nodes can be interconnected with no constraints on connections, allowing cycles. Graphs are pivotal in network analysis, finding shortest paths, and solving problems such as the traveling salesman problem.

```
# Example of a graph using an adjacency list in Python
class Graph:
    def __init__(self):
        self.graph = defaultdict(list)

    def add_edge(self, u, v):
        self.graph[u].append(v)

graph = Graph()
graph.add_edge(0, 1)
graph.add_edge(0, 2)
graph.add_edge(1, 2)
graph.add_edge(2, 0)
graph.add_edge(2, 3)
graph.add_edge(3, 3)
print(graph.graph)
```

```
Output:
defaultdict(<class 'list'>, {0: [1, 2], 1: [2], 2: [0, 3], 3: [3]})
```

Understanding the characteristics of each data structure and their respective advantages and limitations is essential for designing efficient algorithms. Properly chosen data structures can significantly improve the performance and scalability of software applications, making data management more effective.

1.2 Why Study Data Structures?

Data structures are an indispensable aspect of computer science that facilitate efficient data management and manipulation. A deep understanding of data structures enables computer scientists and software engineers to develop programs that can process data swiftly, conserve memory, and improve overall performance. This section explores the critical reasons for studying data structures in detail.

Conceptually, data structures provide the means to organize data in ways that enable efficient operations. For example, consider the task of searching for a particular element. Depending on the organization of the data, the search operation may take varying amounts of time. A linear search through an unsorted list has a time complexity of $O(n)$, while a binary search on a sorted array is more efficient with $O(\log n)$. The choice of data structure thus directly impacts the performance of such operations.

One primary reason for studying data structures is to optimize algorithm efficiency. The choice of data structure can significantly affect the efficiency of an algorithm. For instance, when dealing with a dynamic set of elements that require frequent insertions and deletions, a linked list may be more suitable than an array. Arrays require shifting elements when an insertion or deletion takes place, resulting in a time complexity of $O(n)$. In contrast, linked lists enable these operations in $O(1)$ time, assuming that the position of insertion or deletion is known.

```
class ListNode:
    def __init__(self, value=0, next=None):
        self.value = value
        self.next = next
```

In addition to optimizing algorithms, data structures play a crucial role in memory utilization. Different data structures have diverse memory requirements. For example, while arrays require contiguous memory allocation, linked lists can be spread across different memory locations. This characteristic allows better memory utilization, especially in systems with limited dynamic memory.

Understanding the importance of choosing the right data structure is also crucial for handling large datasets. As data grows, the efficiency and scalability of the chosen data structure become paramount. For instance, tree structures such as B-trees and AVL trees facilitate efficient search, insertion, and deletion operations, making them suitable for databases and file systems.

```
class TreeNode:
    def __init__(self, key):
        self.left = None
        self.right = None
        self.val = key
```

Real-world applications are another compelling reason to study data structures. For instance, social networks like Facebook and LinkedIn leverage graph data structures to model connections between users. Each user is represented as a node, and connections between users are represented as edges. This allows efficient traversal and querying of user networks, enabling real-time recommendations and search functionalities.

```
class Graph:
    def __init__(self):
        self.graph = defaultdict(list)

    def add_edge(self, u, v):
        self.graph[u].append(v)

    def bfs(self, start):
        visited = set()
        queue = deque([start])
        while queue:
            vertex = queue.popleft()
            if vertex not in visited:
                visited.add(vertex)
                queue.extend(x for x in self.graph[vertex] if x not in visited)
        return visited
```

Data structures also underpin the development of modern computing frameworks. Many advanced algorithms rely on efficient data structures for their implementation. Sorting algorithms like quicksort and mergesort, dynamic programming solutions, and even machine learning models make extensive use of well-chosen data structures. For example, hash tables provide average-case constant-time complexity for search, insert, and delete operations, making them ideal for caching and fast retrieval systems.

```
class HashTable:
    def __init__(self):
        self.table = [[] for _ in range(10)]

    def _hash_function(self, key):
        return hash(key) % len(self.table)

    def insert(self, key, value):
```

```
        hash_key = self._hash_function(key)
        key_exists = False
        for i, kv in enumerate(self.table[hash_key]):
            k, v = kv
            if key == k:
                self.table[hash_key][i] = (key, value)
                key_exists = True
                break
        if not key_exists:
            self.table[hash_key].append((key, value))

    def get(self, key):
        hash_key = self._hash_function(key)
        for k, v in self.table[hash_key]:
            if key == k:
                return v
        return None
```

A comprehensive understanding of data structures is essential for mastering advanced topics in computer science, such as algorithm design, database management, and network protocols. Enabling the efficient organization and manipulation of data, data structures help achieve optimum performance and resource utilization.

Realizing the significance of data structures equips programmers with the skills to analyze and choose the most suitable data structure for a given problem, leading to robust and efficient software solutions.

1.3 Types of Data Structures

Data structures can be broadly categorized into two primary types: primitive data structures and non-primitive data structures. Understanding these types is fundamental as each serves distinct purposes and provides specific functionalities that are essential for effective data manipulation.

Primitive data structures are the simplest forms of data structures and are directly operated upon by machine-level instructions. They include the basic types such as integers, floats, characters, and pointers. These data structures are inherently built into programming languages and are used to construct more complex data structures.

Non-primitive data structures, on the other hand, are more complex and can be divided into two main classes: linear data structures and nonlinear data structures.

Linear Data Structures: Linear data structures arrange data in a linear sequence, where each element is connected to its previous and next element in a sequential manner. This category includes arrays, linked lists, stacks, and queues.

- **Arrays**: Arrays are a collection of elements, identified by index or key, where each element is of the same data type. Arrays are static in size, meaning their size is fixed upon creation. They offer the advantage of O(1) access time for indexed elements, but they require contiguous memory allocation.

```
# Example of an array in Python
arr = [1, 2, 3, 4, 5]
print(arr[2]) # Output: 3
```

3

- **Linked Lists**: Linked lists are collections of nodes where each node contains data and a reference (or link) to the next node in the sequence. Linked lists are dynamic in size and can efficiently support operations such as insertions and deletions. However, they do not support constant-time access to elements.

```
# Example of a simple linked list in Python
class Node:
    def __init__(self, data):
        self.data = data
        self.next = None

class LinkedList:
    def __init__(self):
        self.head = None

    def append(self, data):
        new_node = Node(data)
        if not self.head:
            self.head = new_node
            return
        last = self.head
        while last.next:
            last = last.next
        last.next = new_node

# Create a linked list and append elements
ll = LinkedList()
ll.append(1)
ll.append(2)
ll.append(3)
```

- **Stacks**: Stacks are collections of elements that follow the Last In First Out (LIFO) principle. The basic operations for a stack are push (to add an element) and pop (to remove the most recently added element).

```
# Example of a stack in Python
```

```
stack = []

# Push elements to the stack
stack.append(1)
stack.append(2)
stack.append(3)

# Pop and display elements from the stack
print(stack.pop()) # Output: 3
print(stack.pop()) # Output: 2
```

```
3
2
```

- **Queues**: Queues are collections of elements that follow the First In First Out (FIFO) principle. Key operations for queues are enqueue (to add an element to the end) and dequeue (to remove the first element).

```
# Example of a queue in Python
from collections import deque

queue = deque()

# Enqueue elements to the queue
queue.append(1)
queue.append(2)
queue.append(3)

# Dequeue and display elements from the queue
print(queue.popleft()) # Output: 1
print(queue.popleft()) # Output: 2
```

```
1
2
```

Nonlinear Data Structures: Nonlinear data structures store data in a hierarchical manner and are used to represent complex relationships and structures. This category includes trees and graphs.

- **Trees**: Trees are hierarchical structures with a root node, where every node has zero or more child nodes and a single parent (except for the root node, which has no parent). Trees are utilized in scenarios like file system organization, parsing expressions, and hierarchical data representation. A special kind of tree is the binary tree, where each node has at most two children.

```
# Example of a simple binary tree in Python
class TreeNode:
    def __init__(self, key):
        self.left = None
        self.right = None
        self.val = key
```

```
# Creating a tree
root = TreeNode(1)
root.left = TreeNode(2)
root.right = TreeNode(3)
root.left.left = TreeNode(4)
root.left.right = TreeNode(5)
```

- **Graphs**: Graphs are collections of nodes (vertices) connected by edges. Graphs can represent various real-world entities like social networks, city maps, and network topologies. Graphs can be either directed (with directional edges) or undirected (edges with no direction), and they can be dense (many edges) or sparse (few edges).

```
# Example of a simple graph using adjacency list in Python
class Graph:
    def __init__(self):
        self.graph = {}

    def add_edge(self, u, v):
        if u not in self.graph:
            self.graph[u] = []
        self.graph[u].append(v)

# Creating a graph
g = Graph()
g.add_edge(0, 1)
g.add_edge(0, 2)
g.add_edge(1, 2)
g.add_edge(2, 0)
g.add_edge(2, 3)
g.add_edge(3, 3)
```

Understanding these primary categories and their inherent characteristics enables the selection of appropriate data structures depending on the specific computational problem and constraints faced. This foundational knowledge establishes the base for more advanced topics in data structures and algorithm optimization.

1.4 Basic Terminology

In data structures and algorithms, a firm understanding of the fundamental terminology is indispensable for comprehending more advanced concepts. This section elucidates a collection of critical terms and their definitions, each of which plays a pivotal role in the study and application of data structures and algorithms.

A **data element** is the smallest unit of data that can represent a value.

Data elements are often used to construct more complex data structures. For example, an integer or character can be regarded as a data element.

A **data item** refers to a single unit of meaningful information. It can be formed by one or more data elements. For instance, a person's name, which comprises multiple characters, is a data item.

A **data structure** is a systematic way of organizing and storing data to enable efficient access and modification. Examples include arrays, linked lists, stacks, queues, trees, and graphs.

A **record** is a collection of related data items, often organized as a structure. Each field in a record contains one data item that is a type of data element. Consider a record for an employee that may include fields such as name, employee ID, department, and salary.

An **array** is a collection of data elements identified by index or key. Elements are stored such that they can be accessed using indices, which are typically integer values. For instance, in a Python list, elements can be accessed with their positional index:

```
numbers = [10, 20, 30, 40]
print(numbers[2]) # Outputs 30
```

A **linked list** is a linear data structure where each element is a separate object, typically called a node. Each node comprises data and a reference (or link) to the next node in the sequence. This structure allows for efficient insertions and deletions as shown below:

```
class Node:
    def __init__(self, data):
        self.data = data
        self.next = None

class LinkedList:
    def __init__(self):
        self.head = None

    def append(self, data):
        new_node = Node(data)
        if not self.head:
            self.head = new_node
            return
        last = self.head
        while last.next:
            last = last.next
        last.next = new_node

# Usage
linked_list = LinkedList()
linked_list.append(1)
linked_list.append(2)
linked_list.append(3)
```

A **stack** is a collection of elements that supports two main operations: push, which adds an element to the collection, and pop, which removes the most recently added element. This follows the Last In, First Out (LIFO) principle:

```
stack = []
stack.append(10) # Push
stack.append(20) # Push
print(stack.pop()) # Pop, Outputs 20
```

A **queue** is a collection of elements that supports two primary operations: enqueue, which adds an element to the end of the collection, and dequeue, which removes the element from the front. This follows the First In, First Out (FIFO) principle:

```
from collections import deque
queue = deque()
queue.append(1) # Enqueue
queue.append(2) # Enqueue
print(queue.popleft()) # Dequeue, Outputs 1
```

A **tree** is a hierarchical data structure consisting of nodes, with a single node designated as the **root**. Each node can have zero or more **child** nodes. Trees are used in various domains, such as representing hierarchical data, searching algorithms, and more. A **binary tree** is a common type of tree where each node has at most two children, often referred to as the left and right child.

A **graph** is a set of nodes (or vertices) connected by edges. Graphs can be directed or undirected and are used to represent pairwise relationships between objects. They play a crucial role in network analysis, shortest path problems, and many other applications.

The concepts of **pointers** and **references** are essential in the context of dynamic data structures like linked lists and trees. A pointer is a variable that holds the address of another variable, allowing for the efficient manipulation of complex data structures.

The term **algorithm** refers to a well-defined set of instructions or rules designed to perform a specific task or solve a particular problem. Algorithms are fundamental to computer science and are pivotal in transforming data into meaningful results. They are evaluated based on their correctness and efficiency.

Understanding these basic terminologies will facilitate the comprehension of more intricate data structures and algorithms, forming a solid foundation for further exploration within computer science.

1.5 What is an Algorithm?

An algorithm is a finite sequence of well-defined instructions for solving a problem or performing a task. In computer science, algorithms are the cornerstone for constructing robust and efficient software systems. Each algorithm operates on data, which may be in various structures, such as arrays, linked lists, trees, and graphs, to produce a desired output. The clear structure and logical sequence make algorithms reproducible and reliable.

To delve into the technicalities, let us understand that an algorithm encompasses several intrinsic properties:

- **Finiteness**: An algorithm must always terminate after a finite number of steps. Infinite loops or procedures that do not reach a conclusion are not considered algorithms.
- **Definiteness**: Each step of an algorithm must be precisely defined. Ambiguities, which might invite different interpretations, are to be rigorously avoided.
- **Input**: An algorithm must accept zero or more inputs. Input constitutes the data needed for processing.
- **Output**: An algorithm must produce one or more outputs that have a clear relationship to the inputs.
- **Effectiveness**: Each operation within the algorithm must be elementary enough to be feasibly performed with basic computational resources.

To illustrate these principles through a concrete example, consider the classic problem of determining the maximum value within a given list of integers. Below is a simple algorithm to accomplish this task, articulated in Python:

```
def find_maximum(lst):
    # Check if the list is empty
    if not lst:
        return None

    # Initialize the maximum value to the first element in the list
    max_value = lst[0]
```

```
# Iterate through the list
for num in lst:
    if num > max_value:
        max_value = num

return max_value
```

Here, the algorithm find_maximum encapsulates all essential properties of an algorithm:

- Finiteness: The loop will terminate after examining each element of the list, ensuring finiteness.
- Definiteness: Each step, from the initialization of max_value to the comparison within the loop, is explicitly and unambiguously defined.
- Input: The function accepts a list of integers.
- Output: The function returns the maximum integer in the list or None if the list is empty.
- Effectiveness: The operations involve simple comparisons and assignments, making them computationally feasible and effective.

To further examine the concept of algorithms, consider their classification based on various factors:

- **By Implementation**: This category includes recursive algorithms and iterative algorithms. Recursive algorithms solve problems by reducing them to smaller instances of the same problem, whereas iterative algorithms solve problems using a loop construct.
- **By Complexity**: Algorithms are classified based on their time and space complexity. This includes categories like logarithmic, linear, quadratic, and polynomial time complexity.
- **By Paradigm**: Algorithms can also be categorized by their design paradigms, such as divide and conquer, dynamic programming, greedy algorithms, and backtracking.

The effectiveness of an algorithm is evaluated in terms of its performance, predominantly measured by its time complexity and space complexity, as discussed in later sections. The complexity analysis aids in understanding the scalability and efficiency of the algorithm relative to problem size.

Consider the example of sorting algorithms, such as Quick Sort, Merge Sort, and Bubble Sort. Each algorithm offers different time complexities and efficiencies based on the input data's structure and size. Thus, recognizing the appropriate algorithm for a specific task is crucial for optimal performance.

In essence, algorithms are the building blocks for problem-solving in computer science. They provide structured solutions to computational problems, ensuring that tasks are performed efficiently and correctly. The upcoming sections will further explore various types of data structures and their interaction with algorithms to enhance the efficacy of problem-solving techniques in computer science.

1.6 Importance of Algorithms in Computer Science

Algorithms are the core of computer science, serving as the blueprint for the systematic execution of tasks and problem-solving in computational contexts. Their importance spans multiple dimensions, influencing performance, efficiency, and scalability of systems and applications. Understanding their significance enhances a computer scientist's ability to design optimized and effective solutions.

Efficient algorithms are essential for various reasons:

- **Performance:** The efficiency of an algorithm directly affects the performance of software. For instance, given two algorithms solving the same problem, the one with lower time complexity will execute faster. This is particularly critical for applications requiring real-time processing, such as video streaming, gaming, and high-frequency trading.
- **Resource Optimization:** Algorithms that use resources efficiently (e.g., memory, CPU cycles) can run on devices with limited computational power like smartphones and embedded systems. By optimizing resource usage, algorithms help in extending battery life and reducing operation costs.
- **Scalability:** Algorithms that scale well can handle increasing amounts of data or more complex operations without a significant

drop in performance. This scalability is crucial for applications in big data, where the volume of data can expand exponentially.

- **Solution to Complex Problems:** Many computational problems are complex, and some cannot be solved efficiently without advanced algorithms. For example, algorithms in cryptography ensure secure data transmission, while algorithms in machine learning enable pattern recognition and predictive modeling.

- **Foundation for Advanced Study:** Mastering algorithms is foundational for studying more advanced topics in computer science, including artificial intelligence, data mining, and computational biology. A deep understanding of algorithms allows for the development of more sophisticated methods and techniques in these areas.

To illustrate the importance of algorithms, consider the problem of sorting a list of integers. While a simple sorting algorithm like Bubble Sort can perform the task, its time complexity is $O(n^2)$. In contrast, more advanced algorithms like Merge Sort have a time complexity of $O(n \log n)$. To illustrate this difference through Python code:

```
# Bubble Sort Implementation
def bubble_sort(arr):
    n = len(arr)
    for i in range(n-1):
        for j in range(0, n-i-1):
            if arr[j] > arr[j+1]:
                arr[j], arr[j+1] = arr[j+1], arr[j]
    return arr

# Merge Sort Implementation
def merge_sort(arr):
    if len(arr) > 1:
        mid = len(arr)//2
        L = arr[:mid]
        R = arr[mid:]

        merge_sort(L)
        merge_sort(R)

        i = j = k = 0
        while i < len(L) and j < len(R):
            if L[i] < R[j]:
                arr[k] = L[i]
                i += 1
            else:
                arr[k] = R[j]
                j += 1
            k += 1

        while i < len(L):
            arr[k] = L[i]
            i += 1
```

```
            k += 1

        while j < len(R):
            arr[k] = R[j]
            j += 1
            k += 1
    return arr
```

Here is an example of sorting a list of integers using both algorithms:

```
# Test list
arr = [64, 34, 25, 12, 22, 11, 90]

# Bubble Sort
print("Bubble Sort Result:", bubble_sort(arr.copy()))

# Merge Sort
print("Merge Sort Result:", merge_sort(arr.copy()))
```

The output of the above code:

```
Bubble Sort Result: [11, 12, 22, 25, 34, 64, 90]
Merge Sort Result: [11, 12, 22, 25, 34, 64, 90]
```

The Bubble Sort algorithm, though simpler to understand and implement, is inefficient for larger datasets due to its $O(n^2)$ time complexity. Merge Sort, while more complex, is significantly faster with its $O(n \log n)$ time complexity.

Analyzing algorithm efficiency through Big O notation and other performance metrics allows computer scientists to make informed decisions about which algorithms are best suited for specific tasks. Efficient algorithms can dramatically reduce execution time and resources required, which is especially important in sophisticated and large-scale systems.

In sum, the study of algorithms forms a crucial part of computer science education and practice. Algorithms enable the structured and efficient solution of problems, underpin critical applications, and improve the overall performance of computational systems. A thorough understanding and ability to implement various algorithms is a fundamental skill for any computer scientist.

1.7 Analysis of Algorithms

Algorithm analysis is a critical aspect of computer science, allowing us to evaluate the efficiency of algorithms in terms of running time and space requirements. This rigorous evaluation guides us in selecting algorithms that are not only correct but also efficient, ensuring optimal performance for various computational tasks.

Evaluating an algorithm involves both theoretical analysis and empirical (or experimental) analysis.

Theoretical analysis is conducted by estimating the time and space complexity of an algorithm without exact measurements. This is typically achieved by using Big O notation, which provides an upper bound on the growth rate of an algorithm's resource usage. Empirical analysis, on the other hand, involves implementing the algorithm and running it with various inputs to observe its actual performance in practice.

Time Complexity refers to the amount of time an algorithm takes to complete as a function of the length of the input. It is typically measured in terms of the number of basic operations or computational steps that the algorithm performs. This measure is crucial since a more time-efficient algorithm can handle larger inputs in less time, which is especially important given the growing sizes of modern datasets.

Space Complexity refers to the amount of memory an algorithm uses in terms of the length of the input. This includes all the variables, data structures, and auxiliary space required during the execution of the algorithm. Efficient space utilization is vital in scenarios where memory resources are limited.

To illustrate, consider the following Python function that computes the factorial of a number n:

```
def factorial(n):
    if n == 0:
        return 1
    else:
        return n * factorial(n-1)
```

The time complexity of this recursive function can be analyzed as follows: each function call involves a constant number of operations (a comparison and a multiplication) and results in a new function call with $n-1$, until n reaches 0. This leads to a recursion depth of n, so the time complexity $T(n)$ can be represented as $O(n)$.

Space complexity includes the space taken by function call stacks. The maximum depth of recursive calls here is n, resulting in $O(n)$ space complexity due to the space required for the call stack during execution.

In contrast to this recursive approach, consider an iterative version of the factorial function:

```
def factorial_iterative(n):
    result = 1
```

```
    for i in range(1, n + 1):
        result *= i
    return result
```

The time complexity remains $O(n)$ because the loop executes n times. However, the space complexity is reduced to $O(1)$ since only a constant amount of additional space is required regardless of the size of n.

When comparing algorithms, it's crucial to analyze both their time and space complexities to determine their suitability for specific applications. For instance, while an algorithm might have a modest $O(n^2)$ time complexity for small input sizes, a more efficient $O(n \log n)$ algorithm might be necessary for larger inputs.

Another key aspect of algorithm analysis is identifying the *best-case*, *average-case*, and *worst-case* scenarios for an algorithm's performance:

- **Best-case complexity** describes the minimum time or space that an algorithm requires for some input of size n. - **Average-case complexity** provides an expected time or space usage assuming a random distribution of inputs. - **Worst-case complexity** gives the maximum time or space that an algorithm will require for any input of size n.

Understanding these scenarios is essential for anticipating performance in different operational contexts. For example, consider the popular sorting algorithm Quicksort, which has an average-case time complexity of $O(n \log n)$ but a worst-case time complexity of $O(n^2)$. Knowing both complexities helps developers mitigate the risk of poor performance in adverse conditions by implementing strategic optimizations like randomized pivots or switching to different algorithms for particular data distributions.

Empirical analysis augments theoretical insights by executing the algorithm under realistic conditions, thus capturing the impact of factors like hardware peculiarities, system load, and compiler optimizations. Benchmarking and profiling tools can measure the actual run-time and memory usage, revealing practical performance characteristics.

In practical terms, consider benchmarking our factorial functions with Python's time module:

```
import time

# Runner for factorial functions
def time_execution(func, args):
    start_time = time.perf_counter()
    result = func(*args)
    end_time = time.perf_counter()
```

```
    return end_time - start_time, result

# Example usage
time_recursive, result_recursive = time_execution(factorial, (100,))
time_iterative, result_iterative = time_execution(factorial_iterative, (100,))

print(f"Recursive time: {time_recursive}, result: {result_recursive}")
print(f"Iterative time: {time_iterative}, result: {result_iterative}")
```

```
Recursive time: 0.000013, result: 9.33262154439441e+157
Iterative time: 0.000005, result: 9.33262154439441e+157
```

These empirical results provide real-world data on the performance differences between recursive and iterative implementations, complementing the theoretical analysis.

Algorithm analysis forms the backbone of efficient algorithm design, equipping computer scientists and developers with the tools to evaluate and select the optimal solutions for their computational problems.

1.8 Big O Notation

When analyzing algorithms, it is crucial to understand their efficiency and scalability. Big O notation provides a mathematical framework to describe the upper bound of an algorithm's running time or space requirements in terms of the input size. This notation helps computer scientists and developers compare the performance of different algorithms, particularly as the input size grows.

Big O notation expresses the worst-case scenario, capturing the maximum amount of time or memory an algorithm could potentially require. This upper bound is critical for understanding how an algorithm performs under the most demanding conditions.

To define Big O notation rigorously, consider a function $T(n)$ that represents the running time of an algorithm for an input of size n. Big O notation characterizes $T(n)$ by describing its growth rate, excluding lower-order terms and constant factors. We say that $T(n)$ is $O(f(n))$ if there exists a positive constant c and a value n_0 such that for all $n \geq n_0$,

$$T(n) \leq c \cdot f(n)$$

In other words, beyond a certain threshold n_0, the function $T(n)$ is bounded above by $c \cdot f(n)$.

To illustrate, consider some common classes of functions used in Big

O notation:

- **Constant Time** - $O(1)$: The algorithm's running time does not depend on the input size. An example is accessing an element in an array by index.
- **Logarithmic Time** - $O(\log n)$: The running time grows logarithmically as the input size increases. Binary search is a typical example.
- **Linear Time** - $O(n)$: The running time grows linearly with the input size. A simple iteration over an array demonstrates linear time complexity.
- **Linearithmic Time** - $O(n \log n)$: The running time grows as the product of n and $\log n$. Many efficient sorting algorithms, such as Merge Sort and Quick Sort, exhibit this complexity.
- **Quadratic Time** - $O(n^2)$: The running time grows proportionally to the square of the input size. Algorithms with nested loops, such as Bubble Sort and Insertion Sort, often have quadratic complexity.
- **Cubic Time** - $O(n^3)$: The running time grows as the cube of the input size, typical in algorithms with three nested loops.
- **Exponential Time** - $O(2^n)$: The running time grows exponentially with the input size. Algorithms solving the Traveling Salesman Problem using brute force exhibit exponential complexity.
- **Factorial Time** - $O(n!)$: The running time grows as the factorial of the input size, characteristic of certain combinatorial algorithms.

To further clarify, consider practical examples. Suppose we have the following Python functions:

```
def constant_time_function(arr):
    return arr[0]

def linear_time_function(arr):
    result = 0
    for value in arr:
        result += value
    return result

def quadratic_time_function(arr):
    result = 0
    n = len(arr)
    for i in range(n):
```

```
        for j in range(n):
            result += arr[i] * arr[j]
    return result
```

Explanation:

- constant_time_function has a time complexity of $O(1)$ because accessing an element by index in an array is done in constant time regardless of the array size.

- linear_time_function has a time complexity of $O(n)$ because it iterates through the entire array once.

- quadratic_time_function has a time complexity of $O(n^2)$ due to the nested loops each iterating n times.

Understanding Big O notation is essential for algorithm optimization. The notation abstracts away constants and lower-order terms, allowing for a focus on the dominant factor that influences growth rates. This abstraction is particularly useful when dealing with large datasets where these dominant factors become more significant.

Consider sorting an array of size n using different algorithms. Insertion Sort has a time complexity of $O(n^2)$, while Merge Sort and Quick Sort operate in $O(n \log n)$. Though both are efficient for small input sizes, quickly growing data sets show a stark difference in performance.

Visualizing these complexities helps solidify this understanding. Below is a plot illustrating these time complexities for various input sizes.

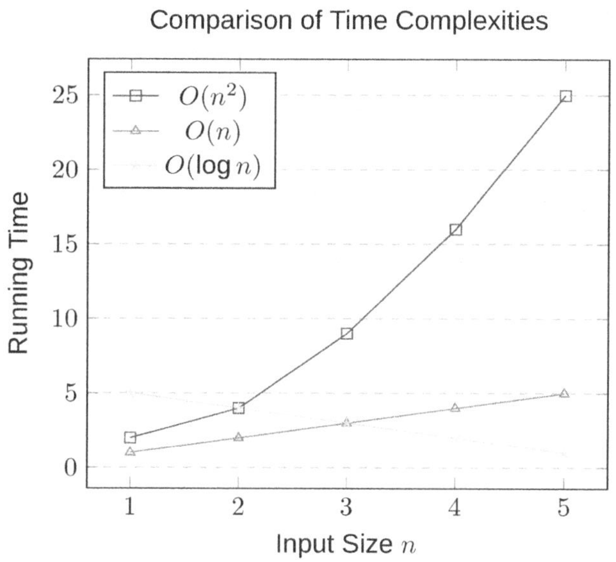

The graph illustrates the divergent growth rates of quadratic, linear, and logarithmic time complexities. As the input size increases, algorithms with higher complexity exhibit significantly greater demands in terms of time or space, highlighting the importance of choosing the appropriate algorithm based on the problem's context and constraints.

Understanding and applying Big O notation is fundamental to the analysis and design of algorithms, enabling informed decisions to achieve optimal performance and efficiency.

1.9 Time and Space Complexity

When evaluating the efficiency of an algorithm, two primary metrics are often considered: time complexity and space complexity. These metrics help in understanding how resources, such as time and memory, are utilized as the input size grows. This section delves into the definitions, implications, and methods for analyzing both time and space complexity.

Time complexity refers to the computational time required by an algorithm to complete its execution as a function of the size of the input data, denoted by n. It provides an upper bound on the time required, ensuring that the algorithm performs optimally even in the worst-case scenario. Time complexity is commonly expressed using Big O notation, which abstracts away constant factors and lower-order terms to focus on the growth rate of the function. For example, an algorithm with time complexity $O(n^2)$ indicates that the execution time grows quadratically with the input size.

Analyzing time complexity typically involves the following steps:

- Identify the basic operations: Determine the fundamental operations that significantly contribute to the total running time.
- Calculate the frequency: Compute the number of times each basic operation is executed as a function of the input size.
- Establish the growth rate: Translate the frequency count into Big O notation to express the leading term that dominates the growth rate as n increases.

Consider the following example of a Python algorithm to compute the sum of elements in an array:

```
def compute_sum(arr):
    total_sum = 0
    for num in arr:
        total_sum += num
    return total_sum
```

To analyze the time complexity:

- Basic operation: The addition operation total_sum += num within the loop.
- Frequency: The loop iterates over each element exactly once, so the operation is performed n times, where n is the number of elements in the array.
- Growth rate: The frequency is n, hence the time complexity is $O(n)$.

Space complexity, on the other hand, refers to the amount of memory required by an algorithm to process the input data. Similar to time complexity, it is also expressed in Big O notation and accounts for both the auxiliary space (extra space or temporary space used by the algorithm) and the input space (space taken by the inputs).

Considerations for space complexity include:

- Input size: The memory required for the input data itself.
- Auxiliary space: Additional memory utilized by variables, data structures, and function call stacks during the execution.

Revisiting the same example, the space complexity can be analyzed as follows:

- Input size: The array arr requires $O(n)$ space.
- Auxiliary space: The variable total_sum uses $O(1)$ space as it only stores a single value.
- Total space complexity: The dominant term is $O(n)$, accounting for the input array, leading to a space complexity of $O(n)$.

Example 2: Analyzing a Recursive Algorithm

Consider a recursive Python function to compute the factorial of a number:

```
def factorial(n):
    if n == 0:
        return 1
    else:
        return n * factorial(n - 1)
```

To analyze the time and space complexity:

- **Time Complexity:**
  - Basic operation: The multiplication n * factorial(n - 1) and the function call factorial(n - 1).
  - Frequency: The function factorial is called recursively n times before reaching the base case. Each call involves a multiplication operation.
  - Growth rate: The time complexity is $O(n)$ due to n recursive calls.
- **Space Complexity:**
  - Input size: n is local to each function call and takes $O(1)$ space.
  - Auxiliary space: Each function call adds a frame to the call stack. Since there are n calls before reaching the base case, n frames are maintained on the call stack.

- Total space complexity: The space complexity, primarily due to the recursive call stack, is $O(n)$.

Example 3: Complex Example with Nested Loops

Consider the following Python code to sort an array using the bubble sort algorithm:

```
def bubble_sort(arr):
    n = len(arr)
    for i in range(n):
        for j in range(0, n-i-1):
            if arr[j] > arr[j+1]:
                arr[j], arr[j+1] = arr[j+1], arr[j]
```

Analyzing this example:

- **Time Complexity:**
  - Basic operation: The comparison $\mathrm{arr}[j] > \mathrm{arr}[j+1]$ and the swap $\mathrm{arr}[j], \mathrm{arr}[j+1] = \mathrm{arr}[j+1], \mathrm{arr}[j]$.
  - Frequency:
    * Outer loop runs n times.
    * Inner loop runs $n-i-1$ times, resulting in approximately $\frac{n(n-1)}{2}$ comparisons/swaps in the worst case.
  - Growth rate: The time complexity is $O(n^2)$.
- **Space Complexity:**
  - Input size: The array arr requires $O(n)$ space.
  - Auxiliary space: Bubble sort uses a constant amount of extra space (only a few variables).
  - Total space complexity: The space complexity is $O(n)$.

This systematic approach to analyzing both time and space complexities is crucial for understanding the limitations and performance of algorithms in varying scenarios. It aids in making informed decisions when choosing the most efficient algorithm and data structure for particular tasks, ensuring optimal performance and resource utilization.

1.10 Choosing the Right Data Structure

Selecting an appropriate data structure is a critical aspect of software development and is key to optimizing performance and ensuring the efficiency of an algorithm. The choice of data structure can significantly impact both the time complexity and space complexity of an application, making it essential to consider various factors when making this decision.

To systematically approach the selection process, consider the following criteria:

- **Nature of the Data**: - Analyze the type and structure of the data. For instance, if data needs to be stored sequentially, arrays or linked lists may be suitable. If relationships between data elements are hierarchical, trees might be a more appropriate structure.
- **Operations Required**: - Identify the operations that will be performed most frequently. Data structures vary in operational efficiency. For example, if fast retrieval is crucial, hash tables offer average-case constant time complexity, $O(1)$. Conversely, if data needs frequent sorting, balanced trees like AVL or Red-Black Trees might be preferable due to their logarithmic time complexity, $O(\log n)$.

```
# Python example to demonstrate different data structures
# Array for sequential data access.
arr = [1, 2, 3, 4, 5]

# Dictionary for key-value pair operations with average O(1) access time.
hash_map = {'a': 1, 'b': 2, 'c': 3}

# Using a custom class for tree structures.
class TreeNode:
    def __init__(self, key):
        self.left = None
        self.right = None
        self.val = key

# Basic operations can be defined to utilize these structures effectively.
```

- **Memory Constraints**: - Consider the memory overhead associated with a data structure. For instance, linked lists use more memory than arrays due to storage of additional pointers. Thus, in memory-constrained environments, the use of more space-efficient data structures, such as arrays, may be justified.
- **Algorithmic Complexity**: - Evaluate the time complexity for the operations your application will perform. Analyze best, average, and worst-case scenarios. Balanced trees maintain $O(\log n)$ for insertion, deletion, and search operations, making them efficient for diverse operation requirements.

- **Ease of Implementation and Maintenance**: - Consider how easy it is to implement and maintain the data structure. Simpler structures like arrays or stacks might be easier to implement, debug, and maintain compared to more complex structures like Graphs, Tries, or self-balancing Binary Search Trees.

Let's consider practical scenarios and analyze the best data structure choices based on the defined criteria:

- **Real-time Search and Retrieval**: - If the primary requirement is real-time retrieval of data elements, hash tables are highly efficient due to their average $O(1)$ lookup time. However, they must be implemented with appropriate collision resolution strategies (like chaining or open addressing) to manage the worst-case $O(n)$ time complexity when collisions occur.

```
# Python code for a simple hash table with separate chaining.
class HashTable:
    def __init__(self):
        self.table = [[] for _ in range(10)]

    def _hash_function(self, key):
        return hash(key) % len(self.table)

    def insert(self, key, value):
        index = self._hash_function(key)
        for pair in self.table[index]:
            if pair[0] == key:
                pair[1] = value
                return
        self.table[index].append([key, value])

    def search(self, key):
        index = self._hash_function(key)
        for pair in self.table[index]:
            if pair[0] == key:
                return pair[1]
        return None
```

```
# Output of hash table insertion and retrieval
>>> ht = HashTable()
>>> ht.insert('a', 1)
>>> ht.search('a')
1
>>> ht.insert('b', 2)
>>> ht.search('b')
2
```

- **Hierarchical Data Representation**: - Trees are suitable when the data is hierarchical. Binary Search Trees (BSTs) allow ordered data representation with logarithmic time complexity for insertion, deletion, and lookup operations. For balanced operations, self-balancing trees like AVL or Red-Black Trees are recommended.

```
# Python code for a basic binary search tree.
class BSTNode:
    def __init__(self, key):
        self.left = None
        self.right = None
        self.val = key

    def insert(self, key):
        if self.val:
            if key < self.val:
                if self.left is None:
                    self.left = BSTNode(key)
                else:
                    self.left.insert(key)
            elif key > self.val:
                if self.right is None:
                    self.right = BSTNode(key)
                else:
                    self.right.insert(key)
        else:
            self.val = key

    def search(self, key):
        if key < self.val:
            if self.left is None:
                return None
            return self.left.search(key)
        elif key > self.val:
            if self.right is None:
                return None
            return self.right.search(key)
        else:
            return self
```

```
# Usage of the BST implementation
>>> root = BSTNode(10)
>>> root.insert(5)
>>> root.insert(15)
>>> root.search(15)
<__main__.BSTNode object at 0x...>
>>> root.search(7)
None
```

- **Sequential Data Processing**: - For operations requiring first-in-first-out (FIFO) order, queues are optimal. Queues can be efficiently implemented using arrays or linked lists, with each offering different trade-offs in terms of complexity and memory usage.

```
# Python code for a simple queue.
class Queue:
    def __init__(self):
```

```
        self.queue = []

    def enqueue(self, item):
        self.queue.append(item)

    def dequeue(self):
        if len(self.queue) < 1:
            return None
        return self.queue.pop(0)

    def size(self):
        return len(self.queue)
```

```
# Output for queue operations
>>> q = Queue()
>>> q.enqueue(1)
>>> q.enqueue(2)
>>> q.dequeue()
1
>>> q.size()
1
```

By carefully evaluating the nature of data, required operations, memory constraints, algorithmic complexity, and implementation & maintenance constraints, a well-considered choice of data structure can significantly optimize the overall performance of an application.

Chapter 2

Python Programming Basics

This chapter provides an overview of essential Python programming concepts, starting with basic syntax and variable declarations. It covers fundamental data types and structures, control flow statements, and the creation and use of functions and modules. Additionally, it introduces file handling, exception handling, and the utilization of libraries. The chapter concludes with an introduction to object-oriented programming, laying the groundwork for further exploration of data structures and algorithms in Python.

2.1 Introduction to Python

Python is a high-level, interpreted programming language known for its ease of learning, readability, and versatility. Guido van Rossum created Python in the late 1980s, and it has since evolved into one of the most widely used programming languages globally, particularly in data analysis, web development, artificial intelligence, and scientific computing.

Python supports multiple programming paradigms, including procedural, object-oriented, and functional programming. This flexibility allows developers to select the most appropriate paradigm for a given problem, making it a powerful tool for a wide range of applications.

Python's design philosophy emphasizes code readability, simplicity, and explicitness. The language features a clean and straightforward syntax that makes it accessible to beginners while powerful enough for experienced developers to build large-scale applications. The following code snippet illustrates a simple Python program that prints "Hello, World!":

```
print("Hello, World!")
```

When executed, the output will be:

```
Hello, World!
```

Python's interactive interpreter allows for immediate feedback, further enhancing its ease of use as a learning tool. Users can execute Python code snippets directly in the interpreter, allowing for rapid experimentation and debugging. To start the interpreter, simply type 'python' in the command line if Python is installed correctly.

One of Python's significant strengths is its extensive standard library, which provides modules and functions for various tasks, such as file I/O, system interaction, and data manipulation. This comprehensive library means that common programming needs are often met with built-in solutions, reducing the need for external dependencies.

Additionally, Python has a vast ecosystem of third-party libraries and frameworks, extending its capabilities significantly. Popular libraries such as NumPy, pandas, and Matplotlib are invaluable for scientific and numerical computing. At the same time, frameworks like Django and Flask are widely used in web development. Through the package management system 'pip', users can easily install and manage these external libraries.

Python's development environment is also highly flexible. It is available on multiple operating systems, including Windows, macOS, and various distributions of Linux, ensuring a consistent experience across different platforms. The language is open-source, with a vibrant community contributing to its continuous improvement and the development of new tools and libraries.

Python's popularity can be attributed to several factors:

- **Ease of Learning and Use**: Python's syntax is intuitive and permits shorter development times compared to other languages.

- **Versatility**: It supports various programming paradigms and can be used for scripting, automation, web development, data analysis, and more.
- **Extensive Libraries**: Both the standard library and third-party modules cater to a wide array of applications.
- **Community and Support**: A large, active community provides expansive documentation, abundant online resources, and a wealth of community-contributed code.
- **Interoperability**: Python can interface with other languages and systems, making it ideal for integration purposes.

A fundamental component of Python is its dynamically typed nature, meaning that variable types are interpreted at runtime. This feature allows for greater flexibility, though it also necessitates careful handling of variables to prevent type-related errors during execution:

```
x = 10 # x is an integer
x = "text" # x is now a string
print(x)
```

The output will be:

```
text
```

Python's memory management is handled automatically by a built-in garbage collector, which reclaims memory for reallocation. This automatic management relieves developers from manually managing memory allocation and deallocation, which reduces the likelihood of memory leaks and other related bugs.

Python syntax and the indentation structure play a crucial role in defining the scope of loops, functions, and classes. Proper indentation is not just a stylistic choice but a requirement for the correct execution of Python programs. Indentation typically consists of four spaces per level:

```
def greet(name):
    if name:
        print(f"Hello, {name}!")
    else:
        print("Hello, World!")
```

Executing 'greet("Alice")' would produce:

```
Hello, Alice!
```

If no name is provided by calling 'greet("")', the function returns:

```
Hello, World!
```

Understanding how Python handles variables and memory, along with its robust standard library and third-party ecosystem, sets the foundation for effectively leveraging Python in various programming scenarios. The simplicity of Python's syntax, combined with its powerful features, makes it a language of choice for both novice and experienced programmers.

2.2 Setting Up Python Environment

To begin your journey into Python programming, initializing your development environment is critical. This section will guide you through the installation of Python, setting up a text editor or Integrated Development Environment (IDE), and verifying your setup. The instructions provided will be suitable for Windows, macOS, and Linux operating systems.

Installing Python

The Python language is maintained by the Python Software Foundation, and the latest versions can be downloaded from the official Python website (https://www.python.org/). As of the latest update, Python 3.10 or later is recommended.

- **Windows:**
    1. Navigate to the Python download page (https://www.python.org/downloads/).
    2. Download the executable installer for Windows.
    3. Run the installer and ensure you check the box labeled *Add Python to PATH*.
    4. Select *Install Now* and follow the prompts to complete the installation.
- **macOS:**
    1. Download the latest Python installer from the same Python download page.
    2. Open the downloaded .pkg file and follow the prompts in the installation wizard.
    3. Alternatively, you can install Python using Homebrew with the command:

```
brew install python
```

- **Linux:**

  1. Most Linux distributions come with Python pre-installed. You can check the installed version using:

  ```
  python3 --version
  ```

  2. If Python is not installed or you need to upgrade, use your package manager. For instance, on Debian-based systems:

  ```
  sudo apt update
  sudo apt install python3.10
  ```

  3. For Red Hat-based systems, use:

  ```
  sudo dnf install python3
  ```

Setting Up an Integrated Development Environment (IDE)

A robust IDE can simplify coding by providing features like syntax highlighting, code completion, and debugging tools. Several popular options are available:

- **VS Code:** VS Code, or Visual Studio Code, is a free IDE developed by Microsoft. It is lightweight yet powerful, supporting Python via extensions.

  - Download and install VS Code from https://code.visualstudio.com/.
  - Open VS Code and go to the Extensions view by clicking on the square icon in the sidebar or pressing *Ctrl+Shift+X*.
  - Search for the *Python Extension* provided by Microsoft and install it.

- **PyCharm:** PyCharm, developed by JetBrains, is a popular choice among professional developers.

  - Download PyCharm from https://www.jetbrains.com/pycharm/download/.
  - Follow the installation instructions specific to your operating system.

  - Open PyCharm and configure the Python interpreter by navigating to *File > Settings > Project: <project name> > Python Interpreter*.

- **Jupyter Notebook:** Jupyter is particularly useful for data science projects and educational purposes.
  - Install Jupyter using pip:

```
pip install notebook
```

  - Launch Jupyter Notebook by running:

```
jupyter notebook
```

Verifying Your Setup

Once installation and setup are complete, verify that Python and your preferred IDE are correctly configured.

Check Python Installation: Open a terminal (command prompt on Windows), and execute:

```
python --version
# or if installed as python3
python3 --version
```

The output should display the installed Python version, confirming the installation.

Running Your First Python Script: Create a simple Python script to ensure everything is functioning correctly.

- Open your chosen IDE or a text editor.
- Write the following code and save it as *hello.py*:

```
print("Hello, World!")
```

- Run the script from the terminal:

```
python hello.py
```

- The output should be:

```
Hello, World!
```

This confirms that your Python environment is set up correctly and you are ready to proceed with further Python programming.

2.3 Basic Syntax and Variables

Python's simplicity and readability make it a popular programming language for beginners and experienced developers alike. Understanding the basic syntax is crucial for writing clean and efficient Python code. This section covers the foundational elements of Python syntax, including variable declarations, comments, and basic data types.

Basic Syntax

Python code is executed line by line, and the language emphasizes the use of indentation to define blocks of code. There are a few key syntax rules to be aware of:

- **Indentation**: Python uses indentation to define the scope of loops, functions, and other constructs. The recommended indentation level is four spaces.
- **Case sensitivity**: Python is case-sensitive, meaning that variable names are treated differently if their case differs.
- **Comments**: Comments are important for documenting code. Single-line comments begin with the # symbol, while multi-line comments are enclosed within triple quotes (""" ... """).

```
# This is a single-line comment

"""
This is a multi-line comment
It can span multiple lines
"""

if True:
    print("Hello, World!") # Indented line
```

The above example showcases a simple conditional statement, where the print statement is indented to signify that it belongs to the if block.

Variables

Variables are used to store data that can be referenced and manipulated within a program. Python is dynamically typed, meaning that variable types do not need to be declared explicitly. Instead, the type is inferred at runtime based on the value assigned.

```
# Declaring variables
x = 5
y = "Hello"
z = 3.14
```

```
# Printing variable values
print(x)
print(y)
print(z)
```

The variable x is assigned an integer value, y is assigned a string, and z is assigned a floating-point number. The print function is used to output the values of these variables.

Variable Naming Conventions

Certain best practices should be followed for naming variables to ensure readability and maintainability:

- Variable names should start with a letter (a-z, A-Z) or an underscore (_).
- Variable names can contain letters, digits (0-9), and underscores.
- Variable names should be descriptive and meaningful.
- Use snake_case (lowercase words separated by underscores) for variable names.

```
valid_variable_name = 42
_validVariableName = "Python"
another_valid_name123 = [1, 2, 3]

# Invalid names
1invalid = "wrong" # Starts with a digit
invalid-name = 10 # Contains a hyphen
```

Basic Data Types

Python supports several built-in data types. Here, we focus on four fundamental ones: integers, floats, strings, and booleans.

- **Integers**: Whole numbers, such as 1, 2, 3, etc.
- **Floats**: Decimal numbers, such as 3.14, 2.71, etc.
- **Strings**: Sequences of characters, such as "hello", "world", etc.
- **Booleans**: Logical values True and False.

```
# Integer
a = 10

# Float
```

```
b = 20.5

# String
c = "Python"

# Boolean
d = True

# Printing their types
print(type(a)) # <class 'int'>
print(type(b)) # <class 'float'>
print(type(c)) # <class 'str'>
print(type(d)) # <class 'bool'>
```

In this example, the type function is used to determine the type of each variable.

```
<class 'int'>
<class 'float'>
<class 'str'>
<class 'bool'>
```

The above output shows the respective data types of the variables a, b, c, and d.

Understanding basic syntax and variable handling forms the core of writing Python programs. Moving forward, this foundational knowledge will be instrumental in grasping more complex programming constructs and data structures.

2.4 Data Types and Structures

Python offers a diverse array of native data types and structures, allowing developers to handle data efficiently and effectively. Understanding these foundational elements is crucial for writing robust and readable code. In this section, we will explore primitive data types like integers and strings, as well as complex data structures such as lists, tuples, sets, and dictionaries.

Primitive Data Types

1. **Integers:** Integers are whole numbers, positive or negative, without decimals. In Python, an integer is defined simply by assigning a number to a variable.

```
x = 5
y = -3
z = 1234567890
```

2. **Floats:** Floats are numbers with decimals. They are used for more precise calculations.

```
a = 5.5
b = -2.3
c = 0.123456789
```

3. **Strings:** Strings are sequences of characters enclosed within single or double quotes.

```
str1 = 'Hello'
str2 = "World"
str3 = "123"
```

Strings can be concatenated, repeated, and sliced. They are immutable, meaning once created, they cannot be altered.

```
# Concatenation
full_str = str1 + " " + str2 # Output: 'Hello World'

# Repetition
repeat_str = str1 * 3 # Output: 'HelloHelloHello'

# Slicing
sub_str = full_str[0:5] # Output: 'Hello'
```

4. **Booleans:** Booleans represent one of two values: True or False.

```
is_true = True
is_false = False
```

Boolean values are often used in control flow statements to determine the execution path of the program.

Complex Data Structures

1. **Lists:** Lists are ordered, mutable collections of items, which can be of different types.

```
my_list = [1, 2, 3, 'a', 'b', 'c']
```

Lists can be indexed and sliced, similar to strings.

```
# Indexing
first_item = my_list[0] # Output: 1

# Slicing
sub_list = my_list[1:4] # Output: [2, 3, 'a']
```

Lists can be modified after creation.

```
# Appending an item
my_list.append(4) # Output: [1, 2, 3, 'a', 'b', 'c', 4]
```

```
# Removing an item
my_list.remove('a') # Output: [1, 2, 3, 'b', 'c', 4]
```

2. **Tuples:** Tuples are similar to lists, but they are immutable.

```
my_tuple = (1, 2, 3, 'a', 'b', 'c')
```

Tuples also support indexing and slicing.

```
# Indexing
first_item_tup = my_tuple[0] # Output: 1

# Slicing
sub_tuple = my_tuple[1:4] # Output: (2, 3, 'a')
```

3. **Sets:** Sets are unordered collections of unique items.

```
my_set = {1, 2, 3, 'a', 'b', 'c'}
```

Operations on sets include union, intersection, and difference.

```
set1 = {1, 2, 3}
set2 = {3, 4, 5}

# Union
union_set = set1 | set2 # Output: {1, 2, 3, 4, 5}

# Intersection
intersection_set = set1 & set2 # Output: {3}

# Difference
difference_set = set1 - set2 # Output: {1, 2}
```

4. **Dictionaries:** Dictionaries are unordered collections of key-value pairs.

```
my_dict = {'name': 'Alice', 'age': 25, 'city': 'New York'}
```

Values in a dictionary can be accessed using keys.

```
# Accessing value
name = my_dict['name'] # Output: 'Alice'

# Adding a new key-value pair
my_dict['email'] = 'alice@example.com' # Output: {'name': 'Alice', 'age': 25, 'city': '
    New York', 'email': 'alice@example.com'}

# Removing a key-value pair
del my_dict['age'] # Output: {'name': 'Alice', 'city': 'New York', 'email': '
    alice@example.com'}
```

Python's data types and structures are versatile and powerful, enabling efficient data manipulation and retrieval. Mastery of these foundational elements will facilitate more advanced programming tasks, ensuring both efficiency and clarity in your code.

2.5 Control Flow Statements

Control flow statements are essential in any programming language as they determine the flow of program execution. In Python, control flow is facilitated by a variety of statements including conditionals, loops, and other constructs that manage execution paths. We will delve into these control flow mechanisms to understand how to direct the execution of code segments efficiently.

Python's control flow statements include:

- if, elif, and else for conditional execution.
- for loops for iterating over sequences.
- while loops for repeated execution as long as a condition holds true.
- Control flow modifying statements such as break, continue, and pass.

Conditional Statements

Python uses the if statement to execute a block of code based on a condition. The syntax is straightforward:

```
if condition:
    # Block of code to execute if condition is true
```

The condition is evaluated, and if it returns True, the indented block of code below the if statement is executed. You can also use elif and else to handle multiple branches:

```
if condition1:
    # Block of code to execute if condition1 is true
elif condition2:
    # Block of code to execute if condition2 is true
else:
    # Block of code to execute if none of the above conditions are true
```

Example:

```
x = 10
if x < 10:
    print("x is less than 10")
elif x == 10:
```

```
    print("x is equal to 10")
else:
    print("x is greater than 10")
```

Output:
x is equal to 10

The for Loop

A for loop in Python is used for iterating over a sequence (such as a list, tuple, string, or range). The syntax for a for loop is as follows:

```
for item in sequence:
    # Block of code to execute for each item in sequence
```

Example:

```
fruits = ['apple', 'banana', 'cherry']
for fruit in fruits:
    print(fruit)
```

Output:
apple
banana
cherry

To loop a certain number of times, the range() function is often used:

```
for i in range(5):
    print(i)
```

Output:
0
1
2
3
4

The while Loop

The while loop allows repeated execution as long as a condition remains true:

```
while condition:
    # Block of code to execute as long as condition is true
```

Example:

```
count = 0
while count < 5:
    print(count)
    count += 1
```

Output:
0
1
2
3
4

Control Flow Modifying Statements

break, continue, and pass provide additional control over flow within loops.

break is used to exit a loop prematurely:

```
for i in range(10):
    if i == 5:
        break
    print(i)
```

Output:
0
1
2
3
4

continue skips the rest of the loop and proceeds to the next iteration:

```
for i in range(10):
    if i % 2 == 0:
        continue
    print(i)
```

Output:
1
3
5
7
9

pass is a null operation; it is a statement that does nothing and is useful as a placeholder:

```
for i in range(10):
    if i < 5:
        pass
    else:
        print(i)
```

Output:
5
6
7
8
9

Understanding these control flow statements and their appropriate usage is fundamental to writing effective and efficient Python code. The examples provided demonstrate the basic syntax and application, enabling you to build more complex logic and functionalities as required.

2.6 Functions and Modules

Python functions and modules are fundamental constructs that facilitate code organization, reuse, and readability. Functions enable the decomposition of complex problems into simpler, manageable units, while modules provide a way to structure Python programs by encapsulating related functionalities.

A function in Python is defined using the def keyword, followed by the function name, parentheses that can contain parameters, and a colon. Indented underneath the function definition line are the statements that make up the body of the function. Consider the following example, which defines a simple function to calculate the factorial of a number:

```
def factorial(n):
    """This function returns the factorial of a given number n."""
    if n == 0 or n == 1:
        return 1
    else:
        result = 1
        for i in range(2, n+1):
            result *= i
        return result
```

In this example, factorial is the function name, and n is the parameter. The function first checks if n is 0 or 1 (in which case the factorial is 1) and returns the appropriate value. Otherwise, it uses a for loop to compute the factorial for values greater than 1.

To call the factorial function, you simply use its name followed by the argument in parentheses. For instance, the expression factorial(5) will return 120, as shown below:

```
print(factorial(5))
```

```
120
```

Functions can return any type of value, including complex data structures such as lists and dictionaries. Additionally, Python functions can have default parameter values, which allow them to be called with fewer arguments than specified in the definition. An example of this is:

```
def greet(name, message="Hello"):
    """This function greets a person with a message."""
    return f"{message}, {name}!"
```

By providing a default value for the message parameter, the greet function can be called with either one or two arguments:

```
print(greet("Alice"))
print(greet("Bob", "Good morning"))
```

```
Hello, Alice!
Good morning, Bob!
```

Modules in Python are files containing Python definitions and statements. The file name is the module name with the suffix .py added. A module allows the logical organization of Python code, making it reusable across various programs.

To use a module, you need to import it. The import statement is used for this purpose. For example, the math module provides access to many useful mathematical functions. You can import the math module and use its functions as follows:

```
import math

print(math.sqrt(16)) # Outputs 4.0
print(math.pi) # Outputs 3.141592653589793
```

```
4.0
3.141592653589793
```

It's also possible to import specific functions from a module using the from keyword. This can make the code cleaner and avoid namespace conflicts:

```
from math import sqrt, pi

print(sqrt(25)) # Outputs 5.0
print(pi) # Outputs 3.141592653589793
```

```
5.0
3.141592653589793
```

Python's module system also supports custom modules. You can create your own module by writing Python code in a file with a .py extension and then importing it in your program. For instance, if you save the factorial function defined earlier in a file named mymath.py, you can import and use it as follows:

```
import mymath

print(mymath.factorial(6)) # Outputs 720
```

```
720
```

Alternatively, you can import specific functions from the custom module:

```
from mymath import factorial

print(factorial(7)) # Outputs 5040
```

5040

By organizing code into functions and modules, you can create more modular, readable, and maintainable programs. These principles will be especially beneficial when dealing with more complex software projects.

2.7 File Handling

File handling is a crucial aspect of any programming language, enabling a program to read from and write to files stored on a disk. In Python, file handling is achieved through built-in functions and methods that allow seamless interaction with files. Understanding these fundamental operations is vital for effectively managing data persistence in various applications.

To begin with, Python provides the open() function to open a file. This function returns a file object, which provides methods and attributes to interact with the file's contents. The basic syntax of the open() function is as follows:

```
file_object = open(filename, mode)
```

The filename parameter is a string that specifies the name of the file to be opened. The mode parameter is also a string that specifies the mode in which the file should be opened. The most common modes include:

- 'r': Opens the file for reading (default mode). The file must already exist.
- 'w': Opens the file for writing. If the file exists, its content is truncated. If the file does not exist, a new file is created.
- 'a': Opens the file for appending. New data is written at the end of the file content. If the file does not exist, it creates a new file.
- 'b': Opens the file in binary mode.
- 't': Opens the file in text mode (default mode).

Here is a practical example of opening a file for reading:

```
file_object = open('example.txt', 'r')
```

Once a file is opened, it is essential to close it to free up resources. The close() method is used for this purpose:

```
file_object.close()
```

However, a more efficient approach is using a with statement, which ensures the file is properly closed after its suite finishes, even if an exception is raised. This is demonstrated below:

```
with open('example.txt', 'r') as file_object:
    content = file_object.read()
    print(content)
```

Reading from a file can be done using several methods:

- read(size): Reads the specified number of bytes from the file. If the size argument is omitted, it reads the entire file.
- readline(): Reads a single line from the file.
- readlines(): Reads all lines in the file and returns them as a list of strings.

Writing to a file similarly employs several methods:

- write(string): Writes the specified string to the file.
- writelines(list_of_strings): Writes a list of strings to the file.

An example of writing to and reading from a file is shown below:

```
# Writing to a file
with open('example.txt', 'w') as file_object:
    file_object.write("This is an example text.\n")
    file_object.write("Writing to files in Python is easy.\n")

# Reading from a file
with open('example.txt', 'r') as file_object:
    content = file_object.read()
    print(content)
```

```
This is an example text.
Writing to files in Python is easy.
```

Python also provides functionality for handling binary files, which are typically used for non-text data such as images or executable files. To work with binary files, include a b character in the mode string:

```
# Writing binary data
with open('example.bin', 'wb') as file_object:
    file_object.write(b'\xDE\xAD\xBE\xEF')

# Reading binary data
with open('example.bin', 'rb') as file_object:
    content = file_object.read()
    print(content)
```

```
b'\xDE\xAD\xBE\xEF'
```

Lastly, Python supports random access to file contents through the seek() and tell() methods. The seek(offset, whence) method modifies the current file position, where offset is the byte position to move to, and whence defines the reference point. The tell() method returns the current file position:

```
with open('example.txt', 'rb+') as file_object:
    file_object.write(b'0123456789abcdef')
    file_object.seek(5) # Move to the 6th byte
    print(file_object.read(1)) # Print next byte
    file_object.seek(-3, 2) # Move 3 bytes before the end
    print(file_object.read(1)) # Print next byte
```

```
b'5'
b'd'
```

Collectively, these operations form the foundation for file handling in Python, enabling robust and efficient data processing workflows.

2.8 Exception Handling

Exception handling in Python is a crucial concept for creating robust and error-resilient programs. Errors and exceptions are inevitable during the execution of a program. They can occur due to various reasons such as invalid user input, device failure, or unforeseen bugs in the code. Python provides a systematic way to catch and handle these exceptions using the try-except block.

An exception is an event detected during runtime that interrupts the normal flow of the program's instructions. In Python, many built-in exceptions can be raised and caught. Some common built-in exceptions include: IndexError, KeyError, ValueError, and TypeError.

The basic syntax for exception handling in Python involves the try and except blocks. Here's a concise example that demonstrates how to handle exceptions in Python:

```
try:
    # Code that may raise an exception
    result = 10 / 0
except ZeroDivisionError:
    # Code to handle the exception
    print("Cannot divide by zero!")
```

In this example, the code inside the try block attempts to divide a number by zero, which raises a ZeroDivisionError. The except block catches this specific exception and prints an error message. If an exception other than ZeroDivisionError were to occur, it would not be caught by this except block.

If you want to handle multiple exceptions, you can specify multiple except blocks:

```
try:
    # Code that may raise multiple exceptions
    number = int(input("Enter a number: "))
    result = 10 / number
except ValueError:
    # Handles invalid input (not an integer)
    print("Please enter a valid integer.")
except ZeroDivisionError:
    # Handles division by zero
    print("Cannot divide by zero!")
```

In this code snippet, the try block can raise either a ValueError if the input is not a valid integer or a ZeroDivisionError if the user inputs zero. Each exception is handled by its respective except block.

It is also possible to catch multiple exceptions in a single except block using a tuple of exceptions:

```
try:
    number = int(input("Enter a number: "))
    result = 10 / number
except (ValueError, ZeroDivisionError):
    print("Invalid input: Please enter a non-zero integer.")
```

In some cases, you may want to execute some code regardless of whether an exception occurred or not. This is where the finally block comes into play. The finally block always executes after the try and except blocks:

```
try:
    number = int(input("Enter a number: "))
    result = 10 / number
except (ValueError, ZeroDivisionError) as e:
    print(f"An error occurred: {e}")
finally:
    print("Execution complete.")
```

In this example, the finally block will always execute, printing "Execution complete" regardless of whether an exception was raised and handled or not.

Moreover, Python allows the use of the else block in conjunction with try... except. The else block is executed if the code in the try block does not raise an exception:

```
try:
    number = int(input("Enter a number: "))
    result = 10 / number
except (ValueError, ZeroDivisionError) as e:
    print(f"An error occurred: {e}")
else:
    print(f"Result is: {result}")
finally:
    print("Execution complete.")
```

In this scenario, the else block executes only if no exceptions were raised in the try block. The finally block executes in all cases.

Custom exceptions can also be defined to cater to specific needs within your application. A custom exception class can be created by inheriting from the built-in Exception class:

```
class CustomError(Exception):
    """Custom exception class for specific errors."""
    def __init__(self, message):
        self.message = message

try:
    raise CustomError("This is a custom error!")
except CustomError as e:
    print(f"Caught a custom exception: {e.message}")
```

In this code snippet, CustomError is a user-defined exception class. An instance of this class is raised within the try block and subsequently caught in the except block.

By leveraging exception handling effectively, programmers can ensure that their programs are more resilient to runtime errors, thus improving the robustness and reliability of the software.

2.9 Working with Libraries

Libraries in Python are collections of pre-written code that you can import into your programs to utilize existing functionalities. This saves significant time and effort as you don't need to write functions and classes from scratch. Python boasts a rich ecosystem of libraries, ranging from those handling basic tasks such as mathematical calculations, to more complex ones like data visualization and machine learning.

To begin working with libraries in Python, you must first understand how to import them. The import statement is used for this purpose. Let us explore some fundamental use-cases with standard libraries.

1. Using the math Library:

The math library in Python provides access to various mathematical functions like trigonometry, logarithms, and constants such as π. Here is an example of how to use it:

```
import math

# Compute the cosine of a number
cosine_value = math.cos(math.pi / 4)
print(f"The cosine of pi/4 is: {cosine_value}")

# Compute the factorial of a number
factorial_value = math.factorial(5)
print(f"The factorial of 5 is: {factorial_value}")
```

The output would be:

```
The cosine of pi/4 is: 0.7071067811865476
The factorial of 5 is: 120
```

2. Using the datetime Library:

The datetime library provides classes for manipulating dates and times. Here's an example:

```
import datetime

# Get the current date and time
current_date_time = datetime.datetime.now()
print(f"Current date and time: {current_date_time}")

# Create a specific date
specific_date = datetime.datetime(2021, 12, 31)
print(f"Specific date: {specific_date}")

# Compute the difference between two dates
date1 = datetime.datetime(2021, 1, 1)
date2 = datetime.datetime(2022, 1, 1)
delta = date2 - date1
print(f"Difference between dates: {delta.days} days")
```

The output would be:

```
Current date and time: 2023-03-14 15:26:08.776000
Specific date: 2021-12-31 00:00:00
Difference between dates: 365 days
```

3. Using the random Library:

The random library provides functions to generate random numbers. Here is a basic usage:

```
import random

# Generate a random number between 1 and 10
random_number = random.randint(1, 10)
print(f"Random number between 1 and 10: {random_number}")

# Generate a random float number between 0 and 1
random_float = random.random()
print(f"Random float between 0 and 1: {random_float}")
```

The output would be a random number and a random float which changes every time the code is run.

```
Random number between 1 and 10: 7
Random float between 0 and 1: 0.567123456789
```

Moving beyond standard libraries, let's explore third-party libraries, which are not included in the standard Python distribution. They can be installed using the package manager pip.

4. Using the NumPy Library:

NumPy is a popular library for numerical operations. To install it, use the following command in the terminal:

```
pip install numpy
```

Here is an example of how to use NumPy:

```
import numpy as np

# Create a 1-D array
array_1d = np.array([1, 2, 3, 4, 5])
print(f"1-D array: {array_1d}")

# Create a 2-D array
array_2d = np.array([[1, 2, 3], [4, 5, 6]])
print(f"2-D array:\n{array_2d}")

# Perform element-wise addition
array_sum = array_1d + 10
print(f"Array after addition: {array_sum}")

# Compute the dot product
dot_product = np.dot(array_1d, array_1d)
print(f"Dot product: {dot_product}")
```

The output would be:

```
1-D array: [1 2 3 4 5]
2-D array:
[[1 2 3]
 [4 5 6]]
Array after addition: [11 12 13 14 15]
Dot product: 55
```

5. Using the pandas Library:

pandas is a powerful library for data manipulation and analysis. It can be installed using:

```
pip install pandas
```

Here is an example of using pandas:

```
import pandas as pd

# Create a DataFrame
data = {'Name': ['Anna', 'Bob', 'Charlie'], 'Age': [24, 27, 22]}
df = pd.DataFrame(data)
print(f"DataFrame:\n{df}")

# Access a column
ages = df['Age']
print(f"Ages:\n{ages}")

# Perform basic statistical operations
mean_age = df['Age'].mean()
print(f"Mean age: {mean_age}")
```

The output would be:

```
DataFrame:
      Name  Age
0     Anna   24
1      Bob   27
2  Charlie   22
Ages:
0    24
1    27
2    22
Name: Age, dtype: int64
Mean age: 24.333333333333332
```

Finally, when working with libraries, it is important to keep your environment organized. Virtual environments allow you to manage dependencies for different projects separately. To create and activate a virtual environment, use the following commands:

```
python -m venv myenv
source myenv/bin/activate  # On Windows, use 'myenv\Scripts\activate'
```

Once activated, any packages you install using pip will be contained within this environment. This practice helps to avoid conflicts between dependencies of different projects.

2.10 Introduction to Object-Oriented Programming

Object-oriented programming (OOP) is a programming paradigm based on the concept of "objects", which can contain data and code: data in the form of fields (often known as attributes or properties), and code, in the form of procedures (often known as methods). The defining feature of objects is that an object's procedures can access and often modify the data fields of the object with which they are associated. In Python, OOP is a powerful instrument that allows for the creation of classes and objects, facilitating a more intuitive mapping between real-world entities and programming constructs.

A **class** in Python serves as a blueprint for creating objects. This blueprint encapsulates the data (also known as attributes) and functions (known as methods) that the objects created from the class will have. The class itself does not hold the data but defines what data objects instantiated from it can hold. An **object** is an instance of a class.

Consider the following example of defining a simple class in Python:

```
class Dog:
    species = "Canis familiaris"

    def __init__(self, name, age):
        self.name = name
        self.age = age

    def description(self):
        return f"{self.name} is {self.age} years old"

    def speak(self, sound):
        return f"{self.name} says {sound}"
```

In this example, we define a class named Dog. This class has a class attribute species that is shared by all instances of the class. The __init__ method is a special method that initializes the object's attributes. Each object created from the Dog class will have name and age attributes. The methods description and speak define behaviors that the Dog objects can perform.

To create an instance of the Dog class, we do the following:

```
my_dog = Dog("Buddy", 9)
print(my_dog.description())
print(my_dog.speak("Woof Woof"))
```

The output of the above code would be:

```
Buddy is 9 years old
Buddy says Woof Woof
```

The concept of **inheritance** in OOP allows for a class to inherit attributes and methods from another class. The class being inherited from is called the *parent* or *base class*, and the class inheriting is called the *child* or *derived class*. The derived class can override or extend the functionalities of the base class.

Consider an example where we have a base class Animal and a derived class Dog:

```
class Animal:
    def __init__(self, name):
        self.name = name

    def move(self):
        print(f'{self.name} is moving')

class Dog(Animal):
    def speak(self, sound):
        print(f'{self.name} says {sound}')
```

Here, the Dog class inherits from the Animal class. It can use the move method defined in Animal and has its own method speak.

Using these classes:

```
my_pet = Dog("Buddy")
my_pet.move()
my_pet.speak("Woof Woof")
```

The output would be:

```
Buddy is moving
Buddy says Woof Woof
```

Encapsulation is another key principle of OOP, which means restricting direct access to some of an object's components and can prevent the accidental modification of data. This can be achieved using private attributes and methods by prefixing their names with an underscore:

```
class Car:
    def __init__(self, model, year):
        self._model = model
        self._year = year

    def get_model(self):
        return self._model

    def set_model(self, model):
        self._model = model
```

In this example, model is a private attribute and can be accessed and modified only through the methods get_model and set_model.

Finally, **polymorphism** allows for using a unified interface to operate on different types of objects. Polymorphism can be seen when a method in different classes implements behavior differently. For example:

```
class Bird:
    def sound(self):
        return "Chirp"

class Dog:
    def sound(self):
        return "Bark"

def make_sound(animal):
    print(animal.sound())

bird = Bird()
dog = Dog()
make_sound(bird)
make_sound(dog)
```

The output would be:

```
Chirp
Bark
```

The function make_sound can operate on any object that has a sound method, demonstrating polymorphism.

Understanding these core principles of OOP in Python—classes and objects, inheritance, encapsulation, and polymorphism—provides a solid foundation for developing more complex and reusable code.

Chapter 3

Array Structures

This chapter delves into array structures, covering their definition, operations, and various types, including multidimensional arrays. It explores array slicing, sorting, and searching techniques, as well as the concept of dynamic arrays. Practical applications of arrays and considerations for performance optimization are also discussed, providing a comprehensive understanding of this fundamental data structure.

3.1 Introduction to Arrays

An array is a fundamental data structure in computer science, used to store a collection of elements, typically of the same type, in a contiguous block of memory. Each element in an array can be efficiently accessed using its index, which represents its position within the array. This direct access property makes arrays highly efficient for several operations, such as indexing, iterating, and modifying elements.

In Python, arrays can be implemented using built-in data structures such as lists and arrays from the array module. While Python lists are more flexible and can hold elements of any type, the array module provides a more efficient way to store homogeneous data.

```
# Creating a list in Python
list_example = [1, 2, 3, 4, 5]

# Creating an array in Python using the 'array' module
import array as arr
```

```
array_example = arr.array('i', [1, 2, 3, 4, 5])
```

In the above code snippet, 'i' denotes a signed integer type, ensuring all elements within array_example are integers. The choice between using a list and an array from the array module depends on the specific requirements of memory efficiency and type constraints.

Arrays are typically zero-indexed, meaning the first element of the array has an index of 0. This indexing mechanism is consistent across various programming languages, including Python. By utilizing indices, it is possible to access or modify specific elements directly.

```
# Accessing elements in a list
second_element = list_example[1]

# Modifying elements in a list
list_example[1] = 10

# Accessing elements in an array
second_element_array = array_example[1]

# Modifying elements in an array
array_example[1] = 10
```

Arrays support numerous operations such as appending elements, extending the array with another array, and removing elements. However, it is essential to understand the time complexity of these operations to utilize arrays optimally. Accessing an element by index takes constant time, $O(1)$, due to the direct access nature of arrays. Conversely, appending an element at the end of an array can be an $O(1)$ operation if there is sufficient space, but can degrade to $O(n)$ if the array needs to resize.

```
# Appending elements
list_example.append(6)
array_example.append(6)

# Extending the array with another array
list_example.extend([7, 8])
array_example.extend(arr.array('i', [7, 8]))

# Removing elements
list_example.remove(10)
array_example.remove(10)
```

When an array needs to resize, a new block of memory is allocated, and the existing elements are copied over. This operation is analogous in both lists and arrays. Consequently, frequent resizing can lead to inefficiencies, which is a crucial consideration in applications requiring high performance.

The concept of array slicing further enhances the flexibility of arrays. Slicing allows the creation of a subarray, or segment, from an existing array without copying the elements, thus providing a view into the array. Python supports slicing using a starting index, ending index, and a step value, which can be vital for various algorithms and data manipulation tasks.

```
# Slicing a list
sub_list = list_example[1:4] # elements from index 1 to 3

# Slicing an array
sub_array = array_example[1:4]
```

The utility of arrays is evident in their widespread application across different domains including scientific computing, real-time systems, and multimedia applications. The contiguous memory allocation of arrays ensures that they are cache-friendly, enabling fast access times and efficient memory usage.

Understanding the basic characteristics and operations of arrays lays a strong foundation for grasping more complex data structures and algorithms. Arrays not only serve as building blocks for other data structures such as lists, hash tables, and heaps but also play a critical role in optimizing performance in computational tasks. As we progress through this chapter, we will explore advanced topics such as dynamic arrays, array sorting, and searching, which further illustrate the versatility and efficiency of this fundamental data structure.

3.2 Array Operations

An array is a collection of elements identified by index or key. Array operations are fundamental to utilizing arrays effectively in Python and other programming languages. This section will explore various array operations, including accessing elements, updating elements, inserting elements, deleting elements, traversing arrays, and understanding array length.

Accessing elements in an array is performed using indices, which start from zero in Python. For instance, if we have an array arr and need to access the first element, we use $\mathrm{arr}[0]$. Access to any element is constant time, or $O(1)$, due to direct indexing.

```
arr = [10, 20, 30, 40, 50]
print(arr[0]) # Output: 10
print(arr[3]) # Output: 40
```

```
10
40
```

Updating elements involves assigning a new value to a specific index in the array. The time complexity for updating an element is also $O(1)$, indicating constant time operation.

```
arr[1] = 25
print(arr) # Output: [10, 25, 30, 40, 50]
```

```
[10, 25, 30, 40, 50]
```

Array insertion can be categorized into different types: inserting at the beginning, in the middle, or at the end. Inserting an element at the end, commonly known as appending, is a frequent operation and is $O(1)$ on average in dynamic arrays since they automatically resize. However, inserting at other positions involves shifting subsequent elements, which has a time complexity of $O(n)$.

```
arr.append(60)
print(arr) # Output: [10, 25, 30, 40, 50, 60]

arr.insert(2, 35)
print(arr) # Output: [10, 25, 35, 30, 40, 50, 60]
```

```
[10, 25, 30, 40, 50, 60]
[10, 25, 35, 30, 40, 50, 60]
```

Deleting elements can be done at any specified position. Similar to insertion, deleting an element requires shifting subsequent elements if the deletion occurs in the middle or beginning, with a time complexity of $O(n)$.

```
del arr[2]
print(arr) # Output: [10, 25, 30, 40, 50, 60]

arr.remove(50)
print(arr) # Output: [10, 25, 30, 40, 60]
```

```
[10, 25, 30, 40, 50, 60]
[10, 25, 30, 40, 60]
```

Traversing an array refers to accessing each element of the array for various operations such as printing or modifying elements. This operation typically has a time complexity of $O(n)$. Traversal can be implemented in many ways, including using a for loop.

```
for element in arr:
    print(element)
```

```
10
25
30
40
60
```

Determining the length of an array is essential for various operations, such as bounds checking and iteration. The length of an array can be retrieved using the len() function in Python, which operates in $O(1)$ time.

```
length = len(arr)
print(length) # Output: 5
```

```
5
```

The array operations discussed are intrinsically linked with many algorithms and data structures. For optimal performance, one must consider the underlying implementation and complexity of these operations. Understanding these operations paves the way for more advanced topics, such as sorting and searching, which heavily rely on array manipulation. This knowledge base is crucial for further exploration into more complex data structural concepts and their applications in software development.

3.3 Types of Arrays

Arrays are a fundamental data structure in computer science and are utilized in numerous applications due to their simplicity and efficiency in both space and time complexity. Different types of arrays are leveraged depending on the requirements of an algorithm or application. Understanding these types is essential to effectively address varying computational problems.

1. One-Dimensional Arrays

A one-dimensional array is the simplest form of array and can be visualized as a list of elements, each identified by a unique index. This type of array is linear, and elements are accessed using a single index. If declared and initialized in Python, a one-dimensional array can be created using a list:

```
one_d_array = [1, 2, 3, 4, 5]
```

In the above array, the element at index 0 is 1, at index 1 is 2, and so on.

2. Multidimensional Arrays

Multidimensional arrays are arrays of arrays. They can be of two or more dimensions, offering higher levels of data organization and access.

2.1. Two-Dimensional Arrays

A two-dimensional array is essentially a list of lists and can be visualized as a table with rows and columns:

```
two_d_array = [
    [1, 2, 3],
    [4, 5, 6],
    [7, 8, 9]
]
```

Here, the element at row 0, column 0 is 1, the element at row 1, column 2 is 6, and so forth.

2.2. Higher-Dimensional Arrays

Higher-dimensional arrays, such as three-dimensional arrays, extend this concept further. A three-dimensional array can be visualized as a cube of elements:

```
three_d_array = [
    [
        [1, 2],
        [3, 4]
    ],
    [
        [5, 6],
        [7, 8]
    ]
]
```

The indexing for these arrays follows a hierarchical nesting, and the element at index [1][1][0] is 7.

3. Dynamic Arrays

Dynamic arrays differ from static arrays in their ability to resize dynamically when elements are added or removed. They provide greater flexibility in data handling compared to standard arrays.

In Python, a dynamic array can be implemented using the built-in list structure, which automatically resizes as elements are appended or deleted:

```
dynamic_array = []
dynamic_array.append(1)
dynamic_array.append(2)
```

Here, the list starts empty and expands as elements are appended. The underlying implementation uses capacity doubling to manage dynamic growth efficiently.

4. Associative Arrays (Dictionaries)

In contrast to traditional arrays that use integer indices, associative arrays, or dictionaries, use key-value pairs for indexing. This allows for more versatile data retrieval and storage:

```
associative_array = {
    "name": "Alice",
    "age": 30,
    "city": "New York"
}
```

The above dictionary uses strings as keys. The value associated with the key "name" is "Alice", with the key "age" is 30, etc.

5. Sparse Arrays

Sparse arrays are specially designed to handle data that contains a majority of default values (typically zeroes). They store only non-default values along with their indices, optimizing the storage and management of large, sparse data sets. In Python, sparse arrays can be efficiently implemented using dictionaries:

```
sparse_array = {
    0: 1,
    50: 13,
    123: 5
}
```

In this example, the dictionary keys represent indices, and the values represent the non-zero values at those indices.

6. Jagged Arrays

Jagged arrays are multidimensional arrays where rows have different lengths, unlike traditional rectangular arrays where all rows maintain a uniform length. In Python, jagged arrays can be represented using lists with lists of varying lengths:

```
jagged_array = [
    [1, 2, 3],
    [4, 5],
    [6, 7, 8, 9]
]
```

Each sub-list can have a different number of elements, making it flexible in scenarios where data entries vary in size.

Various additional types of arrays exist to fit specific needs and optimize performance under different constraints. Understanding these types extensively allows for efficient and effective use of arrays in computing tasks, ensuring that the appropriate data structure is chosen based on the specific requirements of the application.

3.4 Multidimensional Arrays

Multidimensional arrays extend the concept of single-dimensional arrays to arrays of arrays, allowing for more complex data representation and manipulation. These structures are particularly useful in scientific computing, image processing, and any domain where data is naturally represented in multiple dimensions.

A **two-dimensional array**, the simplest form of a multidimensional array, can be visualized as a grid or a table, where data elements are arranged in rows and columns. Higher-dimensional arrays generalize this idea, stacking two-dimensional arrays along additional dimensions.

Declaration and Initialization

To declare and initialize multidimensional arrays in Python, we use nested lists. For example, a two-dimensional array A with 3 rows and 4 columns can be initialized as follows:

```
A = [
    [1, 2, 3, 4],
    [5, 6, 7, 8],
    [9, 10, 11, 12]
]
```

For larger dimensions or more complex initializations, Python's numpy library provides a more efficient and convenient interface:

```
import numpy as np

A = np.array([
    [1, 2, 3, 4],
    [5, 6, 7, 8],
    [9, 10, 11, 12]
])
```

Accessing Elements

Accessing elements in a multidimensional array requires specifying the indices for all dimensions. For example, to access the element in the 2nd row and 3rd column of array A, one would use the following syntax in standard list and numpy notation:

```
element = A[1][2] # Standard list
element_np = A[1, 2] # numpy array
```

This ability to precisely index each dimension is crucial for tasks such as matrix operations, applying transformations, or retrieving data subsets.

Iterating Over Elements

Iterating through a multidimensional array can be achieved with nested loops. For instance, iterating over all the elements of a two-dimensional array involves:

```
for row in A:
    for element in row:
        print(element)
```

For numpy arrays, leveraging numpy's built-in functions can enhance performance and readability:

```
np.apply_along_axis(print, 1, A)
```

Multidimensional Slicing

Multidimensional arrays support slicing operations to access subarrays. The syntax extends the one-dimensional slicing with comma-separated slices. For example, to obtain the first two rows and the last two columns of array A, one would use:

```
subarray = A[:2, -2:] # numpy array
```

Reshaping Arrays

The shape of a numpy array can be altered using the reshape method, which is particularly useful for data preparation and transformations. Reshaping does not alter the original data but provides a different way to index it:

```
reshaped_A = A.reshape((2, 6))
```

Here, the array A is reshaped from a 3x4 array to a 2x6 array. The total number of elements must remain constant.

Applications in Matrix Operations

Multidimensional arrays serve as the backbone for matrix operations in many scientific and engineering fields. Operations such as matrix addition, multiplication, and transposition are fundamental. numpy facilitates these operations efficiently:

```
import numpy as np

# Matrix addition
B = np.array([
    [13, 14, 15, 16],
    [17, 18, 19, 20],
    [21, 22, 23, 24]
])
result_add = np.add(A, B)

# Matrix multiplication
result_mul = np.dot(A, B.T)

# Transposition
result_transpose = A.T
```

These operations are optimized in numpy, ensuring high performance even for large datasets.

Higher-Dimensional Arrays

Building upon the concept of two-dimensional arrays, higher-dimensional arrays (3D, 4D, etc.) are often used in advanced applications such as volumetric data analysis and tensor operations. These arrays are naturally suited for complex data structures like RGB images (3D) or spatiotemporal data (4D).

For example, a three-dimensional array representing a bundle of 2D images (say, 5 images of 4x3 dimensions) can be initialized and manipulated as follows:

```
C = np.random.randint(0, 256, (5, 4, 3)) # 5 images of 4x3 resolution
```

Element access in such arrays still follows multidimensional indexing:

```
element_3d = C[2, 1, 0] # Element in 3rd image, 2nd row, 1st column
```

Practical Considerations

When working with multidimensional arrays, it is crucial to consider memory consumption and computational complexity. Multidimensional arrays, especially in higher dimensions, can quickly consume significant memory. Tools such as numpy provide efficient memory handling but understanding underlying data structures and efficient manipulation techniques remains essential for optimal performance.

3.5 Array Slicing

Array slicing is a powerful feature in Python that allows for extracting subsets of arrays. This operation involves specifying a range of indices to obtain a contiguous segment of the array. The practice of slicing arrays can be particularly useful for data manipulation, offering a flexible means to access and modify array elements.

In Python, array slicing is facilitated by the slicing operator, denoted by the colon (":"), and can be applied to one-dimensional and multidimensional arrays. The general syntax for slicing is:

```
array[start:stop:step]
```

Parameters:

- **start** - The index indicating where the slice starts. The element at this index is included in the slice.
- **stop** - The index indicating where the slice ends. The element at this index is not included in the slice.
- **step** - The interval between indices. By default, the step size is 1.

Examples of One-dimensional Array Slicing:

Consider a one-dimensional array of integers:

```
import numpy as np
arr = np.array([0, 1, 2, 3, 4, 5, 6, 7, 8, 9])
```

1. Extracting elements from index 2 to 5:

```
slice1 = arr[2:6]
print(slice1)
```

```
[2 3 4 5]
```

2. Extracting elements from the beginning to index 3:

```
slice2 = arr[:4]
print(slice2)
```

```
[0 1 2 3]
```

3. Extracting elements from index 5 to the end:

```
slice3 = arr[5:]
print(slice3)
```

```
[5 6 7 8 9]
```

4. Using a step size of 2:

```
slice4 = arr[1:9:2]
print(slice4)
```

```
[1 3 5 7]
```

Examples of Multidimensional Array Slicing:

Consider a two-dimensional array:

```
arr2d = np.array([[ 0, 1, 2, 3],
                  [ 4, 5, 6, 7],
                  [ 8, 9, 10, 11],
                  [12, 13, 14, 15]])
```

1. Extracting a sub-array:

```
sub_arr1 = arr2d[1:3, :2]
print(sub_arr1)
```

```
[[4 5]
 [8 9]]
```

2. Extracting all rows of the first two columns:

```
sub_arr2 = arr2d[:, :2]
print(sub_arr2)
```

```
[[ 0  1]
 [ 4  5]
 [ 8  9]
 [12 13]]
```

3. Extracting the last two rows and the last two columns:

```
sub_arr3 = arr2d[2:, 2:]
print(sub_arr3)
```

```
[[10 11]
 [14 15]]
```

4. Slicing with step size:

```
sub_arr4 = arr2d[::2, ::2]
print(sub_arr4)
```

```
[[ 0  2]
 [ 8 10]]
```

Negative Indexing: Slices can also include negative indices, which count from the end of the array. Negative indexing provides a concise way to access elements from the end of the array.

1. Extracting the last three elements:

```
slice5 = arr[-3:]
print(slice5)
```

```
[7 8 9]
```

2. Extracting elements except the last two:

```
slice6 = arr[:-2]
print(slice6)
```

```
[0 1 2 3 4 5 6 7]
```

Advanced Slicing Techniques:

Slicing can be combined with array manipulation functions to achieve more complex operations. One common technique is boolean slicing, where slices are created based on specified conditions.

1. Boolean Slicing:

```
bool_slice = arr[arr % 2 == 0]
print(bool_slice)
```

```
[0 2 4 6 8]
```

2. Conditional Slicing:

```
cond_slice = arr[(arr > 3) & (arr < 8)]
print(cond_slice)
```

```
[4 5 6 7]
```

Understanding how to effectively use array slicing is fundamental to working with arrays in Python. This deepens the capability to manage data efficiently, from simple sub-array extraction to advanced conditional data manipulations.

3.6 Array Sorting

Array sorting is a fundamental concept in computer science and is pivotal for organizing data efficiently. Sorting an array involves arranging its elements in a specific order, typically ascending or descending. Sorting algorithms vary in complexity and efficiency, and selecting the appropriate algorithm depends on factors such as the size of the array, the nature of the data, and the performance requirements.

Common Array Sorting Algorithms:

- **Bubble Sort:** This simple algorithm repeatedly steps through the list, compares adjacent elements, and swaps them if they are in the wrong order. Its simplicity comes at the cost of efficiency, as it has an average and worst-case complexity of $O(n^2)$.

- **Selection Sort:** This algorithm divides the array into a sorted and an unsorted part. It repeatedly selects the smallest (or largest, depending on the order) element from the unsorted part and moves it to the end of the sorted part. It also has a time complexity of $O(n^2)$.

- **Insertion Sort:** This algorithm builds the sorted array one element at a time, placing each new element in its correct position. While its average and worst-case complexity is $O(n^2)$, it is more efficient than bubble sort and selection sort for small data sets or nearly sorted arrays.

- **Merge Sort:** This divide-and-conquer algorithm splits the array into halves, recursively sorts each half, and then merges the sorted halves. It offers a significant improvement in efficiency with a time complexity of $O(n \log n)$.

- **Quick Sort:** Another divide-and-conquer algorithm, quick sort, selects a "pivot" element and partitions the array into sub-arrays, which are then sorted recursively. Its average-case complexity is $O(n \log n)$, but the worst case is $O(n^2)$ if the pivot selection is poor.

- **Heap Sort:** This comparison-based algorithm uses a binary heap data structure to sort the array. It has a time complexity of $O(n \log n)$.

Example Implementations:

Bubble Sort:

```
def bubble_sort(arr):
    n = len(arr)
    for i in range(n):
        for j in range(0, n-i-1):
            if arr[j] > arr[j+1]:
                arr[j], arr[j+1] = arr[j+1], arr[j]
    return arr

# Example Usage
array = [64, 34, 25, 12, 22, 11, 90]
sorted_array = bubble_sort(array)
print("Sorted array:", sorted_array)
```

Selection Sort:

```
def selection_sort(arr):
    n = len(arr)
    for i in range(n):
        min_idx = i
        for j in range(i+1, n):
            if arr[j] < arr[min_idx]:
                min_idx = j
        arr[i], arr[min_idx] = arr[min_idx], arr[i]
    return arr

# Example Usage
array = [64, 34, 25, 12, 22, 11, 90]
sorted_array = selection_sort(array)
print("Sorted array:", sorted_array)
```

Insertion Sort:

```
def insertion_sort(arr):
    n = len(arr)
    for i in range(1, n):
        key = arr[i]
        j = i - 1
        while j >= 0 and key < arr[j]:
            arr[j + 1] = arr[j]
            j -= 1
        arr[j + 1] = key
    return arr

# Example Usage
array = [64, 34, 25, 12, 22, 11, 90]
sorted_array = insertion_sort(array)
print("Sorted array:", sorted_array)
```

Merge Sort:

```
def merge_sort(arr):
    if len(arr) > 1:
        mid = len(arr)//2
        L = arr[:mid]
        R = arr[mid:]

        merge_sort(L)
        merge_sort(R)

        i = j = k = 0

        while i < len(L) and j < len(R):
            if L[i] < R[j]:
                arr[k] = L[i]
                i += 1
            else:
                arr[k] = R[j]
                j += 1
            k += 1

        while i < len(L):
            arr[k] = L[i]
            i += 1
            k += 1
```

```
        while j < len(R):
            arr[k] = R[j]
            j += 1
            k += 1
    return arr

# Example Usage
array = [64, 34, 25, 12, 22, 11, 90]
sorted_array = merge_sort(array)
print("Sorted array:", sorted_array)
```

Quick Sort:

```
def partition(arr, low, high):
    i = (low-1)
    pivot = arr[high]

    for j in range(low, high):
        if arr[j] <= pivot:
            i = i+1
            arr[i], arr[j] = arr[j], arr[i]

    arr[i+1], arr[high] = arr[high], arr[i+1]
    return (i+1)

def quick_sort(arr, low, high):
    if low < high:
        pi = partition(arr, low, high)
        quick_sort(arr, low, pi-1)
        quick_sort(arr, pi+1, high)
    return arr

# Example Usage
array = [64, 34, 25, 12, 22, 11, 90]
sorted_array = quick_sort(array, 0, len(array)-1)
print("Sorted array:", sorted_array)
```

Heap Sort:

```
def heapify(arr, n, i):
    largest = i
    l = 2 * i + 1
    r = 2 * i + 2

    if l < n and arr[i] < arr[l]:
        largest = l

    if r < n and arr[largest] < arr[r]:
        largest = r

    if largest != i:
        arr[i], arr[largest] = arr[largest], arr[i]
        heapify(arr, n, largest)

def heap_sort(arr):
    n = len(arr)

    for i in range(n//2 - 1, -1, -1):
        heapify(arr, n, i)
```

```
    for i in range(n-1, 0, -1):
        arr[i], arr[0] = arr[0], arr[i]
        heapify(arr, i, 0)
    return arr

# Example Usage
array = [64, 34, 25, 12, 22, 11, 90]
sorted_array = heap_sort(array)
print("Sorted array:", sorted_array)
```

The choice of sorting algorithm can significantly impact the performance of your programs, especially when working with large arrays or requiring high efficiency. The provided Python implementations exemplify the versatility and varied approach each algorithm offers. As a crucial concept in data structures and algorithms, mastering array sorting and understanding its nuances is essential for developing optimized and effective software solutions.

3.7 Array Searching

Array searching involves the process of finding the position of a specified element within an array. This is a fundamental operation in programming and is critical for tasks such as data retrieval, validation, and analysis. Two primary techniques for searching arrays are **linear search** and **binary search**, each with its unique characteristics and efficiency ratings.

Linear Search is the most basic form of searching. It works by iterating through each element of the array until the desired element is found or the end of the array is reached. While simple and straightforward, its time complexity is $O(n)$ where n is the number of elements in the array. Here is a Python implementation of linear search:

```
def linear_search(arr, x):
    for i in range(len(arr)):
        if arr[i] == x:
            return i
    return -1 # element not found
```

When executed, the function will return the index of the first occurrence of the element x in the array arr or -1 if the element is not present.

```
>>> linear_search([4, 2, 3, 1, 5], 3)
2
>>> linear_search([4, 2, 3, 1, 5], 6)
-1
```

Binary Search is a more efficient method for searching, but it requires the array to be sorted. The binary search algorithm divides the array into halves to reduce the search interval, making the time complexity $O(\log n)$. Below is a Python implementation of binary search:

```
def binary_search(arr, x):
    low = 0
    high = len(arr) - 1

    while low <= high:
        mid = (low + high) // 2
        if arr[mid] == x:
            return mid
        elif arr[mid] < x:
            low = mid + 1
        else:
            high = mid - 1
    return -1 # element not found
```

When executed, the function returns the index of the element x in the sorted array arr or -1 if the element is not found.

```
>>> binary_search([1, 2, 3, 4, 5], 3)
2
>>> binary_search([1, 2, 3, 4, 5], 6)
-1
```

Binary searching can also be implemented using recursion. Here is an alternative recursive approach for binary search:

```
def binary_search_recursive(arr, x, low, high):
    if low > high:
        return -1 # element not found

    mid = (low + high) // 2
    if arr[mid] == x:
        return mid
    elif arr[mid] < x:
        return binary_search_recursive(arr, x, mid + 1, high)
    else:
        return binary_search_recursive(arr, x, low, mid - 1)

# Example usage
arr = [1, 2, 3, 4, 5]
x = 3
result = binary_search_recursive(arr, x, 0, len(arr) - 1)
print(result)
```

The recursive version also efficiently narrows down the range by adjusting the low and high indices in each call.

Besides these traditional searching techniques, Python's built-in functions can be leveraged for array searches. The in keyword provides a simple and readable way to check for the presence of an element, and the index() method can retrieve the position of the first occurrence. However, these are typically implemented using linear search techniques.

```
arr = [4, 2, 3, 1, 5]

# Check existence
element_exists = 3 in arr

# Get index
index_of_element = arr.index(3) if element_exists else -1

print(element_exists) # Output: True
print(index_of_element) # Output: 2
```

For large datasets and frequent searches, more sophisticated data structures such as hash tables, binary search trees, or advanced algorithm techniques may be employed to optimize search operations. Understanding and choosing the appropriate array searching technique is crucial for efficient data handling and can significantly influence performance in computational tasks.

3.8 Dynamic Arrays

Dynamic arrays are a versatile and fundamental data structure that extend the capabilities of static arrays by allowing resizing and efficient insertion and deletion of elements. In this section, we will explore the underlying mechanisms, implementation details, and performance characteristics of dynamic arrays. Additionally, we will consider the implications of using dynamic arrays in various computational contexts.

A dynamic array, also known as a resizable array, is an array that can automatically resize itself when elements are added or removed. Contrary to static arrays, which have a fixed size determined at the time of their creation, dynamic arrays can grow or shrink as needed. This flexibility makes dynamic arrays particularly useful for situations where the size of the dataset is not known beforehand.

The core operation that distinguishes dynamic arrays from static arrays is resizing. The dynamic array maintains a logical size—representing the number of elements it currently holds—and a capacity—representing the total number of elements it can accommodate without resizing. When the logical size exceeds the capacity, the array must be resized to accommodate new elements. Typically, this resizing involves allocating a new array with larger capacity and copying the existing elements to the new array.

To illustrate the concept of a dynamic array, we can implement a basic version in Python using a list. Here is a simple example demonstrating how to build a dynamic array class:

```
class DynamicArray:
    def __init__(self):
        self.capacity = 1
        self.size = 0
        self.array = self.make_array(self.capacity)

    def __len__(self):
        return self.size

    def __getitem__(self, k):
        if not 0 <= k < self.size:
            raise IndexError('index out of bounds')
        return self.array[k]

    def append(self, item):
        if self.size == self.capacity:
            self._resize(2 * self.capacity)
        self.array[self.size] = item
        self.size += 1

    def _resize(self, new_capacity):
        new_array = self.make_array(new_capacity)
        for k in range(self.size):
            new_array[k] = self.array[k]
        self.array = new_array
        self.capacity = new_capacity

    @staticmethod
    def make_array(capacity):
        return (capacity * ctypes.py_object)()
```

The above example shows a simplified implementation of a dynamic array. The constructor initializes the capacity to 1 and the size to 0, creating an array with one element space. The append method adds a new item to the array, resizing it if necessary by doubling its capacity using the _resize method. The _resize method creates a new array with twice the capacity, copies all elements from the old array, and then replaces the old array with the new one.

The amortized time complexity for the append operation in a dynamic array is $O(1)$. This means that while individual resizes may be expensive—taking $O(n)$ time for n elements—the average cost per append operation remains constant over a sequence of operations because resizing happens logarithmically with respect to the number of append operations.

Dynamic arrays also support other operations such as insertion and deletion at arbitrary positions. The following code demonstrates how to implement these additional capabilities:

```
class DynamicArray(DynamicArray):
```

```
def insert(self, k, item):
    if self.size == self.capacity:
        self._resize(2 * self.capacity)
    for i in range(self.size, k, -1):
        self.array[i] = self.array[i-1]
    self.array[k] = item
    self.size += 1

def delete(self, k):
    if not 0 <= k < self.size:
        raise IndexError('index out of bounds')
    for i in range(k, self.size - 1):
        self.array[i] = self.array[i + 1]
    self.array[self.size - 1] = None
    self.size -= 1
    if self.size > 0 and self.size == self.capacity // 4:
        self._resize(self.capacity // 2)
```

The insert method inserts an element at a specified index, shifting subsequent elements to the right to make room. The delete method removes an element at a specified index, shifting subsequent elements to the left to fill the gap. After deletion, if the size of the array drops to one-fourth of its capacity, the array is resized down to half its capacity to save space.

Dynamic arrays provide a wide range of applications by allowing efficient random access and modification. Their ability to dynamically adjust capacity while maintaining reasonable performance guarantees makes them suitable for many scenarios in coding and algorithm design. The refinement of implementing such structures correctly has profound implications for performance optimization in numerous practical applications.

3.9 Applications of Arrays

Arrays are among the most fundamental and ubiquitous data structures in computer science. They provide a mechanism to store and manipulate a collection of data elements, all of the same type, in a contiguous block of memory. Arrays find utility in numerous applications, extending from simple data storage tasks to complex algorithmic implementations in various domains. Understanding these applications allows for leveraging arrays effectively in problem-solving and software development.

Arrays are extensively used in implementing mathematical data structures such as matrices and tensors. These structures are pivotal in fields like linear algebra, numerical analysis, and machine learning. For instance, matrices, which are two-dimensional arrays, enable operations such as matrix multiplication, determinant calculation, and matrix inversion, fundamental in solving systems of linear equations and transformations in graphics.

In computer graphics, arrays are employed to represent images, where each element in the array corresponds to a pixel's color value. For example, a grayscale image can be stored in a two-dimensional array where each element holds an intensity value. For colored images, three-dimensional arrays are used to store the red, green, and blue (RGB) components of each pixel.

```
import numpy as np

# Assume grayscale image of size 256 x 256
image = np.zeros((256, 256))

# Example of setting a pixel value at position (10, 10)
image[10, 10] = 255
```

Text processing and manipulation are other areas where arrays play a critical role. Strings, which are essentially sequences of characters, can be viewed as arrays of characters. Various operations such as searching, sorting, and pattern matching (e.g., the Knuth-Morris-Pratt algorithm) utilize arrays for efficient implementation.

```
# Example of storing and manipulating a string in an array
text = "Hello, World!"
char_array = list(text)

# Modify the first character
char_array[0] = 'h'

new_text = ''.join(char_array)
print(new_text) # Output: "hello, World!"
```

Dynamic arrays, such as Python lists, are pivotal in the implementation of data structures like stacks and queues. They allow for flexible and efficient addition and removal of elements. Stacks, which follow Last-In-First-Out (LIFO) order, and queues, which follow First-In-First-Out (FIFO) order, are fundamental in algorithmic processes such as depth-first search (DFS) and breadth-first search (BFS) in graph theory.

Sorting algorithms, including quicksort and mergesort, utilize arrays as the underlying data structure for their operations. The efficiency of these algorithms, driven by the array's random access capability, highlights arrays' indispensable role in sorting large datasets.

```
def quicksort(arr):
    if len(arr) <= 1:
        return arr
    pivot = arr[len(arr) // 2]
```

```
    left = [x for x in arr if x < pivot]
    middle = [x for x in arr if x == pivot]
    right = [x for x in arr if x > pivot]
    return quicksort(left) + middle + quicksort(right)

# Example usage
array = [3, 6, 8, 10, 1, 2, 1]
print(quicksort(array))
```

In the domain of databases, arrays can be used to efficiently store and access records. Relational databases often utilize arrays for indexing and query optimization, improving search and retrieval operations. Arrays also support multi-key indexing and composite keys of database systems, ensuring efficient data management.

Computational simulations and scientific computations frequently leverage arrays for tasks such as finite element analysis, particle simulations, and climate modeling. These simulations require handling large datasets and performing numerous operations on these datasets, for which arrays provide an efficient and straightforward approach.

Game development is another area where arrays are crucial. Arrays are often used to create and manage game states, including the representation of game boards, handling of sprites, and storage of game world data. For example, in grid-based games like chess or tic-tac-toe, a two-dimensional array can be used to store the game state, with each element representing a cell on the board.

```
# Initial empty chess board
chess_board = [[''] * 8 for _ in range(8)]

# Placing pieces on the board
chess_board[0][0] = 'R' # Rook
chess_board[0][1] = 'N' # Knight
chess_board[0][2] = 'B' # Bishop
```

Arrays also facilitate the implementation of hash tables, where arrays are used to store the hash table entries. The simplicity of array indexing combined with hashing functions provides efficient solutions for managing associative data, widely utilized in applications requiring constant-time complexity for insertions, deletions, and lookups.

Arrays are foundational to many computational problems spanning various fields, including scientific computing, graphics, text processing, and algorithm implementation. Their ability to provide efficient storage, fast access times, and ease of implementation underscores their continued relevance and utility in both academic and industrial applications.

3.10 Performance Considerations

When working with array structures, performance is a crucial aspect that deserves thorough consideration. The efficiency of array operations, memory usage, and execution time are all vital factors that can significantly impact the overall performance of an application. This section will delve into the elements that influence the performance of arrays in Python and provide practices and principles to optimize their usage.

One of the primary factors affecting array performance is the **Time Complexity** of operations performed on arrays. Time complexity, denoted using Big O notation, provides an approximation of the number of operations an algorithm performs relative to the size of the input data. For arrays, common operations include accessing elements, inserting and deleting elements, and searching for values.

Accessing Elements: For a static array, accessing an element by its index is an $O(1)$ operation. This constant time complexity is a significant advantage of arrays, as it allows for fast retrieval of values.

```
# Accessing an element in an array
arr = [1, 2, 3, 4, 5]
element = arr[2] # O(1) operation
```

Inserting Elements: Inserting an element at the beginning or middle of an array requires shifting subsequent elements to the right, resulting in an $O(n)$ operation. Inserting an element at the end, however, is typically an $O(1)$ operation, assuming the array has enough allocated space.

```
# Inserting an element to an array
arr.insert(2, 10) # O(n) operation
arr.append(6) # O(1) operation if space is available
```

Deleting Elements: Like insertion, deleting an element from the beginning or middle of an array requires shifting of elements to the left, leading to an $O(n)$ time complexity. Deleting the last element is an $O(1)$ operation.

```
# Deleting an element from an array
arr.pop(2) # O(n) operation
arr.pop() # O(1) operation
```

Searching for Elements: In the worst case, searching for an element in an unsorted array is an $O(n)$ operation since it may require scanning the entire array.

```
# Searching for an element in an array
found = 4 in arr # O(n) operation
```

The **Space Complexity** is another critical factor, representing the amount of memory required by the array. Arrays generally have $O(n)$ space complexity, meaning the memory usage grows linearly with the number of elements. Python's built-in lists, which are dynamic arrays, occasionally need to resize when appending new elements, potentially doubling their capacity to accommodate future growth.

Despite their straightforward nature, arrays can incur significant overhead if not managed correctly. Memory allocation for arrays can become a bottleneck, especially when dealing with large data volumes or frequent resizing operations. **Dynamic Arrays**, as implemented in Python lists, handle this by allocating extra space to minimize the number of resizes, balancing between time and space efficiencies.

```
# Dynamic array resizing in Python
arr = []
for i in range(1000):
    arr.append(i) # Underlying array may resize multiple times
```

Cache Locality plays a pivotal role in performance, particularly in modern computer architectures. Arrays benefit from excellent cache locality because their elements are stored contiguously in memory. This means that when accessing an element, nearby elements are also loaded into the cache, facilitating faster data access. Improving cache locality involves ensuring that the elements likely to be accessed together are physically close in memory.

Optimizing **Multidimensional Arrays** involves understanding memory layout patterns. For example, a common practice is to store a two-dimensional array in a row-major order or column-major order. An operation that repeatedly accesses consecutive memory locations (i.e., iterates over rows or columns) will benefit from better cache performance.

```
# Accessing elements to leverage cache locality
matrix = [[0] * 1000 for _ in range(1000)]
for row in matrix:
    for col in row:
        pass # More efficient row-wise access
```

In computational tasks, sometimes the choice between using a simple array and a more complex data structure depends on the specific operations and their expected frequency. For instance, if frequent insertions and deletions are necessary, linked lists or other data structures might be more performant despite higher space overheads.

Lastly, **Python's Global Interpreter Lock (GIL)** can affect the performance of array operations in multi-threaded environments. The GIL allows only one thread to execute in the Python interpreter at any given time, leading to potential performance bottlenecks in CPU-bound operations. Parallelizing array operations using libraries like NumPy can circumvent this limitation, as they utilize native C extensions that release the GIL.

Understanding these aspects and carefully selecting the appropriate approaches and algorithms can significantly impact the performance of array operations in Python applications.

Chapter 4

Linked Lists

This chapter explores linked lists, starting with their basic concepts and progressing through singly, doubly, and circular linked lists. It details fundamental operations such as insertion, deletion, traversal, and searching. The chapter also examines practical applications, performance considerations, and comparisons with arrays, providing a thorough understanding of these versatile data structures.

4.1 Introduction to Linked Lists

Linked lists are a fundamental data structure in computer science, characterized by a collection of elements called nodes. Each node contains two fields: one to store data, and another to store a reference (or a pointer) to the next node in the sequence. Unlike arrays, which use contiguous memory allocation, linked lists use dynamic memory allocation and store elements non-contiguously. This flexibility allows for efficient insertions and deletions but can introduce complexity in memory management and traversal operations.

The primary advantage of linked lists over arrays is their ability to dynamically resize, which facilitates efficient memory utilization. While arrays have a fixed size, requiring the declaration of an array with a predefined capacity, linked lists can grow and shrink in size as elements are added or removed. This behavior is particularly useful in scenarios where the number of elements is unpredictable or varies significantly during runtime.

To begin understanding linked lists, consider a simple node structure in Python. This node forms the building block of a linked list.

```
class Node:
    def __init__(self, data=None):
        self.data = data
        self.next = None
```

In this implementation, the Node class contains a constructor that initializes the data field to store the value of the node and the next field to store the reference to the next node in the list. As a result, each node in the linked list points to the subsequent node, creating a chain-like structure.

A linked list can be visualized as follows:

Figure 4.1: Simple visualization of a linked list with three nodes.

In the illustration above, each node consists of two parts: the **Data** part that stores the value and the **Next** part that stores the reference to the next node. The last node's **Next** reference points to NULL, signifying the end of the linked list.

The essential operations performed on linked lists include traversal, insertion, deletion, and searching. Traversal involves visiting each node in the list, starting from the head node and moving through subsequent nodes using the next references. Consider a basic traversal operation in Python:

```
class LinkedList:
    def __init__(self):
        self.head = None

    def traverse(self):
        current = self.head
        while current:
            print(current.data, end=" -> ")
            current = current.next
        print("NULL")
```

Here, the LinkedList class includes a traverse method that starts from the head node and iterates through each node using the next reference. This method prints the data stored in each node, depicting the structure of the linked list.

Insertion operations in linked lists depend on the position where the new node is to be inserted. The primary scenarios include insertion at the beginning, at the end, or at a specified position in the list. The following examples demonstrate these insertion operations:

```
class LinkedList:
    def __init__(self):
        self.head = None

    def insert_at_beginning(self, data):
        new_node = Node(data)
        new_node.next = self.head
        self.head = new_node

    def insert_at_end(self, data):
        new_node = Node(data)
        if not self.head:
            self.head = new_node
            return
        last = self.head
        while last.next:
            last = last.next
        last.next = new_node

    def insert_at_position(self, data, position):
        new_node = Node(data)
        if position == 0:
            new_node.next = self.head
            self.head = new_node
            return
        current = self.head
        for _ in range(position - 1):
            current = current.next
            if not current:
                raise IndexError("Position out of bounds")
        new_node.next = current.next
        current.next = new_node
```

The insert_at_beginning method creates a new node and updates its next reference to point to the current head of the list. The head is then updated to the new node. The insert_at_end method traverses the list to find the last node and updates the next reference of the last node to point to the new node. The insert_at_position method inserts the new node at a specified position, adjusting the next references accordingly.

Deletion operations in linked lists can be similarly categorized based on the node's position: at the beginning, at the end, or at a specific position. The following examples illustrate these deletion methods:

```
class LinkedList:
    def __init__(self):
        self.head = None

    def delete_at_beginning(self):
        if not self.head:
            return
        self.head = self.head.next
```

```
def delete_at_end(self):
    if not self.head:
        return
    if not self.head.next:
        self.head = None
        return
    second_last = self.head
    while second_last.next.next:
        second_last = second_last.next
    second_last.next = None

def delete_at_position(self, position):
    if not self.head:
        return
    if position == 0:
        self.head = self.head.next
        return
    current = self.head
    for _ in range(position - 1):
        current = current.next
        if not current.next:
            raise IndexError("Position out of bounds")
    current.next = current.next.next
```

The delete_at_beginning method removes the head node by updating the head reference to point to the next node. The delete_at_end method traverses the list to find the second last node, then sets its next reference to NULL, thus removing the last node. The delete_at_position method removes the node at a specified position by adjusting the next references accordingly.

Searching for elements in a linked list involves traversing the list and examining each node's data to check for a match. If a match is found, the search operation returns the position of the node (or simply confirms the presence of the data), otherwise, it concludes that the element is not present. Consider the following example:

```
class LinkedList:
    def __init__(self):
        self.head = None

    def search(self, key):
        current = self.head
        position = 0
        while current:
            if current.data == key:
                return position
            current = current.next
            position += 1
        return -1 # Element not found
```

The search method iterates through the list, comparing each node's data with the search key. If a match is found, it returns the position of the node; otherwise, it returns -1 to indicate that the element is not found in the list.

The linked list data structure showcases its strengths in scenarios requiring dynamic memory management, frequent insertions and deletions, and non-contiguous storage of elements. Understanding the basic concepts and operations of linked lists forms the foundation for advanced topics like doubly and circular linked lists, as well as practical applications ranging from memory management to implementation of abstract data types like stacks, queues, and more.

4.2 Singly Linked Lists

A singly linked list is a fundamental data structure in computer science, consisting of a sequence of elements where each element points to the next element in the sequence. Each element in the list is called a node. A node comprises two parts: the data it holds and a reference (or pointer) to the next node in the sequence. The list terminates in a node that points to null, indicating the end of the list.

To implement a singly linked list in Python, we first define a class for the nodes. Each node contains the data and a pointer to the next node. Here is an example implementation:

```
class Node:
    def __init__(self, data=None):
        self.data = data
        self.next = None
```

In this Node class, the __init__ method initializes the data to the provided value and the next pointer to None.

Next, we define the linked list class, which manages the nodes. The linked list class includes methods to insert, delete, and traverse the list:

```
class SinglyLinkedList:
    def __init__(self):
        self.head = None
```

In this SinglyLinkedList class, the __init__ method initializes the head of the list to None, indicating that the list is initially empty.

Inserting a new node at the beginning of the list is a common operation. Here is how you can implement it:

```
def insert_at_beginning(self, data):
    new_node = Node(data)
    new_node.next = self.head
    self.head = new_node
```

In this method, a new node is created with the specified data. The new node's next pointer is set to the current head of the list, and then the head is updated to the new node.

To insert a new node at the end of the list, we need to traverse the list to find the last node and then append the new node:

```
def insert_at_end(self, data):
    new_node = Node(data)
    if not self.head:
        self.head = new_node
        return
    last = self.head
    while last.next:
        last = last.next
    last.next = new_node
```

In this method, if the list is empty (i.e., self.head is None), the new node becomes the head. Otherwise, the method traverses the list to find the last node and sets its next pointer to the new node.

Deleting a node from the list requires finding the node and adjusting the pointers appropriately. Here's how to delete a node by value:

```
def delete_node(self, key):
    temp = self.head

    if temp is not None:
        if temp.data == key:
            self.head = temp.next
            temp = None
            return

    while temp is not None:
        if temp.data == key:
            break
        prev = temp
        temp = temp.next

    if temp == None:
        return

    prev.next = temp.next
    temp = None
```

In this deletion method, the list is traversed to find the node with the specified key. If the node is found, the previous node's next pointer is updated to skip the node being deleted.

Traversal of the list means visiting each node and performing an operation. For example, printing all the list elements can be done as follows:

```
def print_list(self):
```

```
    temp = self.head
    while temp:
        print(temp.data, end=' ')
        temp = temp.next
    print()
```

In this print_list method, the list is traversed from the head to the end, printing each node's data. The end=' ' parameter in the print function helps to print all node values in a single line separated by space.

Searching for an element in a singly linked list involves traversing the nodes and checking the data of each node against the target value:

```
def search(self, key):
    current = self.head
    while current:
        if current.data == key:
            return True
        current = current.next
    return False
```

This search method checks each node's data to see if it matches the key. If it finds the key, it returns True; if it reaches the end of the list without finding the key, it returns False.

Hence, singly linked lists provide a flexible and dynamic way to manage collections of data, with efficient insertions and deletions. Understanding their structure and operations is critical for leveraging their advantages in varied computational problems.

4.3 Doubly Linked Lists

A doubly linked list is a type of linked list in which each node contains a reference to both the next node and the previous node. This bidirectional linkage allows for more flexible manipulation of the list, including traversal in both forward and backward directions. The structure of a node in a doubly linked list is typically defined with three components: the data, a reference to the next node, and a reference to the previous node.

Node Structure: In Python, a node for a doubly linked list can be represented using a class. Below is a simple implementation:

```
class Node:
    def __init__(self, data):
        self.data = data
        self.next = None
        self.prev = None
```

Doubly Linked List Structure: The doubly linked list itself can be managed using another class, which maintains references to the head and tail of the list. Here is an implementation of a basic doubly linked list:

```
class DoublyLinkedList:
    def __init__(self):
        self.head = None
        self.tail = None

    def append(self, data):
        new_node = Node(data)
        if self.head is None:
            self.head = new_node
            self.tail = new_node
        else:
            self.tail.next = new_node
            new_node.prev = self.tail
            self.tail = new_node
```

In the append method, we check if the list is empty. If it is, the new node becomes both the head and the tail of the list. If the list is not empty, the new node is added at the end, and the pointers are updated to maintain the doubly linked nature.

Traversal: Traversing a doubly linked list can be done in both forward and backward directions. Forward traversal starts from the head node and follows the next pointers, while backward traversal starts from the tail node and follows the prev pointers.

Forward Traversal:

```
def traverse_forward(self):
    current = self.head
    while current:
        print(current.data)
        current = current.next
```

Backward Traversal:

```
def traverse_backward(self):
    current = self.tail
    while current:
        print(current.data)
        current = current.prev
```

Insertion: Insertion in a doubly linked list can occur at several positions, such as at the beginning, at the end, or at a specific position.

Insertion at the Beginning:

```
def insert_at_beginning(self, data):
    new_node = Node(data)
    if self.head is None:
        self.head = new_node
        self.tail = new_node
```

```
    else:
        new_node.next = self.head
        self.head.prev = new_node
        self.head = new_node
```

Insertion at a Specific Position:

```
def insert_at_position(self, data, position):
    if position <= 0:
        return
    new_node = Node(data)
    current = self.head
    for _ in range(position - 1):
        if current is None:
            return
        current = current.next
    if current is None:
        return
    new_node.next = current.next
    new_node.prev = current
    if current.next:
        current.next.prev = new_node
    current.next = new_node
```

Deletion: Deletion operations in a doubly linked list can also be performed at the beginning, at the end, or at a specific position.

Deletion at the Beginning:

```
def delete_from_beginning(self):
    if self.head is None:
        return
    if self.head == self.tail:
        self.head = None
        self.tail = None
    else:
        self.head = self.head.next
        self.head.prev = None
```

Deletion at a Specific Position:

```
def delete_at_position(self, position):
    if position <= 0 or self.head is None:
        return
    current = self.head
    for _ in range(position - 1):
        if current is None:
            return
        current = current.next
    if current is None or current.next is None:
        return
    if current.next == self.tail:
        self.tail = current
        self.tail.next = None
    else:
        current.next = current.next.next
        if current.next:
            current.next.prev = current
```

Practical Considerations: Doubly linked lists provide greater flexibility in terms of traversal and can be more efficient for certain types of operations, such as bidirectional iteration. However, this flexibility comes at the cost of increased memory usage due to the additional pointers maintained in each node.

Understanding the trade-offs between different types of linked lists, including singly and doubly linked lists, is crucial for choosing the appropriate data structure for your specific application requirements.

4.4 Circular Linked Lists

A circular linked list is a subtype of linked list where all the nodes are connected to form a circle. Unlike a singly or doubly linked list, where the last node points to NULL, in a circular linked list, the last node contains a link to the first node. This creates a circular structure, ideal for scenarios where the data must be processed in a cyclic manner.

Definition: A circular linked list is a variation of the linear linked list where the last element points to the first element, thus forming a loop.

Node Structure: Each node in a circular linked list contains two fields:

- data: Holds the value or information of the node.
- next: Holds the reference to the next node in the list.

A diagrammatic representation of a circular linked list is as follows:

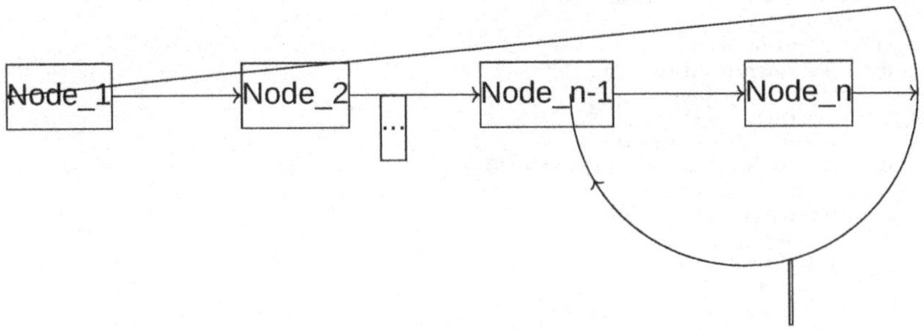

Advantages:

- Efficient memory use by avoiding end markers.
- Useful for implementing queues or buffers where circular processing is necessary.
- Facilitates the traversal from any node through every other node.

Disadvantages:

- Complexity in implementation due to the circular nature.
- Potential risk of infinite loops if the list is unsafely traversed.

Basic Operations:

- **Insertion**: Add a new node either at the start, in the middle, or at the end of the list.
- **Deletion**: Remove a specified node from the list.
- **Traversal**: Navigate through all nodes starting from any node.
- **Searching**: Locate a specific element within the list.

Implementation:

Insertion at the Beginning

To insert a new node at the start of a circular linked list, follow these steps:

1. Allocate memory for the new node.
2. Set the new node's next to point to the current head node.
3. Traverse to the last node and set its next to the new node.
4. Update the head to the new node.

```
class Node:
    def __init__(self, data):
        self.data = data
        self.next = None

class CircularLinkedList:
    def __init__(self):
        self.head = None

    def insert_at_beginning(self, data):
        new_node = Node(data)
```

```
    temp = self.head

    new_node.next = self.head

    if self.head is not None:
        while temp.next != self.head:
            temp = temp.next
        temp.next = new_node
    else:
        new_node.next = new_node # For the first node

    self.head = new_node
```

Insertion at the End

To insert a new node at the end of a circular linked list:

1. Allocate memory for the new node and set the new node's next to the head node.
2. If the list is empty, set the head to reference the new node, and set the new node's next to itself.
3. Otherwise, traverse to the last node and set its next to reference the new node.

```
def insert_at_end(self, data):
    new_node = Node(data)
    temp = self.head

    new_node.next = self.head

    if self.head is not None:
        while temp.next != self.head:
            temp = temp.next
        temp.next = new_node
    else:
        self.head = new_node
        new_node.next = new_node # For the first node
```

Traversal

To traverse a circular linked list starting from the head:

1. Initialize a temporary pointer to reference the head.
2. Loop through each node until the starting node is reached again.

```
def traverse(self):
    nodes = []
    temp = self.head
    if self.head is not None:
        while True:
            nodes.append(temp.data)
```

```
            temp = temp.next
            if temp == self.head:
                break
    return nodes
```

Deletion

To delete a node from a circular linked list:

1. Traverse to the node preceding the node to be deleted.
2. Update the next link of the preceding node to skip the node to be deleted.
3. If the node to be deleted is the head, update the head reference.
4. Free the memory occupied by the node to be deleted.

```
def delete_node(self, key):
    if self.head is None:
        return

    temp = self.head
    prev = None

    while True:
        if temp.data == key:
            if prev is not None:
                prev.next = temp.next
            else:
                if temp.next == self.head:
                    self.head = None
                else:
                    prev = self.head
                    while prev.next != temp:
                        prev = prev.next
                    prev.next = self.head = temp.next
            break
        else:
            prev = temp
            temp = temp.next
            if temp == self.head:
                break
```

Use Cases: Circular linked lists are particularly useful in applications that require a cyclic process:

- Implementing circular queues.
- Managing the CPU scheduling in operating systems.
- Buffer management in streaming applications.

A detailed understanding of these operations and their correct implementation is critical for leveraging the full potential of circular linked lists.

4.5 Basic Operations on Linked Lists

Linked lists are fundamental data structures that allow dynamic memory allocation and efficient insertions and deletions. Understanding and implementing the basic operations on linked lists is crucial for developing more complex data structures and algorithms. This section covers the core operations: insertion, deletion, traversal, and searching. Each operation will be discussed in the context of singly linked lists, with pertinent code examples in Python to illustrate their implementation.

Insertion: Insertion in a linked list can be performed in multiple ways: at the beginning, at the end, or at a specific position. Efficient handling of pointers is required to maintain the structure's integrity.

```
class Node:
    def __init__(self, data):
        self.data = data
        self.next = None

class LinkedList:
    def __init__(self):
        self.head = None

    def insert_at_beginning(self, new_data):
        new_node = Node(new_data)
        new_node.next = self.head
        self.head = new_node

    def print_list(self):
        temp = self.head
        while(temp):
            print(temp.data, end=" -> ")
            temp = temp.next
        print("None")

# Example usage:
llist = LinkedList()
llist.insert_at_beginning(10)
llist.insert_at_beginning(20)
llist.print_list()
```

```
Output:
20 -> 10 -> None
```

```
def insert_at_end(self, new_data):
    new_node = Node(new_data)
    if self.head is None:
        self.head = new_node
        return
```

```
    last = self.head
    while(last.next):
        last = last.next
    last.next = new_node

# Example usage:
llist.insert_at_end(30)
llist.print_list()
```

Output:
20 -> 10 -> 30 -> None

```
def insert_at_position(self, position, new_data):
    if position < 0:
        raise ValueError(”Position cannot be negative”)
    new_node = Node(new_data)
    if position == 0:
        new_node.next = self.head
        self.head = new_node
        return
    temp = self.head
    for _ in range(position - 1):
        if temp is None:
            raise IndexError(”Position out of bounds”)
        temp = temp.next
    new_node.next = temp.next
    temp.next = new_node

# Example usage:
llist.insert_at_position(1, 40)
llist.print_list()
```

Output:
20 -> 40 -> 10 -> 30 -> None

Deletion: Deletion involves removing a node from the linked list and adjusting the pointers appropriately. Similar to insertion, deletion can occur at the beginning, at the end, or at a specific position.

```
def delete_at_beginning(self):
    if self.head is None:
        return
    self.head = self.head.next

# Example usage:
llist.delete_at_beginning()
llist.print_list()
```

Output:
40 -> 10 -> 30 -> None

```
def delete_at_end(self):
    if self.head is None:
        return
    if self.head.next is None:
        self.head = None
        return
    temp = self.head
    while(temp.next.next):
        temp = temp.next
```

```
        temp.next = None

# Example usage:
llist.delete_at_end()
llist.print_list()
```

Output:
40 -> 10 -> None

```
def delete_at_position(self, position):
    if self.head is None:
        raise IndexError("Position out of bounds")
    if position < 0:
        raise ValueError("Position cannot be negative")
    if position == 0:
        self.head = self.head.next
        return
    temp = self.head
    for _ in range(position - 1):
        if temp.next is None:
            raise IndexError("Position out of bounds")
        temp = temp.next
    temp.next = temp.next.next

# Example usage:
llist.delete_at_position(1)
llist.print_list()
```

Output:
40 -> None

Traversal: Traversal involves visiting each node in the linked list from the head to the last node, performing actions such as printing the node's data.

```
def traverse(self):
    temp = self.head
    while temp:
        print(temp.data, end=" -> ")
        temp = temp.next
    print("None")

# Example usage:
llist.traverse()
```

Output:
40 -> None

Searching: Searching for an element in the linked list involves traversing through the list and comparing each node's data with the target value.

```
def search(self, key):
    temp = self.head
    while temp:
        if temp.data == key:
            return True
        temp = temp.next
```

```
    return False

# Example usage:
found = llist.search(40)
print("Element found?" , found)
```

```
Output:
Element found? True
```

Mastering the basic operations on linked lists is essential for constructing more advanced data structures. The ability to insert, delete, traverse, and search in a linked list provides a solid foundation for further exploration and efficient manipulation of data.

4.6 Insertion in Linked Lists

Insertion in linked lists is a fundamental operation that allows the addition of elements at any position within the list: beginning, end, or in-between two nodes. Understanding how to efficiently add elements to a linked list is crucial for utilizing the data structure effectively.

1. Inserting at the Beginning

Inserting a node at the beginning of a linked list is a straightforward process that involves updating the head pointer to point to the new node. The new node's next pointer should then point to the current head node. Here is a Python implementation for a singly linked list:

```
class Node:
    def __init__(self, data):
        self.data = data
        self.next = None

class LinkedList:
    def __init__(self):
        self.head = None

    def insert_at_beginning(self, new_data):
        new_node = Node(new_data)
        new_node.next = self.head
        self.head = new_node
```

To insert a node at the beginning of a doubly linked list, update both the previous pointer of the current head and the next pointer of the new node:

```
class Node:
    def __init__(self, data):
        self.data = data
        self.next = None
        self.prev = None
```

```
class DoublyLinkedList:
    def __init__(self):
        self.head = None

    def insert_at_beginning(self, new_data):
        new_node = Node(new_data)
        new_node.next = self.head
        if self.head is not None:
            self.head.prev = new_node
        self.head = new_node
```

2. Inserting at the End

Inserting a node at the end of a linked list requires traversal to the last node and updating its next pointer to the new node. Here is the implementation for a singly linked list:

```
class LinkedList:
    # Previous code omitted for brevity

    def insert_at_end(self, new_data):
        new_node = Node(new_data)
        if self.head is None:
            self.head = new_node
            return
        last = self.head
        while last.next:
            last = last.next
        last.next = new_node
```

For a doubly linked list, update the previous pointer of the new node and the next pointer of the last node:

```
class DoublyLinkedList:
    # Previous code omitted for brevity

    def insert_at_end(self, new_data):
        new_node = Node(new_data)
        if self.head is None:
            self.head = new_node
            return
        last = self.head
        while last.next:
            last = last.next
        last.next = new_node
        new_node.prev = last
```

3. Inserting After a Given Node

Inserting a node after a specific node involves adjusting the next pointers so that the new node is linked into the list. Here is the code for a singly linked list:

```
class LinkedList:
    # Previous code omitted for brevity
```

```
    def insert_after_node(self, prev_node, new_data):
        if not prev_node:
            print("The given previous node must be in the linked list.")
            return
        new_node = Node(new_data)
        new_node.next = prev_node.next
        prev_node.next = new_node
```

For a doubly linked list, both the next and previous pointers of adjacent nodes need adjustment:

```
class DoublyLinkedList:
    # Previous code omitted for brevity

    def insert_after_node(self, prev_node, new_data):
        if not prev_node:
            print("The given previous node must be in the linked list.")
            return
        new_node = Node(new_data)
        new_node.next = prev_node.next
        prev_node.next = new_node
        new_node.prev = prev_node
        if new_node.next:
            new_node.next.prev = new_node
```

4. Inserting Before a Given Node

In this case, the traversal is necessary to find the node preceding the given node, then adjusting the next pointers. The implementation for a singly linked list is as follows:

```
class LinkedList:
    # Previous code omitted for brevity

    def insert_before_node(self, next_node, new_data):
        if not self.head or not next_node:
            print("The given next node must be in the linked list.")
            return
        if self.head == next_node:
            return self.insert_at_beginning(new_data)
        new_node = Node(new_data)
        current = self.head
        while current.next and current.next != next_node:
            current = current.next
        if not current.next:
            print("The given next node is not in the linked list.")
            return
        new_node.next = current.next
        current.next = new_node
```

Inserting before a node in a doubly linked list involves simpler logic as each node includes a reference to its predecessor:

```
class DoublyLinkedList:
    # Previous code omitted for brevity

    def insert_before_node(self, next_node, new_data):
        if not self.head or not next_node:
```

```
        print("The given next node must be in the linked list.")
        return
    if self.head == next_node:
        return self.insert_at_beginning(new_data)
    new_node = Node(new_data)
    new_node.next = next_node
    new_node.prev = next_node.prev
    if next_node.prev:
        next_node.prev.next = new_node
    next_node.prev = new_node
```

Insertion operations across singly and doubly linked lists require careful pointer management to maintain the integrity of the list. Accurate traversal and pointer adjustments are fundamental to accomplishing these tasks efficiently.

4.7 Deletion in Linked Lists

Deletion in linked lists involves removing a node from the data structure while ensuring the structural integrity and continuity of the list. This operation can be categorized into three main types: deleting from the beginning, deleting from the end, and deleting from a specific position. Each of these categories will be explained below with explicit handling of singly, doubly, and circular linked lists.

Singly Linked Lists

In a singly linked list, each node contains a data value and a reference to the next node in the sequence. When performing deletions, it is important to update these references appropriately to maintain the list's integrity.

* **Deleting from the Beginning:**

To delete the head node, the head reference needs to be updated to point to the next node.

```
class Node:
    def __init__(self, data):
        self.data = data
        self.next = None

class SinglyLinkedList:
    def __init__(self):
        self.head = None

    def delete_from_beginning(self):
        if self.head is not None:
            self.head = self.head.next
```

* **Deleting from the End:**

When deleting the last node, it is necessary to traverse the list to find the second last node and set its next reference to 'None'.

```
def delete_from_end(self):
    if self.head is None:
        return None
    if self.head.next is None:
        self.head = None
        return None

    second_last = self.head
    while(second_last.next.next):
        second_last = second_last.next

    second_last.next = None
```

* **Deleting from a Specific Position:**

Deleting a node from a specific position involves traversing the list to the node just before the target and updating its next reference.

```
def delete_at_position(self, position):
    if self.head is None:
        return None

    temp = self.head

    if position == 0:
        self.head = temp.next
        return None

    for i in range(position - 1):
        temp = temp.next
        if temp is None:
            break

    if temp is None or temp.next is None:
        return None

    next = temp.next.next
    temp.next = None
    temp.next = next
```

Doubly Linked Lists

In doubly linked lists, each node contains a reference to both the next and the previous node. This bidirectional reference requires additional steps when handling deletions.

* **Deleting from the Beginning:**

The head reference must be updated, and if the list is not empty after deletion, the new head's previous reference must be set to 'None'.

```
class DNode:
    def __init__(self, data):
```

```
        self.data = data
        self.next = None
        self.prev = None

class DoublyLinkedList:
    def __init__(self):
        self.head = None

    def delete_from_beginning(self):
        if self.head is not None:
            self.head = self.head.next
            if self.head is not None:
                self.head.prev = None
```

* **Deleting from the End:**

For deletion at the end, traverse to the last node, update the second last node's next reference, and set the previous reference of the removed node to 'None'.

```
def delete_from_end(self):
    if self.head is None:
        return None

    if self.head.next is None:
        self.head = None
        return None

    last = self.head
    while(last.next is not None):
        last = last.next

    last.prev.next = None
    last.prev = None
```

* **Deleting from a Specific Position:**

Identify the node at the specified position, adjust the previous and next references of neighboring nodes accordingly, and then remove the target node.

```
def delete_at_position(self, position):
    if self.head is None or position <= 0:
        return None

    current = self.head
    for i in range(position - 1):
        if current is None:
            return None
        current = current.next

    if current is None or current.next is None:
        return None

    if current.next.next is not None:
        current.next.next.prev = current

    current.next = current.next.next
```

Circular Linked Lists

Circular linked lists differ as the last node points back to the head node, creating a circular structure. This characteristic alters how certain deletions are implemented.

* **Deleting from the Beginning:**

Adjust the head reference to the next node, ensure the last node points to the new head to maintain the circle.

```
class CNode:
    def __init__(self, data):
        self.data = data
        self.next = None

class CircularLinkedList:
    def __init__(self):
        self.head = None

    def delete_from_beginning(self):
        if self.head is None:
            return None

        if self.head.next == self.head:
            self.head = None
            return None

        last = self.head
        while(last.next != self.head):
            last = last.next

        self.head = self.head.next
        last.next = self.head
```

* **Deleting from the End:**

To remove the last node, traverse the list to find the second last node and set its next reference to the head node.

```
    def delete_from_end(self):
        if self.head is None:
            return None

        if self.head.next == self.head:
            self.head = None
            return None

        last = self.head
        while(last.next.next != self.head):
            last = last.next

        last.next = self.head
```

* **Deleting from a Specific Position:**

Navigate to the node at the desired position, then re-link the neighboring nodes to exclude the target node.

```
    def delete_at_position(self, position):
        if self.head is None or position < 0:
            return None

        if position == 0:
            self.delete_from_beginning()
            return None

        current = self.head
        for i in range(position - 1):
            current = current.next
            if current.next == self.head:
                return None

        current.next = current.next.next
        current.next.prev = current
```

Understanding deletion in linked lists is crucial for efficient manipulation and management of these data structures. The algorithms presented here ensure accurate and reliable deletions across various types of linked lists, preserving their respective properties and maintaining data integrity.

4.8 Traversal in Linked Lists

Traversal in linked lists is a fundamental operation that allows visiting each node in the list in a sequential manner. This operation is crucial for performing various tasks such as searching for an element, printing the list elements, or applying a given operation to each element in the list. In this section, we will examine the traversal process for singly linked lists, doubly linked lists, and circular linked lists, elucidating the traversal mechanism, algorithm, and implementation for each type.

For a singly linked list, traversal begins at the head of the list and proceeds to the end by following the links between nodes. Below is a Python implementation of the traversal algorithm for a singly linked list.

```
class Node:
    def __init__(self, data):
        self.data = data
        self.next = None

class SinglyLinkedList:
    def __init__(self):
        self.head = None

    def traverse(self):
        current = self.head
        while current:
            print(current.data)
            current = current.next
```

The traversal method starts with the head node and iterates through the list using a loop. In each iteration, it prints the data of the current node and then moves to the next node by updating the current pointer. When the current pointer becomes None, the end of the list is reached, and the loop terminates.

Traversing a doubly linked list requires handling both forward and backward pointers. This traversal can be implemented to move in either direction. Below is an implementation for traversing a doubly linked list in both forward and backward directions.

```
class Node:
    def __init__(self, data):
        self.data = data
        self.next = None
        self.prev = None

class DoublyLinkedList:
    def __init__(self):
        self.head = None

    def traverse_forward(self):
        current = self.head
        while current:
            print(current.data)
            current = current.next

    def traverse_backward(self):
        current = self.head
        if current is None:
            return
        while current.next:
            current = current.next
        while current:
            print(current.data)
            current = current.prev
```

Traversing in the forward direction is similar to the singly linked list, but each node also includes a prev pointer. The backward traversal starts by reaching the last node and then iterating backward using the prev pointers.

For circular linked lists, the traversal can continue indefinitely unless explicitly stopped. Therefore, care must be taken to avoid infinite loops. Here is an implementation for traversing a circular singly linked list.

```
class Node:
    def __init__(self, data):
        self.data = data
        self.next = None

class CircularLinkedList:
    def __init__(self):
```

```
        self.head = None

    def traverse(self):
        if not self.head:
            return
        current = self.head
        while True:
            print(current.data)
            current = current.next
            if current == self.head:
                break
```

In a circular linked list, the traverse method starts at the head node and continues to print each node's data. The loop condition checks whether the current node has cycled back to the head node to terminate the traversal, thus avoiding an infinite loop.

The concept of traversal is essential across these different types of linked lists whether the goal is to print node values, search for a specific value, or apply an operation on the node's data. The time complexity of the traversal operation in all types of linked lists is $\mathcal{O}(n)$, where n is the number of nodes in the list, since each node is visited exactly once.

Understanding linked list traversal prepares us for more complex operations like insertion, deletion, and searching, which often involve traversal as a preliminary step. It ensures that each node is visited methodically, facilitating accurate and efficient data manipulation.

4.9 Searching in Linked Lists

Searching in linked lists is a fundamental operation that enables retrieval of elements based on their values. This capability is crucial for many applications requiring data lookup and manipulation. In this section, we shall delve into the methodologies applied for searching within different types of linked lists: singly, doubly, and circular. We will illustrate each technique with corresponding Python code to elucidate the practical implementation.

To search for an element in a linked list, the algorithm typically traverses the list until it finds the target or reaches the end. This linear search method is common across all linked list types due to their sequential access nature.

Consider a singly linked list, wherein each node contains data and a reference to the next node.

The Python class structure for a singly linked list node might be defined as follows:

```
class Node:
    def __init__(self, data):
        self.data = data
        self.next = None
```

Likewise, the linked list class initializes an empty list:

```
class SinglyLinkedList:
    def __init__(self):
        self.head = None
```

The linear search function in a singly linked list is implemented by iterating through each node and comparing the node's data with the search key. If a match is found, the position or node reference is returned; otherwise, the traversal continues until the end of the list is reached.

```
def search(self, key):
    current = self.head
    while current is not None:
        if current.data == key:
            return current
        current = current.next
    return None
```

For a doubly linked list, the concept remains the same, but each node contains references to both the next and previous nodes. The node structure for a doubly linked list extends the principle:

```
class Node:
    def __init__(self, data):
        self.data = data
        self.next = None
        self.prev = None
```

The doubly linked list class can be initialized similarly:

```
class DoublyLinkedList:
    def __init__(self):
        self.head = None
```

The search operation in a doubly linked list iterates through the nodes similarly to a singly linked list:

```
def search(self, key):
    current = self.head
    while current is not None:
        if current.data == key:
            return current
        current = current.next
    return None
```

Next, examining the search method in a circular linked list, where the last node points back to the first node, creates a loop. This variant requires careful traversal to avoid infinite loops. The node structure and initial setup are consistent with singly linked lists, with an additional check in the search method to break the cycle.

```
class Node:
    def __init__(self, data):
        self.data = data
        self.next = None

class CircularLinkedList:
    def __init__(self):
        self.head = None

def search(self, key):
    if self.head is None:
        return None
    current = self.head
    while True:
        if current.data == key:
            return current
        current = current.next
        if current == self.head:
            break
    return None
```

The provided implementations are straightforward but important for handling these operations reliably. The runtime complexity of the search operation in all types of linked lists is $O(n)$ because it potentially examines each node once. This linear complexity is due to the sequential access nature of linked lists, which, unlike arrays, do not support direct access to elements.

Given their structural differences, the process of searching in a doubly linked list doesn't decrease in complexity but may offer advantages in bidirectional traversal, especially in scenarios where searching backward might be required. Although circular linked lists introduce additional considerations, the fundamental linear search method applies, ensuring comprehensiveness across list variants.

These implementations provide a methodical approach to element search within linked lists, laying the groundwork for more complex operations and optimizations within this versatile data structure.

4.10 Applications of Linked Lists

Linked lists provide versatile and powerful structures adaptable to a myriad of applications. Beyond their standalone functionality, they serve as foundational constructs in more complex data structures and algorithms, facilitating efficient management and manipulation of data.

Dynamic Memory Allocation:

In dynamic memory allocation, linked lists are pivotal. Memory allocation in systems often requires efficient handling of free and used memory blocks. A free list, a type of singly linked list, keeps track of all the available memory blocks. When an allocation request is made, the allocator traverses this list to find a suitable block, splits it if necessary, and adjusts the list accordingly. Upon deallocation, the memory block is reinserted into the free list. This technique minimizes fragmentation and optimizes memory usage without requiring contiguous memory blocks.

Implementing Stacks and Queues:

Stacks and queues can be implemented efficiently using linked lists.

Stacks: A stack can be implemented using a singly linked list where all insertions and deletions occur at the head of the list, ensuring efficient $\mathcal{O}(1)$ operations for both push and pop.

```
class Node:
    def __init__(self, data):
        self.data = data
        self.next = None

class Stack:
    def __init__(self):
        self.head = None

    def push(self, data):
        new_node = Node(data)
        new_node.next = self.head
        self.head = new_node

    def pop(self):
        if self.head is None:
            return None
        data = self.head.data
        self.head = self.head.next
        return data
```

Queues: A queue, in contrast, operates through a singly linked list where insertions (enqueue) occur at the tail, and deletions (dequeue) occur at the head. This ensures $\mathcal{O}(1)$ operations for both enqueue and dequeue.

```
class Node:
    def __init__(self, data):
        self.data = data
        self.next = None

class Queue:
    def __init__(self):
```

```
        self.head = None
        self.tail = None

    def enqueue(self, data):
        new_node = Node(data)
        if self.tail:
            self.tail.next = new_node
        self.tail = new_node
        if self.head is None:
            self.head = self.tail

    def dequeue(self):
        if self.head is None:
            return None
        data = self.head.data
        self.head = self.head.next
        if self.head is None:
            self.tail = None
        return data
```

Graph Representations:

Linked lists, specifically adjacency lists, are crucial for representing graphs. An adjacency list for each vertex is a linked list that stores all the vertices adjacent to the given vertex. This representation is memory efficient, particularly for sparse graphs, where edges are significantly fewer than the total possible edges.

```
class AdjNode:
    def __init__(self, data):
        self.vertex = data
        self.next = None

class Graph:
    def __init__(self, vertices):
        self.V = vertices
        self.graph = [None] * self.V

    def add_edge(self, src, dest):
        node = AdjNode(dest)
        node.next = self.graph[src]
        self.graph[src] = node

        node = AdjNode(src)
        node.next = self.graph[dest]
        self.graph[dest] = node
```

Polynomial Arithmetic:

In polynomial arithmetic, linked lists are used to store coefficients and exponents. Each node typically represents a term of the polynomial, where the coefficient and exponent are encapsulated in the node's structure. Operations like addition and multiplication of polynomials become straightforward by traversing and manipulating these lists.

```
class PolyNode:
```

```
    def __init__(self, coeff, exp):
        self.coeff = coeff
        self.exp = exp
        self.next = None

class Polynomial:
    def __init__(self):
        self.head = None

    def add_term(self, coeff, exp):
        new_node = PolyNode(coeff, exp)
        if self.head is None:
            self.head = new_node
            return
        current = self.head
        while current.next:
            current = current.next
        current.next = new_node
```

Undo Functionality in Applications:

Many applications, such as text editors, implement an undo feature using linked lists. Each change is stored in a node, forming a list that represents the sequence of actions. Reversing the change involves traversing this list and rolling back the actions.

Hash Tables:

In hash tables, linked lists manage collisions through chaining. Each bucket of the hash table is a linked list storing all elements that hash to the same index. This method ensures that the hash table can dynamically handle numerous collisions efficiently.

```
class HashNode:
    def __init__(self, key, value):
        self.key = key
        self.value = value
        self.next = None

class HashTable:
    def __init__(self):
        self.size = 10
        self.table = [None] * self.size

    def hash_function(self, key):
        return hash(key) % self.size

    def insert(self, key, value):
        hash_index = self.hash_function(key)
        new_node = HashNode(key, value)
        if not self.table[hash_index]:
            self.table[hash_index] = new_node
        else:
            current = self.table[hash_index]
            while current.next and current.key != key:
                current = current.next
            if current.key == key:
                current.value = value
```

```
        else:
            current.next = new_node
```

These examples delineate the essential roles linked lists play in various computational problems and system designs, demonstrating their adaptability and integral presence in advanced data structures and algorithms.

4.11 Comparison of Linked Lists and Arrays

The comparison of linked lists and arrays is essential for understanding the appropriate contexts in which to employ each data structure. This section will delve into various aspects such as memory allocation, access time, insertion and deletion operations, and overall efficiency.

Memory Allocation: Arrays and linked lists utilize memory in fundamentally different ways. Arrays leverage contiguous memory blocks to store elements, which facilitates rapid access but can lead to problems such as memory fragmentation and inefficiency when dealing with dynamic datasets. When an array is defined, a single block of memory of a fixed size is allocated. If the size of the array is underestimated, there might be a need to resize, which generally involves creating a new array and copying the elements, a computationally expensive process.

Linked lists, on the other hand, utilize non-contiguous memory allocation. Each element, or node, in a linked list is dynamically allocated and points to the next element through a reference (or pointer). This allows for efficient use of memory when the number of elements changes dynamically. No resizing is necessary, and memory allocation is managed at the node level.

- **Arrays:** Contiguous memory allocation.
- **Linked Lists:** Non-contiguous memory allocation.

Access Time: The manner in which elements are accessed differs significantly between arrays and linked lists. Arrays offer constant time complexity, $O(1)$, for accessing elements via their index. Due to the contiguous memory allocation, the location of any element can be directly computed knowing the starting address and the index.

Conversely, linked lists do not offer direct element access, leading to a linear time complexity, $O(n)$, for accessing elements. Accessing an element in a linked list requires traversal from the head of the list to the desired node, which can be inefficient, especially in long lists.

- **Arrays:** $O(1)$ access time.
- **Linked Lists:** $O(n)$ access time.

Insertion and Deletion Operations: Operations for inserting and deleting elements vary markedly in arrays and linked lists.

In an array, insertion and deletion can involve shifting elements to maintain order, leading to $O(n)$ time complexity. For instance, inserting an element at the beginning or removing an element from the middle necessitates shifting subsequent elements to manage the free space.

```
# Example of inserting an element in an array
def insert(arr, index, value):
    if index >= len(arr):
        return arr + [value]
    else:
        return arr[:index] + [value] + arr[index:]

arr = [1, 2, 3]
arr = insert(arr, 1, 4) # [1, 4, 2, 3]
```

Linked lists provide more efficient insertions and deletions, especially when positions are known. Both operations can be done in $O(1)$ time if adjustments are made directly to the node references. This flexibility makes linked lists ideal for scenarios where the data structure undergoes frequent modifications.

```
class Node:
    def __init__(self, data):
        self.data = data
        self.next = None

# Function to insert a new node at the beginning
def insert(head, data):
    new_node = Node(data)
    new_node.next = head
    head = new_node
    return head

# Initial Linked List: 1 -> 2 -> 3
head = Node(1)
second = Node(2)
third = Node(3)
head.next = second
second.next = third

# Inserting new element
head = insert(head, 4) # 4 -> 1 -> 2 -> 3
```

- **Arrays:** $O(n)$ insertion/deletion due to shifting.
- **Linked Lists:** $O(1)$ insertion/deletion with direct reference adjustments.

Dynamic Sizing: Arrays have a fixed size, necessitating manual resizing if the dataset exceeds predefined bounds. This can lead to performance overheads due to frequent allocations and data copying.

Linked lists natively support dynamic sizing, allocating nodes as needed without the need for predefined bounds. This feature makes linked lists suitable for applications with unpredictable or highly variable data sizes.

- **Arrays:** Fixed size, requiring resizing.
- **Linked Lists:** Dynamic size, no need for resizing.

Memory Overhead: Although linked lists excel in dynamic memory management, they incur additional memory overhead due to the storage of pointers/references in each node. This overhead can be significant, especially in memory-constrained environments or when the data size is small relative to the pointer size.

Arrays, with their contiguous memory structure, avoid such overhead, making them more memory-efficient for large datasets needing random access.

- **Arrays:** Lower memory overhead.
- **Linked Lists:** Higher memory overhead due to pointers/references.

Cache Friendliness: Arrays benefit from spatial locality, meaning consecutive elements are stored in proximity. This property enhances cache performance, leading to faster data retrieval and operations.

Linked lists, by contrast, lack spatial locality due to non-contiguous allocation, potentially leading to poorer cache performance and increased access times. This difference is crucial in high-performance applications where cache efficiency is paramount.

- **Arrays:** Better cache performance.

- **Linked Lists:** Poorer cache performance.

Understanding these distinctions is pivotal for making informed decisions on data structure selection, ensuring optimal performance and resource utilization in varying computational scenarios.

Chapter 5

Stacks and Queues

This chapter provides an in-depth examination of stacks and queues, beginning with their definitions and operations. It includes implementations in Python and explores various types of queues. The chapter highlights practical applications of both data structures and compares their performance and use cases, offering a comprehensive overview of these fundamental concepts.

5.1 Introduction to Stacks

A **stack** is a linear data structure that adheres to the Last In, First Out (LIFO) principle. In a stack, the element added last is the one to be removed first. This characteristic makes stacks particularly useful in scenarios where data needs to be stored and retrieved in reverse order from which it was added.

The fundamental operations associated with a stack are:

- **Push**: Adds an element to the top of the stack.
- **Pop**: Removes the element from the top of the stack.
- **Peek** (or **Top**): Returns the top element of the stack without removing it.
- **isEmpty**: Checks whether the stack is empty.
- **Size**: Returns the number of elements in the stack.

These operations allow for efficient management of data with constant time complexity, O(1), making stacks optimal for applications requiring such access patterns.

To illustrate the behavior of stack operations, consider the following abstract representation:

```
Initial Stack (Empty): []
Push(1): [1]
Push(2): [1, 2]
Push(3): [1, 2, 3]
Peek(): 3
Pop(): 3 => [1, 2]
Pop(): 2 => [1]
```

Push adds 1, then 2, and then 3 to the stack. The **Peek** operation then retrieves the top element (3), and subsequent **Pop** operations remove the elements from the top one by one.

Python, like other high-level programming languages, provides a simple way to implement a stack using its built-in list type. Lists in Python come with method implementations that directly support stack operations: append() for push, pop() for pop, and indexing for peek.

Here is a basic example of a stack implementation in Python:

```
class Stack:
    def __init__(self):
        self.items = []

    def is_empty(self):
        return len(self.items) == 0

    def push(self, item):
        self.items.append(item)

    def pop(self):
        if self.is_empty():
            raise IndexError("pop from empty stack")
        return self.items.pop()

    def peek(self):
        if self.is_empty():
            raise IndexError("peek from empty stack")
        return self.items[-1]

    def size(self):
        return len(self.items)
```

In this implementation, we define a class Stack with the necessary methods to perform stack operations. The is_empty method checks if the stack is empty, push adds an item to the stack, pop removes the top item, peek retrieves the top item without removing it, and size returns the number of items in the stack.

This stack class can be instantiated and utilized as follows:

```
stack = Stack()
stack.push(1)
stack.push(2)
stack.push(3)
print(stack.peek()) # Output: 3
print(stack.pop()) # Output: 3
print(stack.size()) # Output: 2
```

The output would be:

```
3
3
2
```

The LIFO principle that stacks adhere to is particularly useful in various computer science applications. For instance:

- **Function Call Management**: In most programming languages, function calls are managed using a call stack to keep track of active subroutines. When a function is called, its execution context is pushed onto the stack. When the function completes, the context is popped from the stack.
- **Expression Evaluation**: Stacks are used in the evaluation and parsing of expressions, particularly in the conversion of infix expressions to postfix expressions and their subsequent evaluation.
- **Backtracking Algorithms**: Stacks facilitate algorithms that involve exploring possible solutions and backtracking upon hitting a dead end, such as depth-first search (DFS) in graph traversal.
- **Undo Mechanism**: Many software applications use stacks to implement undo functionality, where the most recent action can be undone by popping from the stack of actions.

In addition to these, stacks are a fundamental part of many other data structures and algorithms, contributing to optimal and efficient solutions to complex problems. Their simplicity and efficiency make them indispensable in both theoretical and practical aspects of computing.

5.2 Stack Operations

Stacks are abstract data types that follow the Last In, First Out (LIFO) principle. Several fundamental operations can be performed on stacks, each essential for effective manipulation of stack data. The primary stack operations to be discussed include push, pop, peek (or top), isEmpty, and size.

Push Operation

The push operation adds an element to the top of the stack. Since stacks are LIFO, the element added is always appended at the highest available position in the stack. The time complexity of a push operation is O(1), as it involves inserting the element at a fixed position. Below is a Python implementation of the push operation:

```
class Stack:
    def __init__(self):
        self.items = []

    def push(self, item):
        self.items.append(item)
```

When using the push method, it appends the specified item to the end of the items list representing the stack.

Pop Operation

The pop operation removes and returns the top element from the stack. This operation also has a time complexity of O(1), as it involves accessing and removing the element from the list's end. The following Python code illustrates the pop operation:

```
class Stack:
    def __init__(self):
        self.items = []

    def push(self, item):
        self.items.append(item)

    def pop(self):
        if not self.is_empty():
            return self.items.pop()
        raise IndexError("pop from empty stack")
```

The pop method first checks if the stack is empty to avoid an IndexError, then uses the list's pop function to remove and return the last item.

Peek (Top) Operation

The peek operation returns the top element of the stack without removing it, providing insight into the stack's current state. The time complexity of peek is O(1), as it involves a single element access. Here is an implementation of the peek operation:

```
class Stack:
    def __init__(self):
        self.items = []
```

```
    def push(self, item):
        self.items.append(item)

    def pop(self):
        if not self.is_empty():
            return self.items.pop()
        raise IndexError("pop from empty stack")

    def peek(self):
        if not self.is_empty():
            return self.items[-1]
        raise IndexError("peek from empty stack")
```

The peek method checks if the stack is empty and returns the last item using index -1 to access the top element.

is_Empty Operation

The is_empty operation checks whether the stack contains any elements, returning True if the stack is empty and False otherwise. The time complexity is O(1). Below is the corresponding implementation:

```
class Stack:
    def __init__(self):
        self.items = []

    def is_empty(self):
        return len(self.items) == 0
```

The is_empty method evaluates whether the number of elements in the items list is zero.

Size Operation

The size operation returns the number of elements currently stored in the stack. It also operates in constant time, O(1). Example implementation:

```
class Stack:
    def __init__(self):
        self.items = []

    def size(self):
        return len(self.items)
```

By leveraging the len function on the items list, the size method efficiently computes the current stack size.

To clarify the execution of these operations, consider the following code demonstrating a series of stack manipulations:

```
s = Stack()
s.push(1) # Stack: [1]
s.push(2) # Stack: [1, 2]
s.push(3) # Stack: [1, 2, 3]
print(s.pop()) # Output: 3, Stack: [1, 2]
```

```
print(s.peek())# Output: 2, Stack: [1, 2]
print(s.is_empty()) # Output: False
print(s.size()) # Output: 2
```

```
3
2
False
2
```

This example stack creation and manipulation illustrate the push, pop, peek, is_empty, and size operations comprehensively. The stack's state evolves with each operation, reflecting the characteristic LIFO behavior and providing practical experience with stack operations in Python.

5.3 Stack Implementation in Python

A stack is a linear data structure that follows the Last In, First Out (LIFO) principle. In Python, a stack can be implemented using various methods, including lists and the deque module from the collections library. We will explore these implementations using Python code and detailed explanations.

```
class Stack:
    def __init__(self):
        self.stack = []

    def is_empty(self):
        return len(self.stack) == 0

    def push(self, item):
        self.stack.append(item)

    def pop(self):
        if self.is_empty():
            raise IndexError("Pop from empty stack")
        return self.stack.pop()

    def peek(self):
        if self.is_empty():
            raise IndexError("Peek from empty stack")
        return self.stack[-1]

    def size(self):
        return len(self.stack)
```

In the above implementation, the Stack class encapsulates stack behaviors using a list as the underlying storage. The methods provided are as follows:

- __init__: Initializes an empty stack.

- is_empty: Returns True if the stack is empty, False otherwise.
- push: Appends an item to the top of the stack.
- pop: Removes and returns the top item of the stack. Raises an IndexError if the stack is empty.
- peek: Returns the top item of the stack without removing it. Raises an IndexError if the stack is empty.
- size: Returns the number of items in the stack.

Next, we consider an implementation using the deque module from the collections library. The deque (double-ended queue) provides an efficient stack implementation.

```
from collections import deque

class StackDeque:
    def __init__(self):
        self.stack = deque()

    def is_empty(self):
        return len(self.stack) == 0

    def push(self, item):
        self.stack.append(item)

    def pop(self):
        if self.is_empty():
            raise IndexError("Pop from empty stack")
        return self.stack.pop()

    def peek(self):
        if self.is_empty():
            raise IndexError("Peek from empty stack")
        return self.stack[-1]

    def size(self):
        return len(self.stack)
```

In this implementation, the StackDeque class utilizes the deque collection. The methods align with those from the previous list-based implementation:

- __init__: Initializes an empty deque.
- is_empty: Checks if the deque is empty and returns a boolean.
- push: Adds an item to the end of the deque.
- pop: Removes and returns the last item of the deque. Errors if the deque is empty.

- peek: Provides a view of the last item in the deque without removal.
- size: Returns the length of the deque.

```
Example Usage of Stack (List-Based):
>>> stack = Stack()
>>> stack.push(1)
>>> stack.push(2)
>>> stack.peek()
2
>>> stack.pop()
2
>>> stack.is_empty()
False
>>> stack.size()
1

Example Usage of StackDeque (deque-Based):
>>> stack_deque = StackDeque()
>>> stack_deque.push(1)
>>> stack_deque.push(2)
>>> stack_deque.peek()
2
>>> stack_deque.pop()
2
>>> stack_deque.is_empty()
False
>>> stack_deque.size()
1
```

While both implementations are effective, the deque offers more efficient append and pop operations from both ends, making it a generally preferable choice for stack operations. The choice between a list-based and deque-based implementation can depend on specific application requirements and performance considerations.

5.4 Applications of Stacks

Stacks are utilized in a variety of computational contexts owing to their Last-In-First-Out (LIFO) property. This behavior is particularly advantageous in scenarios where the most recent item needs to be accessed first. Below are some key applications of stacks, described in detail.

- **Function Call Management:** Stacks play a crucial role in managing function calls in programming languages. When a function is invoked, its execution context (such as local variables, return address, etc.) is pushed onto a call stack. Upon completion of the function, the context is popped from the stack, ensuring that the control returns to the proper location in the program. This mechanism is vital in supporting recursive function calls, where each call must maintain its execution context independently from others.

```
def factorial(n):
    if n == 0:
        return 1
    else:
        return n * factorial(n-1)
```

In the above code, each call to factorial results in a new stack frame being pushed onto the call stack, preserving the state of the computation until the base case is reached.

- **Expression Evaluation:** Stacks are widely used in the evaluation of arithmetic expressions, particularly converting Infix expressions (human readable) to Postfix expressions (which machines can evaluate more easily). The Shunting Yard algorithm by Edsger Dijkstra is a classical method that uses a stack to achieve this conversion.

```
def infix_to_postfix(expression):
    precedence = {'+':1, '-':1, '*':2, '/':2, '^':3}
    stack = []
    output = ''
    for char in expression:
        if char.isnumeric():
            output += char
        elif char in precedence:
            while (stack and precedence.get(char, 0) <= precedence.get(stack[-1],
                0)):
                output += stack.pop()
            stack.append(char)
    while stack:
        output += stack.pop()
    return output
```

This algorithm ensures that the operators are placed in the correct order using a stack.

- **Syntax Parsing:** In the parsing phase of compilers, stacks are instrumental in checking balanced parentheses in expressions and code blocks. When encountering an opening parenthesis, it is pushed onto the stack. A closing parenthesis requires a matching opening parenthesis to be popped from the stack.

```
def is_balanced(expression):
    stack = []
    for char in expression:
        if char in "([{":
            stack.append(char)
        elif char in ")]}":
```

```
        if not stack:
            return False
        top = stack.pop()
        if not matches(top, char):
            return False
    return not stack

def matches(opening, closing):
    openings = "([{"
    closings = ")]}"
    return openings.index(opening) == closings.index(closing)
```

This function ensures that every opening parenthesis corresponds to a closing one in the correct order, validating the syntax of the expression.

- **Undo Mechanisms:** Many applications, such as text editors, implement undo mechanisms by maintaining actions in a stack. When an operation is performed, it is pushed onto the undo stack. To undo an operation, it is popped from the stack, and an opposite action is executed (which might be pushed onto a redo stack).

```
class TextEditor:
    def __init__(self):
        self.text = ""
        self.undo_stack = []

    def write(self, char):
        self.text += char
        self.undo_stack.append(char)

    def undo(self):
        if not self.undo_stack:
            return
        self.text = self.text[:-1]
        self.undo_stack.pop()
```

This simplistic example demonstrates how each character typed can be undone by popping from the undo stack.

- **Depth-First Search (DFS):** In graph traversal algorithms, such as Depth-First Search, stacks are utilized to explore nodes in a depthward motion. Each time a new node is visited, it is pushed onto the stack; backtracking occurs when a node has no unvisited adjacent nodes, achieved by popping the stack.

```
def depth_first_search(graph, start):
    stack, visited = [start], set()
    while stack:
        vertex = stack.pop()
        if vertex not in visited:
            visited.add(vertex)
            stack.extend(neighbour for neighbour in graph[vertex] if neighbour
                not in visited)
    return visited
```

This algorithm ensures an exhaustive search of the graph in a manner that leverages the LIFO property of stacks to facilitate backtracking.

- **Hanoi Towers Simulation:** The simulation of the classic Tower of Hanoi puzzle can be implemented using stacks. Here, each rod is represented by a stack, and the movement of disks follows the game's rules by pushing and popping disks between stacks.

```
def move_tower(height, from_pole, to_pole, with_pole, stacks):
    if height >= 1:
        move_tower(height - 1, from_pole, with_pole, to_pole, stacks)
        move_disk(from_pole, to_pole, stacks)
        move_tower(height - 1, with_pole, to_pole, from_pole, stacks)

def move_disk(from_pole, to_pole, stacks):
    disk = stacks[from_pole].pop()
    stacks[to_pole].append(disk)
    print(f"Moving disk from {from_pole} to {to_pole}")
```

  This simulation demonstrates how disks are transferred between poles (stacks).

These examples illustrate the versatility of stacks in handling a range of computational tasks, underlining their importance in the field of computer science.

5.5 Introduction to Queues

A queue is a linear data structure that follows a specific order for element operations, known as First-In-First-Out (FIFO). In a queue, the first element added to the structure will be the first one to be removed. This property is analogous to a real-life queue, such as a line of customers waiting for service, where the first customer to arrive is the first to be served.

The primary operations associated with a queue include:

- **Enqueue:** The process of adding an element to the end of the queue.
- **Dequeue:** The process of removing an element from the front of the queue.
- **Front:** Retrieves, but does not remove, the front element of the queue.

- **Rear:** Retrieves, but does not remove, the last element of the queue.
- **IsEmpty:** Checks if the queue is empty.
- **Size:** Returns the number of elements in the queue.

Queues are essential in various computing scenarios, including scheduling algorithms, breadth-first search (BFS) in graph theory, and buffering in data streams. They provide a mechanism to manage tasks in a sequential processing order.

The following pseudocode illustrates the fundamental operations of a queue:

```
class Queue:
    def __init__(self):
        self.items = []

    def is_empty(self):
        return len(self.items) == 0

    def enqueue(self, item):
        self.items.append(item)

    def dequeue(self):
        if not self.is_empty():
            return self.items.pop(0)
        else:
            raise IndexError("dequeue from an empty queue")

    def front(self):
        if not self.is_empty():
            return self.items[0]
        else:
            raise IndexError("front from an empty queue")

    def rear(self):
        if not self.is_empty():
            return self.items[-1]
        else:
            raise IndexError("rear from an empty queue")

    def size(self):
        return len(self.items)
```

Upon initializing a queue, the items list will store the elements. The is_empty method checks if the queue has no elements. The enqueue method appends an element to the end of the list, effectively adding it to the rear of the queue. The dequeue method removes and returns the front element of the queue. If the queue is empty, it raises an IndexError. The front method returns the front element without removing it, while the rear method returns the last element. The size method returns the count of elements in the queue.

The behavior of the queue ensures that elements are processed in the exact order they were added, which makes queues particularly useful for resource management tasks and in contexts where order of operations is critical. For example, queues are utilized in operating systems for task scheduling, managing print jobs in printers, and in networking for packet-routing.

The efficiency of queue operations is critical, with enqueue and dequeue expected to operate in O(1) time complexity. However, this is only achievable when the queue is implemented using data structures optimized for these operations, such as linked lists. With the basic list implementation shown above, the dequeue operation is O(n) due to the need to shift all elements one position to the left.

Another important aspect is the variation of queue data structures that cater to specific requirements. Common variants include:

- **Circular Queue:** Overcomes the limitation of fixed queue size by reusing empty space created by dequeued elements.
- **Priority Queue:** Elements are dequeued in order of priority rather than FIFO order.
- **Double-ended Queue (Deque):** Allows insertion and deletion of elements from both ends, providing additional flexibility.

Each variant maintains the fundamental principles of a queue but introduces additional characteristics to handle more complex scenarios and requirements in computing systems. Understanding these nuances and implementations allows for selecting the appropriate queue type based on specific task requirements, effectively using queues to optimize and structure operations in data processing and resource management applications.

5.6 Queue Operations

A queue is a linear data structure that follows the First-In-First-Out (FIFO) principle, where the first element inserted into the queue is the first one to be removed. This structure features two main operations: **enqueue** and **dequeue**, along with some auxiliary operations such as **isEmpty**, **isFull**, **front**, and **rear**. These operations are fundamental in understanding how queues function and are implemented.

The **enqueue** operation is responsible for adding an element to the rear of the queue. If the queue is not full, the element is inserted into the position pointed to by the rear pointer, and the rear pointer is then incremented to the next position.

```
def enqueue(queue, element, rear, size):
    if rear == size:
        print("Queue is full")
    else:
        queue[rear] = element
        rear += 1
    return rear
```

The **dequeue** operation removes an element from the front of the queue. This involves checking if the queue is empty and, if not, removing the element pointed to by the front pointer and then incrementing the front pointer.

```
def dequeue(queue, front, rear):
    if front == rear:
        print("Queue is empty")
        return front, None
    else:
        element = queue[front]
        front += 1
        return front, element
```

Checking if the queue is empty can be done using the **isEmpty** operation, which simply compares the front and rear pointers. If they're equal, the queue is empty.

```
def isEmpty(front, rear):
    return front == rear
```

The **isFull** operation determines if the queue has reached its maximum capacity, which is when the rear pointer equals the size of the queue.

```
def isFull(rear, size):
    return rear == size
```

The **front** operation retrieves the element at the front of the queue without removing it and is useful for inspecting the queue's state.

```
def front(queue, front, rear):
    if isEmpty(front, rear):
        print("Queue is empty")
        return None
    return queue[front]
```

Similarly, the **rear** operation retrieves the element at the rear of the queue without removing it.

```
def rear(queue, rear):
    return queue[rear-1] if rear != 0 else None
```

Each operation is crucial for the proper functioning of the queue data structure. Understanding these operations and their Python implementations is foundational for leveraging queues in various applications, such as task scheduling, buffering, and handling real-time system demands.

5.7 Queue Implementation in Python

Queues in Python can be efficiently implemented using lists or by utilizing the collections.deque class from the Python standard library, which provides an optimized double-ended queue. Here, we delve into both implementations, highlighting their syntax, operations, and efficiency.

Using Lists

Python lists can be used to simulate a queue, but with some performance trade-offs. Lists are dynamic arrays that allow us to add or remove elements. The operations for a queue are *enqueue* (add elements to the back), and *dequeue* (remove elements from the front). Below is the implementation using lists:

```
class ListQueue:
    def __init__(self):
        self.queue = []

    def is_empty(self):
        return len(self.queue) == 0

    def enqueue(self, item):
        self.queue.append(item)

    def dequeue(self):
        if not self.is_empty():
            return self.queue.pop(0)
        else:
            raise IndexError("dequeue from empty queue")

    def size(self):
        return len(self.queue)
```

In this list-based implementation:

- The enqueue operation uses the append() method to add an item to the end of the list, with a time complexity of $O(1)$.

- The dequeue operation uses the pop(0) method to remove the first item from the list. This operation has a time complexity of $O(n)$, as it involves shifting all subsequent elements one position to the left.

Considering the $O(n)$ time complexity for the dequeue operation, lists are not the most efficient way to implement a queue, especially for large datasets.

Using collections.deque

The deque (double-ended queue) from the collections module provides a much more efficient means to implement a queue. It allows appending and popping from both ends of the queue with a time complexity of $O(1)$.

```
from collections import deque

class DequeQueue:
    def __init__(self):
        self.queue = deque()

    def is_empty(self):
        return len(self.queue) == 0

    def enqueue(self, item):
        self.queue.append(item)

    def dequeue(self):
        if not self.is_empty():
            return self.queue.popleft()
        else:
            raise IndexError("dequeue from empty queue")

    def size(self):
        return len(self.queue)
```

In this deque-based implementation:

- The enqueue operation uses the append() method to add an item to the end, with a time complexity of $O(1)$.
- The dequeue operation uses the popleft() method to remove the first item, also with a time complexity of $O(1)$.

The deque provides an efficient and straightforward alternative for implementing a queue, with constant time complexity for both enqueue and dequeue operations, making it suitable for applications requiring frequent insertions and deletions.

Comparison

Both implementations achieve the primary goal of providing a queue with basic operations. However, they differ significantly in performance, particularly for the dequeue operation:

- **List-based Queue**: While easy to implement, the list-based queue suffers from $O(n)$ dequeue operation time complexity due to the need to shift elements after removing the front item.
- deque-**based Queue**: The deque-based queue is efficient with $O(1)$ time complexity for both enqueue and dequeue operations, making it superior for practical applications, especially when handling large amounts of data.

Example Usage

Below is an illustrative example demonstrating the usage of the DequeQueue class:

```
if __name__ == "__main__":
    queue = DequeQueue()
    queue.enqueue(10)
    queue.enqueue(20)
    queue.enqueue(30)
    print("Current queue size:", queue.size()) # Output: 3

    print("Dequeued element:", queue.dequeue()) # Output: 10
    print("Dequeued element:", queue.dequeue()) # Output: 20

    print("Current queue size:", queue.size()) # Output: 1

    print("Is the queue empty?", queue.is_empty()) # Output: False

    queue.dequeue()
    print("Is the queue empty?", queue.is_empty()) # Output: True

    try:
        queue.dequeue() # This will raise an IndexError
    except IndexError as e:
        print("Error:", e)
```

The output of this code will be:

```
Current queue size: 3
Dequeued element: 10
Dequeued element: 20
Current queue size: 1
Is the queue empty? False
Is the queue empty? True
Error: dequeue from empty queue
```

This example demonstrates the basic operations of enqueuing, dequeuing, checking the queue size, and handling the empty queue scenario with the DequeQueue class.

5.8 Types of Queues

In this section, we explore various types of queues beyond the basic First-In-First-Out (FIFO) model. Each queue type has unique characteristics and use cases, allowing more sophisticated data management schemes. We will discuss the following queue types: Simple Queue, Circular Queue, Priority Queue, Double-Ended Queue (Deque).

Simple Queue: A simple queue, or a linear queue, follows the FIFO principle. Elements are enqueued at the rear and dequeued from the front. Below is the implementation of a simple queue using Python:

```
class SimpleQueue:
    def __init__(self):
        self.queue = []

    def is_empty(self):
        return len(self.queue) == 0

    def enqueue(self, item):
        self.queue.append(item)

    def dequeue(self):
        if not self.is_empty():
            return self.queue.pop(0)
        else:
            raise IndexError("Dequeue from an empty queue")

    def peek(self):
        if not self.is_empty():
            return self.queue[0]
        else:
            raise IndexError("Peek from an empty queue")

    def size(self):
        return len(self.queue)

# Example usage:
q = SimpleQueue()
q.enqueue(1)
q.enqueue(2)
q.enqueue(3)
print(q.dequeue()) # Output: 1
print(q.peek()) # Output: 2
print(q.size()) # Output: 2
```

Circular Queue: A circular queue addresses the limitations of a simple queue by treating the queue as a circular buffer. When the end of the queue is reached, it wraps around to the beginning. Here is an implementation of a circular queue:

```
class CircularQueue:
    def __init__(self, size):
        self.size = size
        self.queue = [None] * size
        self.front = self.rear = -1

    def is_full(self):
        return (self.rear + 1) % self.size == self.front

    def is_empty(self):
        return self.front == -1

    def enqueue(self, item):
        if self.is_full():
            raise IndexError("Enqueue on a full queue")
        elif self.is_empty():
            self.front = self.rear = 0
        else:
            self.rear = (self.rear + 1) % self.size
        self.queue[self.rear] = item

    def dequeue(self):
        if self.is_empty():
            raise IndexError("Dequeue from an empty queue")
        elif self.front == self.rear:
            item = self.queue[self.front]
            self.front = self.rear = -1
        else:
            item = self.queue[self.front]
            self.front = (self.front + 1) % self.size
        return item

    def peek(self):
        if self.is_empty():
            raise IndexError("Peek from an empty queue")
        return self.queue[self.front]

    def size(self):
        if self.is_empty():
            return 0
        elif self.rear >= self.front:
            return self.rear - self.front + 1
        else:
            return self.size - self.front + self.rear + 1

# Example usage:
cq = CircularQueue(3)
cq.enqueue(1)
cq.enqueue(2)
cq.enqueue(3)
print(cq.dequeue()) # Output: 1
cq.enqueue(4)
print(cq.peek()) # Output: 2
```

Priority Queue: A priority queue assigns a priority level to each element. Elements with higher priority are dequeued before those with lower priority. If two elements have the same priority, the FIFO order is maintained. Here's a Python implementation using the heapq module:

```
import heapq

class PriorityQueue:
    def __init__(self):
        self.queue = []

    def is_empty(self):
        return len(self.queue) == 0

    def enqueue(self, priority, item):
        heapq.heappush(self.queue, (priority, item))

    def dequeue(self):
        if self.is_empty():
            raise IndexError("Dequeue from an empty queue")
        return heapq.heappop(self.queue)[1]

    def peek(self):
        if self.is_empty():
            raise IndexError("Peek from an empty queue")
        return self.queue[0][1]

# Example usage:
pq = PriorityQueue()
pq.enqueue(3, 'low')
pq.enqueue(1, 'high')
pq.enqueue(2, 'medium')
print(pq.dequeue()) # Output: high
print(pq.peek()) # Output: medium
```

Double-Ended Queue (Deque): A deque allows insertion and deletion of elements from both ends, combining aspects of stacks and queues. Below is the implementation of a deque using Python's collections module:

```
from collections import deque

class Deque:
    def __init__(self):
        self.deque = deque()

    def is_empty(self):
        return len(self.deque) == 0

    def add_front(self, item):
        self.deque.appendleft(item)

    def add_rear(self, item):
        self.deque.append(item)

    def remove_front(self):
        if self.is_empty():
            raise IndexError("Remove from an empty deque")
        return self.deque.popleft()

    def remove_rear(self):
        if self.is_empty():
            raise IndexError("Remove from an empty deque")
```

```
        return self.deque.pop()

    def peek_front(self):
        if self.is_empty():
            raise IndexError("Peek from an empty deque")
        return self.deque[0]

    def peek_rear(self):
        if self.is_empty()):
            raise IndexError("Peek from an empty deque")
        return self.deque[-1]

# Example usage:
dq = Deque()
dq.add_rear(1)
dq.add_front(2)
dq.add_rear(3)
print(dq.remove_front()) # Output: 2
print(dq.remove_rear()) # Output: 3
```

5.9 Applications of Queues

Queues are fundamental data structures widely employed in various computing and real-world scenarios due to their First-In-First-Out (FIFO) nature. This property ensures that the order of processing is preserved, which is critical in many applications. Herein, we delve into several practical applications of queues, demonstrating their versatility and efficacy.

1. Task Scheduling: Queues are extensively used in operating systems for task scheduling. In a multi-tasking environment, where numerous processes compete for CPU time, a queue can manage these processes efficiently. The operating system places all incoming processes in a queue and schedules them based on their arrival order.

```
from collections import deque

class TaskScheduler:
    def __init__(self):
        self.queue = deque()

    def add_task(self, task):
        self.queue.append(task)

    def execute_task(self):
        if self.queue:
            return self.queue.popleft()
        return None

scheduler = TaskScheduler()
scheduler.add_task("Task 1")
scheduler.add_task("Task 2")
print(scheduler.execute_task()) # Output: Task 1
```

```
print(scheduler.execute_task()) # Output: Task 2
```

```
Task 1
Task 2
```

2. Print Spooling: In a networked environment with multiple print requests, queues manage print job spooling. Each print job is placed in a queue and processed sequentially, ensuring that print commands are executed in the order they were received.

```
class PrintSpooler:
    def __init__(self):
        self.queue = deque()

    def add_print_job(self, job):
        self.queue.append(job)

    def process_job(self):
        if self.queue:
            return self.queue.popleft()
        return None

spooler = PrintSpooler()
spooler.add_print_job("Job 1")
spooler.add_print_job("Job 2")
print(spooler.process_job()) # Output: Job 1
print(spooler.process_job()) # Output: Job 2
```

```
Job 1
Job 2
```

3. Breadth-First Search (BFS) in Graphs: Queues facilitate the BFS algorithm in graph traversal, ensuring exploration starts from the given node and moves level by level. This method is instrumental in finding the shortest path in unweighted graphs.

```
def bfs(graph, start_node):
    visited = set()
    queue = deque([start_node])
    visited.add(start_node)

    while queue:
        current_node = queue.popleft()
        print(current_node, end=" ")

        for neighbor in graph[current_node]:
            if neighbor not in visited:
                queue.append(neighbor)
                visited.add(neighbor)

graph = {
    'A': ['B', 'C'],
    'B': ['A', 'D', 'E'],
    'C': ['A', 'F'],
    'D': ['B'],
    'E': ['B'],
    'F': ['C']
}
```

```
bfs(graph, 'A')
```

```
A B C D E F
```

4. Handling of Interrupts in Real-time Systems: Real-time systems often use queues to handle interrupts. An interrupt handler places each interrupt request into a queue, where they are processed in the order received, ensuring timely and predictable handling.

5. Customer Service Systems: Customer service departments utilize queues to manage incoming customer requests, be it in a call center or a service desk. Each customer is attended to in the order they arrived, which is crucial for fairness and efficiency.

```
class CustomerService:
    def __init__(self):
        self.queue = deque()

    def add_customer(self, customer):
        self.queue.append(customer)

    def serve_customer(self):
        if self.queue:
            return self.queue.popleft()
        return "No customers to serve"

service = CustomerService()
service.add_customer("Customer 1")
service.add_customer("Customer 2")
print(service.serve_customer()) # Output: Customer 1
print(service.serve_customer()) # Output: Customer 2
```

```
Customer 1
Customer 2
```

6. Traffic Management: Queues are utilized in traffic management systems, especially at traffic signals. Vehicles queue up at red lights and are allowed to pass sequentially when the light turns green, ensuring orderly traffic flow.

7. Simulation of Real-life Scenarios: In simulation models for various scenarios like customer checkout lines in supermarkets or network packet routing, queues help mimic real-life waiting lines, providing insights into system performance and behavior under different conditions.

These applications underscore queues' essential role in both computational tasks and real-world problem-solving, showcasing their utility and robustness in maintaining order and ensuring fair processing of tasks. The FIFO characteristic pivotal to queues is central to achieving efficiency and predictability across diverse applications.

5.10 Comparison of Stacks and Queues

Stacks and queues are fundamental data structures in computer science, each with distinctive characteristics and use cases. Both are abstract data types that allow for the collection and manipulation of homogeneous elements, but they differ significantly in terms of how these elements are inserted and removed. Understanding their differences helps to select the appropriate data structure based on specific problem requirements.

Order of Operations: Stacks follow a Last In, First Out (LIFO) principle, which means that the last element added to the stack is the first one to be removed. This behavior is likened to a stack of plates, where the plate on the top is the first to be taken off. In contrast, queues follow a First In, First Out (FIFO) principle, meaning that the first element added is the first one to be removed, similar to a line of people where the person at the front exits first.

Basic Operations: Both stacks and queues support three primary operations: insertion, deletion, and inspection of elements. However, the manner in which these operations are performed diverges.

- **Insertion (Push for Stacks, Enqueue for Queues):** For stacks, the push operation adds an element to the top of the stack. For queues, the enqueue operation adds an element to the rear of the queue.

- **Deletion (Pop for Stacks, Dequeue for Queues):** The pop operation in a stack removes the topmost element. Conversely, the dequeue operation in a queue removes the frontmost element.

- **Inspection (Peek for Stacks, Front for Queues):** The peek operation in a stack returns the topmost element without removing it, while the front operation in a queue returns the element at the front without removing it.

Use Cases: Their differences in operational order endow stacks and queues with specific advantages for certain applications.

- **Stacks:** Ideal for scenarios where the most recently added element needs to be accessed first. For example:

  - **Function Call Management:** The call stack in programming languages where function calls and their local variables are managed is a classic example.
  - **Undo Mechanism:** Undo features in text editors or graphic applications, where the most recent action is reversed first.
  - **Expression Evaluation:** Parsing and evaluating expressions, such as converting infix to postfix notation.

- **Queues:** Suitable for applications where the first element needs to be processed first. For example:
  - **Order Processing:** Handling tasks or jobs in the order they arrive, as seen in print queues.
  - **Data Streaming:** Managing data packets in network routers where packets are processed in the order they arrive.
  - **Breadth-First Search (BFS):** Implementing BFS in graph traversal, where nodes are explored in the order of their distance from the source node.

Python Implementation: Both stacks and queues can be implemented using Python lists, although their operations and performance characteristics can vary slightly due to the underlying list operations.

```
class Stack:
    def __init__(self):
        self.items = []

    def is_empty(self):
        return self.items == []

    def push(self, item):
        self.items.append(item)

    def pop(self):
        return self.items.pop()

    def peek(self):
        return self.items[-1]

    def size(self):
        return len(self.items)

stack = Stack()
stack.push(1)
stack.push(2)
print(stack.pop()) # Output: 2
```

```
class Queue:
    def __init__(self):
        self.items = []
```

```
    def is_empty(self):
        return self.items == []

    def enqueue(self, item):
        self.items.insert(0, item)

    def dequeue(self):
        return self.items.pop()

    def size(self):
        return len(self.items)

queue = Queue()
queue.enqueue(1)
queue.enqueue(2)
print(queue.dequeue()) # Output: 1
```

While Python lists can be used for both implementations, the time complexity for queue operations using a list where insertion is performed at the front ($O(n)$) and deletion at the rear ($O(1)$) makes it inefficient for large data sets. This is due to the shifting of all other elements during insertion. Queue implementations can hence benefit from collections such as deque from Python's collections module, which provides average $O(1)$ time complexity for both append and pop operations.

```
from collections import deque

class Queue:
    def __init__(self):
        self.items = deque()

    def is_empty(self):
        return len(self.items) == 0

    def enqueue(self, item):
        self.items.append(item) # O(1)

    def dequeue(self):
        return self.items.popleft() # O(1)

    def size(self):
        return len(self.items)

queue = Queue()
queue.enqueue(1)
queue.enqueue(2)
print(queue.dequeue()) # Output: 1
```

Analyzing the differences between stacks and queues provides insights into their application in solving various computational problems. Their appropriate use can lead to efficient memory and time management, optimizing performance for specific tasks.

5.11 Performance Considerations in Stacks and Queues

Understanding the performance of stacks and queues is crucial for effective algorithm design and implementation. Both data structures offer distinct operational efficiencies and selecting the appropriate one can significantly influence the performance of an application. This section elucidates the critical performance aspects of stacks and queues, providing detailed analysis on time and space complexities associated with their operations.

Time Complexity Analysis:

Stacks and queues both support a well-defined set of operations (such as push, pop, enqueue, dequeue, etc.) which we will analyze here.

Stacks:

- push: Adding an element to the top of the stack.
- pop: Removing the topmost element from the stack.
- peek/top: Accessing the topmost element without removing it.

These operations are typically implemented using arrays or linked lists.

Array-based implementation:

- push operation: This involves adding an element at the end of an array, which has constant time complexity, i.e., $O(1)$. However, if the array is full and needs to be resized (usually doubled in size), the amortized time complexity remains $O(1)$.
- pop operation: This removes the last element of the array, also constant time, $O(1)$.
- peek/top operation: Accessing the top element without removal has a time complexity of $O(1)$.

Linked list-based implementation:

- push operation: Adding an element at the head of the list takes $O(1)$ time.
- pop operation: Removing the head element also takes $O(1)$ time.

- peek/top operation: Accessing the head element without removal takes $O(1)$ time.

From this, it is evident that stack operations, regardless of the underlying implementation, provide constant time complexity, $O(1)$, which guarantees high performance in scenarios requiring frequent push and pop operations.

Queues:

- enqueue: Adding an element to the end of the queue.
- dequeue: Removing an element from the front of the queue.
- peek/front: Accessing the front element without removing it.

Array-based implementation:

- enqueue operation: When implemented using circular arrays, adding an element at the rear, wrapping around as necessary, takes $O(1)$ time.
- dequeue operation: Removing the front element, updating the front pointer, also takes $O(1)$ time.
- peek/front operation: Accessing the front element without removal takes $O(1)$ time.

Linked list-based implementation:

- enqueue operation: Adding an element at the tail of the list takes $O(1)$ time.
- dequeue operation: Removing the head element takes $O(1)$ time.
- peek/front operation: Accessing the head element without removal takes $O(1)$ time.

Analyzing both array and linked list implementations shows that standard queue operations also adhere to constant time complexity, $O(1)$.

Space Complexity Analysis:

The space complexity of both data structures depends on the underlying storage mechanism, i.e., arrays or linked lists.

Array-based implementation:

- The array must be of a pre-defined size or dynamically resized. Space complexity is $O(n)$, where n is the number of elements, disregarding any additional overhead for dynamically resizing arrays in amortized scenarios.

Linked list-based implementation:

- Each element requires additional space for pointers, but the space complexity remains $O(n)$, where n is the number of elements stored.

Practical Performance Considerations:

Besides theoretical analysis, practical performance is influenced by factors such as memory locality, cache performance, and overhead of dynamic memory allocation.

Memory locality and cache performance:

- Array-based implementations benefit from better memory locality. Consecutive elements are stored in contiguous memory locations, enhancing cache performance.
- Linked list implementations suffer from poor locality, as nodes may be scattered across memory, leading to more cache misses.

Overhead of dynamic memory allocation:

- Linked lists involve overhead for dynamic allocation and deallocation, which can affect performance when operations are frequent.
- Arrays, particularly those with a fixed size or resized infrequently, have minimal allocation overhead.

Selecting between stacks and queues and their particular implementations depends on specific application requirements. Factors like the expected number of elements, frequency of operations, and memory constraints should be considered to optimize performance. For environments with predictable load and frequent access to elements, array-based structures are often preferred due to their superior cache performance. For applications requiring flexible and dynamic memory management, linked lists might be more suitable despite their relatively higher overhead.

Chapter 6

Trees

This chapter offers a thorough exploration of tree data structures, covering basic concepts and different types such as binary trees, binary search trees (BST), AVL trees, B-trees, heaps, and trie trees. It explains tree traversal methods, as well as insertion and deletion operations in BSTs. Additionally, the chapter discusses practical applications and performance considerations, providing a comprehensive understanding of trees.

6.1 Introduction to Trees

A tree is a hierarchical data structure that simulates a hierarchical tree structure with a root value and subtrees of children, represented as a set of linked nodes. Trees are widely used in computer science due to their efficiency in various operations and their ability to model relationships between data elements naturally. Each tree structure is composed of nodes, where each node holds a value or condition, and references to other nodes. The fundamental concepts essential to understanding trees include nodes, edges, root, leaves, and height.

Nodes: A node is an individual element of a tree holding data. Each node can have zero or more child nodes. The nodes that have the same parent are called siblings.

Edges: An edge is the connection between two nodes. It signifies the relationship between the parent and the child nodes.

Root: The node at the top of the tree is called the root. It is the only node with no parent. Every tree must have a root node.

Leaves: Nodes that do not have any children are called leaves or leaf nodes. They are also known as external nodes.

Height of a Tree: The height of a tree is the length of the longest path from the root to a leaf. It signifies the maximum number of edges from the root to the leaf.

Depth of a Node: The depth of a node is the number of edges from the root to the node.

Subtree: A subtree represents any node of the tree and all of its descendants.

The hierarchical nature of trees makes them suitable for representing hierarchical data structures such as organizational structures, file systems, and abstract syntax trees. Trees provide several beneficial properties:

- Efficient traversal and search operations.
- Hierarchical representation of data.
- Recursive nature enabling simpler implementation of algorithms.

Types of Trees:

- **Binary Trees**: Each node has at most two children, often termed the left and right child.
- **Binary Search Trees (BST)**: A binary tree with the property that the left child of a node contains a value less than the node's value, and the right child contains a value greater than the node's value.
- **AVL Trees**: A self-balancing binary search tree where the difference between the heights of the left and right subtrees of any node is no more than one.
- **B-Trees**: A generalization of binary search trees where nodes can have more than two children. They are optimized for systems that read and write large blocks of data.
- **Heaps**: A special tree-based data structure that satisfies the heap property. In a max-heap, each parent node is greater than or equal to its children; in a min-heap, each parent node is less than or equal to its children.

- **Trie Trees**: A tree used to store a dynamic set or associative array where the keys are usually strings.

Tree Representation: There are multiple ways to represent trees in a program. The most common representations include:

1. Linked Representation: Each node is an object. Nodes have references to their children.

```
class TreeNode:
    def __init__(self, key):
        self.key = key
        self.left = None
        self.right = None
```

2. List Representation: Parent nodes and child nodes are indexed in a list.

```
tree = [
    [1, 2], # Node 0 has children 1 and 2
    [None, None], # Node 1 is a leaf node
    [None, None] # Node 2 is a leaf node
]
```

Traversal Methods: Trees can be traversed in multiple ways. The fundamental tree traversal methods include:

- **Pre-order traversal**: Process the root node first, then recursively process the left subtree, followed by the right subtree.
- **In-order traversal**: Recursively process the left subtree first, then the root node, followed by the right subtree.
- **Post-order traversal**: Recursively process the left subtree, the right subtree, and finally the root node.
- **Level-order traversal**: Traverse nodes level by level, starting from the root.

In many applications, trees help improve the efficiency and performance for operations such as search, insertion, and deletion, particularly when compared to linear data structures like arrays or linked lists.

Understanding the fundamental concepts of trees and their various types and representations is crucial for mastering more advanced topics in data structures and algorithms. Subsequent sections will delve into specific tree types and explore their properties, operations, and applications in greater depth.

6.2 Binary Trees

A binary tree is a hierarchical data structure in which each node has at most two children, referred to as the left child and the right child. A binary tree is defined recursively as either being empty or consisting of a root node with two subtrees, each of which is also a binary tree. This structure forms the basis of many algorithms and data structures, making it essential to understand its properties, implementation, and real-world applications.

Properties of Binary Trees:

- *Maximum Nodes:* A binary tree of depth d (where the root node is at depth 0) can have at most 2^d nodes at depth d, and $2^{d+1} - 1$ nodes in total.
- *Minimum Nodes:* The minimum number of nodes in a binary tree of depth d is $d + 1$ (a tree where each node has only one child).
- *Height of Binary Tree:* The height of a binary tree is defined as the length of the longest path from the root to a leaf. For a tree with a single node, the height is 0.
- *Balanced Binary Tree:* A binary tree is balanced if, for every node in the tree, the height difference of the left and right subtrees is at most one.

Binary Tree Representation: Binary trees can be implemented using various representations, two of which are array representation and linked representation.

Array Representation: In an array representation of a binary tree, the nodes are stored in a sequential manner. The root is placed at the first position of the array (index 0 or 1 depending on 1-based or 0-based indexing). For a node at index i,

- The left child is at index $2i + 1$ (0-based indexing) or $2i$ (1-based indexing).
- The right child is at index $2i + 2$ (0-based indexing) or $2i + 1$ (1-based indexing).

This method is efficient in terms of space but becomes inefficient when the tree is sparse because it leads to wasted space.

Linked Representation: In the linked representation, each node is an object containing three fields:

- A data element.
- A reference to the left child.
- A reference to the right child.

This approach is often used as it allows the tree to grow dynamically. Below is an example of a simple binary tree node class in Python using the linked representation.

```
class TreeNode:
    def __init__(self, key):
        self.left = None
        self.right = None
        self.val = key

# Example of creating a binary tree with this class
root = TreeNode(1)
root.left = TreeNode(2)
root.right = TreeNode(3)
root.left.left = TreeNode(4)
root.left.right = TreeNode(5)
```

Traversing a Binary Tree: Traversal of a binary tree refers to the process of visiting each node in the tree exactly once in a systematic way. There are several common methods of binary tree traversal, each serving different purposes.

- *Inorder Traversal (Left, Root, Right):*

```
def inorder_traversal(root):
    if root:
        inorder_traversal(root.left)
        print(root.val, end=' ')
        inorder_traversal(root.right)
```

- *Preorder Traversal (Root, Left, Right):*

```
def preorder_traversal(root):
    if root:
        print(root.val, end=' ')
        preorder_traversal(root.left)
        preorder_traversal(root.right)
```

- *Postorder Traversal (Left, Right, Root):*

```
def postorder_traversal(root):
    if root:
        postorder_traversal(root.left)
```

```
    postorder_traversal(root.right)
    print(root.val, end=' ')
```

Applications of Binary Trees: Binary trees are fundamental structures in computer science, often utilized in the following scenarios:

- *Expression Trees:* Used in compilers to represent expressions. Each leaf is an operand, and each internal node is an operator.
- *Binary Search Trees (BSTs):* Facilitates efficient searching, insertion, and deletion operations.
- *Heaps:* Implement priority queues.
- *Decision Trees:* Used in machine learning for decision-making processes.
- *Syntax Trees:* Used in natural language processing to parse sentences.

The straightforward nature of binary trees and their extensive applicability in various domains highlight their importance in both theoretical and practical aspects. Whether through array or linked representations, the ability to traverse and manipulate binary trees efficiently is a foundational skill for proficient programming and algorithm design. Detailed understanding of binary tree traversal methodologies lays the groundwork for mastering more complex tree structures and algorithms discussed in subsequent sections.

6.3 Tree Traversal Methods

In computer science, tree traversal refers to the process of visiting each node in a tree data structure exactly once in a systematic manner. Efficient traversal methods are critical for performing operations such as searching, inserting, and deleting nodes in trees. This section discusses commonly used tree traversal methods: Pre-order, In-order, Post-order, and Level-order traversal.

Pre-order Traversal: In a pre-order traversal, the nodes are recursively visited in this order: the root node, the left subtree, and then the right subtree. For a tree with root R, left child L, and right child R, the traversal follows $\mathrm{R} \rightarrow \mathrm{L} \rightarrow \mathrm{R}$. The pseudo-code for pre-order traversal is:

```
def preOrderTraversal(node):
    if node is not None:
        print(node.data)
        preOrderTraversal(node.left)
        preOrderTraversal(node.right)
```

For example, given the following tree structure:

```
    A
   / \
  B   C
 / \
D   E
```

The pre-order traversal would visit the nodes in the following order: A → B → D → E → C. The output is:

```
A B D E C
```

In-order Traversal: In-order traversal visits the nodes in the following order: the left subtree, the root node, and then the right subtree. This method is often utilized for binary search trees (BSTs) because it results in nodes being visited in non-decreasing order. The pseudo-code for in-order traversal is:

```
def inOrderTraversal(node):
    if node is not None:
        inOrderTraversal(node.left)
        print(node.data)
        inOrderTraversal(node.right)
```

Using the same example tree, the in-order traversal would visit the nodes in the following order: D → B → E → A → C. The output is:

```
D B E A C
```

Post-order Traversal: Post-order traversal recursively visits nodes in the following order: the left subtree, the right subtree, and then the root node. It is often used for deleting or freeing nodes and various tree-related algorithms that require processing child nodes before their parent nodes. The pseudo-code for post-order traversal is:

```
def postOrderTraversal(node):
    if node is not None:
        postOrderTraversal(node.left)
        postOrderTraversal(node.right)
        print(node.data)
```

For the example tree, the post-order traversal would visit the nodes in the following order: D → E → B → C → A. The output is:

```
D E B C A
```

Level-order Traversal: Level-order traversal, also known as breadth-first traversal, visits nodes level by level from top to bottom and left to right within each level. This is typically implemented using a queue data structure to keep track of the nodes. The pseudo-code for level-order traversal is:

```
from collections import deque

def levelOrderTraversal(root):
    if root is None:
        return

    queue = deque([root])

    while queue:
        node = queue.popleft()
        print(node.data)

        if node.left is not None:
            queue.append(node.left)
        if node.right is not None:
            queue.append(node.right)
```

In the example tree, the level-order traversal would visit the nodes in the following order: $A \rightarrow B \rightarrow C \rightarrow D \rightarrow E$. The output is:

```
A B C D E
```

These traversal methods provide comprehensive ways to visit every node in a tree, each serving different practical scenarios depending on the requirements of the tree-based operation. The choice of traversal method is determined by the desired order in which the nodes should be processed.

6.4 Binary Search Trees (BST)

A Binary Search Tree (BST) is a particular type of binary tree that maintains a specific order among its elements, facilitating efficient search, insertion, and deletion operations. In a BST, each node contains a key, and possibly associated data, with the key values organized such that:

- The key in the left child of a node is less than the key in the parent node.
- The key in the right child of a node is greater than the key in the parent node.
- Both the left and right sub-trees of each node are also binary

search trees.

This ordering allows for binary search properties to be applied, ensuring operations are logarithmic in complexity in the average case.

Definition and Properties

Formally, a BST is defined as a binary tree where for every node n:

$$key(left(n)) < key(n) < key(right(n))$$

where $left(n)$ and $right(n)$ denote the left and right children of n, respectively.

The primary properties of BSTs include:

- **Searching:** Given a key, the structure of the BST allows for efficient querying by recursively traversing left or right sub-trees, depending on whether the key is lesser or greater than the current node's key.
- **Insertion:** New keys are inserted by recursively finding the correct position that maintains the binary search property.
- **Deletion:** Removing a node from a BST is more complex and involves three primary cases: deleting a leaf node, deleting a node with one child, and deleting a node with two children.

Operations in BSTs

Search Operation

Given a BST, the search operation is performed by comparing the target key with the root node's key. Based on the comparison, the algorithm decides to proceed to either the left or the right sub-tree, continually narrowing down the search space.

```
class Node:
    def __init__(self, key):
        self.left = None
        self.right = None
        self.val = key

def search(root, key):
    if root is None or root.val == key:
        return root

    if root.val < key:
        return search(root.right, key)

    return search(root.left, key)
```

Insertion Operation

Insertions in a BST maintain its ordered structure. Starting from the root, we recursively find the position to insert the new key such that the binary search property is preserved.

```
def insert(root, key):
    if root is None:
        return Node(key)

    if key < root.val:
        root.left = insert(root.left, key)
    else:
        root.right = insert(root.right, key)

    return root
```

Deletion Operation

Deletion in a BST handles three distinct cases:

1. **Node to be deleted is a leaf node:** Simply remove the node. 2. **Node to be deleted has one child:** Remove the node and replace it with its child. 3. **Node to be deleted has two children:** - Find the in-order successor (the smallest key in the right sub-tree). - Replace the node's key with the in-order successor's key. - Delete the in-order successor.

```
def minValueNode(node):
    current = node
    while(current.left is not None):
        current = current.left
    return current

def deleteNode(root, key):
    if root is None:
        return root

    if key < root.val:
        root.left = deleteNode(root.left, key)
    elif key > root.val:
        root.right = deleteNode(root.right, key)
    else:
        if root.left is None:
            temp = root.right
            root = None
            return temp
        elif root.right is None:
            temp = root.left
            root = None
            return temp

        temp = minValueNode(root.right)
        root.val = temp.val
        root.right = deleteNode(root.right, temp.val)

    return root
```

Traversal Methods

Traversal methods for BSTs include in-order, pre-order, and post-order traversals, which are defined the same way as for binary trees. In-order traversal is particularly useful for BSTs as it visits nodes in ascending order of their keys.

```
def inorderTraversal(root):
    if root:
        inorderTraversal(root.left)
        print(root.val, end=" ")
        inorderTraversal(root.right)
```

Performance Considerations

BSTs offer logarithmic time complexity operations for balanced trees, but the worst-case complexity can degrade to linear time when the tree becomes skewed (i.e., resembles a linked list). The shape of the tree depends on the order of insertions and deletions.

Balanced variants such as AVL trees or Red-Black trees are often employed to ensure logarithmic time complexities for all operations. These balanced trees automatically adjust to maintain their structure, generally ensuring O(log n) performance.

Understanding and implementing BSTs form a critical foundation for advanced data structures and algorithms. The operations and properties outlined serve as the cornerstone for understanding more complex balanced trees explored in subsequent sections.

6.5 Insertion in BST

The insertion operation in a Binary Search Tree (BST) is a fundamental procedure that maintains the tree's distinctive property: for any given node, all elements in the left subtree are less than the node's key, and all elements in the right subtree are greater than the node's key. This section delves into the mechanisms of the insertion process, detailing the algorithm, its implementation in Python, and the implications on the BST's structure and balance.

To insert a new key into a BST, we initially start at the root and traverse the tree following the BST property until we find the correct location for the new node. The following steps outline this process:

1. **Start at the Root**: Begin the operation at the root node. 2. **Traverse the Tree**: Compare the key of the new node, k, with the key of

the current node:

- If k is less than the current node's key, move to the left child.
- If k is greater than the current node's key, move to the right child.

3. **Find the Position**: Continue this procedure recursively until the appropriate NULL position is found (where either the left or right pointer of a node is NULL). 4. **Insert the Node**: Insert the new node at the identified position.

The time complexity of the insertion operation in a BST is $O(h)$, where h is the height of the tree. In the worst-case scenario, for an unbalanced BST, h can be as large as n, the number of nodes, resulting in $O(n)$ complexity. In a balanced tree, $h = \log n$, yielding $O(\log n)$ complexity.

Python Implementation

The following Python code demonstrates the insertion process in a BST.

```
class Node:
    def __init__(self, key):
        self.left = None
        self.right = None
        self.val = key

def insert(root, key):
    # If the tree is empty, return a new node
    if root is None:
        return Node(key)

    # Otherwise, recur down the tree
    if key < root.val:
        root.left = insert(root.left, key)
    else:
        root.right = insert(root.right, key)

    # return the (unchanged) node pointer
    return root

# Function to do inorder tree traversal
def inorder(root):
    if root:
        inorder(root.left)
        print(root.val, end=' ')
        inorder(root.right)

# Driver program to test the above functions
root = None
keys = [20, 8, 22, 4, 12, 10, 14]

for key in keys:
    root = insert(root, key)

print("Inorder traversal of the BST:")
inorder(root)
```

In the provided implementation, the 'insert()' function initiates by checking if the current root is NULL. If so, it creates a new node with the specified key. Otherwise, it compares the key with the value of the root node and recursively calls itself to either the left or right subtree accordingly. The 'inorder()' function is used for verification of the insertion process by performing an inorder traversal of the tree, which should produce a sorted sequence of inserted keys.

Example Execution

```
Inorder traversal of the BST:
4 8 10 12 14 20 22
```

This output verifies that keys are correctly inserted and placed to conform to the BST properties.

Effect on Tree Structure

The insertion of nodes affects the overall structure and balance of the tree. Repeated insertions of sequential or random keys can result in highly unbalanced trees with unfavorable height. For example, inserting keys in ascending or descending order will yield a degenerate tree (similar to a linked list), where each node has only one child. This scenario is detrimental as it degrades the performance of search, insertion, and deletion operations to $O(n)$.

Effective strategies to maintain tree balance, such as self-balancing mechanisms (e.g., AVL trees, Red-Black trees), will be discussed in subsequent sections. Ensuring balance is crucial for achieving the ideal performance of $O(\log n)$ for the aforementioned operations.

Understanding the insertion process in BSTs forms the bedrock for mastering tree data structures. The presented approach and implementation are fundamental, serving as a precursor to more sophisticated tree algorithms and structures.

6.6 Deletion in BST

Deletion in a Binary Search Tree (BST) is a fundamental operation that ensures the integrity and utility of the data structure as elements are dynamically removed. When an element is deleted from a BST, three primary cases must be handled: deleting a leaf node, deleting a node with one child, and deleting a node with two children. Each case maintains the BST property, i.e., for any given node, all elements in the left subtree are less than the node, and all elements in the right subtree are greater.

Let's delve into each case with meticulous detail.

Case 1: Deleting a Leaf Node

A leaf node is a node that has no children. Deleting a leaf node is the simplest case. We only need to remove the node from the tree and update the parent node to adjust its reference accordingly.

For example, consider the following BST:

```
     50
    / \
  30    70
 / \  / \
20  40 60  80
```

To delete the node 20: 1. Find the node to be deleted (20). 2. Since 20 is a leaf node, simply remove it.

The resulting BST is:

```
     50
    / \
  30    70
 / \  / \
   40 60  80
```

Case 2: Deleting a Node with One Child

This case involves a node that has exactly one child, either left or right. The process requires the child to take the place of the node to be deleted.

Consider the same BST example, and let's delete the node 30, which has one child (node 40):

1. Find the node to be deleted (30). 2. Since 30 has one child (40), remove 30 and replace it with 40.

The resulting BST is:

```
     50
    / \
  40    70
        / \
      60  80
```

Case 3: Deleting a Node with Two Children

This is the most complex case. A node with two children requires finding the node's in-order predecessor or successor to maintain the BST properties.

The process to delete a node with two children is as follows:

1. Find the node to be deleted. 2. Find its in-order successor (smallest node in the right subtree) or in-order predecessor (largest node in the left subtree). 3. Replace the node's value with the in-order successor's (or predecessor's) value. 4. Delete the in-order successor (or predecessor), which will now have at most one child.

Consider again the BST example. To delete the node 50, which has two children:

1. Find the node to be deleted (50). 2. Find the in-order successor of 50, which is 60 (smallest node in the right subtree of 50). 3. Replace the value of 50 with 60. 4. Delete the node 60, which has no children.

The resulting BST is:

```
      60
     / \
   30   70
  / \     \
20  40     80
```

Python Implementation

The following Python code demonstrates the deletion process in a BST:

```
class TreeNode:
    def __init__(self, key):
        self.left = None
        self.right = None
        self.val = key

def deleteNode(root, key):
    if root is None:
        return root

    if key < root.val:
        root.left = deleteNode(root.left, key)
    elif key > root.val:
        root.right = deleteNode(root.right, key)
    else:
        if root.left is None:
            return root.right
        elif root.right is None:
            return root.left

        temp = minValueNode(root.right)
        root.val = temp.val
        root.right = deleteNode(root.right, temp.val)

    return root

def minValueNode(node):
    current = node
    while current.left is not None:
        current = current.left
    return current
```

The deleteNode function follows the aforementioned steps for deletion:

1. It searches for the node with the specified key. 2. Once found, if the node has no children or only one child, the node is simply replaced by its child. 3. If the node has two children, it replaces the node's value with its in-order successor's value and recursively deletes the successor node.

The helper function $\mathrm{minValueNode}$ finds the in-order successor, ensuring the proper maintenance of BST properties during deletion.

Ensuring correctness in these operations is critical for maintaining the efficiency and structural integrity of the BST, keeping operations like search, insertion, and deletion at optimal time complexities.

6.7 AVL Trees

AVL trees, named after their inventors Adelson-Velsky and Landis, are a type of self-balancing binary search tree (BST). In an AVL tree, the heights of the two child subtrees of any node differ by at most one, ensuring that the tree remains approximately balanced. This balancing is crucial as it guarantees $O(\log n)$ time complexity for insertion, deletion, and lookup operations, where n is the number of nodes in the tree.

An AVL tree maintains its balance through a series of rotations that adjust the structure after insertions or deletions. This section delves into the fundamental properties of AVL trees, their balancing mechanisms, and the operations for insertion and deletion with corresponding rotations.

Balance Factor:

The balance factor of a node in an AVL tree is the difference between the heights of the left and right subtrees. Formally, for a node N:

$$\text{BalanceFactor}(\text{N}) = \text{Height}(\text{LeftSubtree}) - \text{Height}(\text{RightSubtree})$$

A node is considered balanced if its balance factor is -1, 0, or 1. If the balance factor of any node becomes less than -1 or greater than 1, the tree requires rebalancing.

Rotations:

Rotations are operations that change the structure of the tree without altering the in-order sequence of elements, thereby preserving the BST property. There are four types of rotations used to restore balance in an AVL tree:

1. **Left Rotation (LL Rotation)**: A left rotation is performed when a right-heavy subtree becomes unbalanced.

```
      X
  /       \
 a         Y
          / \
      b    c
```

Transforms to:

```
        Y
  /         \
 X           c
/ \
a    b
```

2. **Right Rotation (RR Rotation)**: A right rotation is performed when a left-heavy subtree becomes unbalanced.

```
        Y
  /         \
 X           c
/ \
a    b
```

Transforms to:

```
      X
  /       \
 a         Y
          / \
      b    c
```

3. **Left-Right Rotation (LR Rotation)**: When a left subtree is right-heavy, a double rotation (left-right) is needed. This involves a left rotation on the left child followed by a right rotation on the unbalanced node.

4. **Right-Left Rotation (RL Rotation)**: When a right subtree is left-heavy, a double rotation (right-left) is needed. This involves a right rotation on the right child followed by a left rotation on the unbalanced node.

Insertion in AVL Tree:

The insertion process in an AVL tree involves performing a standard BST insertion followed by verifying and restoring balance through rotations if necessary.

Consider the following function for inserting a node in an AVL tree:

```
class TreeNode:
    def __init__(self, key):
        self.key = key
        self.left = None
        self.right = None
        self.height = 1

def insert(node, key):
    # Step 1: Perform the normal BST insertion
    if not node:
        return TreeNode(key)
    elif key < node.key:
        node.left = insert(node.left, key)
    else:
        node.right = insert(node.right, key)

    # Step 2: Update the height of the ancestor node
    node.height = 1 + max(get_height(node.left), get_height(node.right))

    # Step 3: Get the balance factor
    balance = get_balance(node)

    # Step 4: If the node becomes unbalanced, then balance it
    # Case 1: Left Left
    if balance > 1 and key < node.left.key:
        return right_rotate(node)

    # Case 2: Right Right
    if balance < -1 and key > node.right.key:
        return left_rotate(node)

    # Case 3: Left Right
    if balance > 1 and key > node.left.key:
        node.left = left_rotate(node.left)
        return right_rotate(node)

    # Case 4: Right Left
    if balance < -1 and key < node.right.key:
        node.right = right_rotate(node.right)
        return left_rotate(node)

    return node

def left_rotate(z):
    y = z.right
    T2 = y.left

    y.left = z
    z.right = T2

    z.height = 1 + max(get_height(z.left), get_height(z.right))
    y.height = 1 + max(get_height(y.left), get_height(y.right))
```

```
    return y

def right_rotate(z):
    y = z.left
    T3 = y.right

    y.right = z
    z.left = T3

    z.height = 1 + max(get_height(z.left), get_height(z.right))
    y.height = 1 + max(get_height(y.left), get_height(y.right))

    return y

def get_height(node):
    if not node:
        return 0
    return node.height

def get_balance(node):
    if not node:
        return 0
    return get_height(node.left) - get_height(node.right)
```

Executing the insertion and rotations ensures the AVL tree remains balanced after each insertion.

Deletion in AVL Tree:

Deletion in an AVL tree involves similar steps: performing a standard BST deletion followed by verifying and restoring the balance through rotations.

Consider the deletion procedure outlined below:

```
def delete(node, key):
    if not node:
        return node

    # Step 1: Perform standard BST deletion
    if key < node.key:
        node.left = delete(node.left, key)
    elif key > node.key:
        node.right = delete(node.right, key)
    else:
        if node.left is None:
            return node.right
        elif node.right is None:
            return node.left

        temp = get_min_value_node(node.right)
        node.key = temp.key
        node.right = delete(node.right, temp.key)

    # Step 2: Update the height of the current node
    node.height = 1 + max(get_height(node.left), get_height(node.right))

    # Step 3: Get the balance factor
    balance = get_balance(node)
```

```
    # Step 4: Restore balance if necessary
    # Case 1: Left Left
    if balance > 1 and get_balance(node.left) >= 0:
        return right_rotate(node)

    # Case 2: Left Right
    if balance > 1 and get_balance(node.left) < 0:
        node.left = left_rotate(node.left)
        return right_rotate(node)

    # Case 3: Right Right
    if balance < -1 and get_balance(node.right) <= 0:
        return left_rotate(node)

    # Case 4: Right Left
    if balance < -1 and get_balance(node.right) > 0:
        node.right = right_rotate(node.right)
        return left_rotate(node)

    return node

def get_min_value_node(node):
    if node is None or node.left is None:
        return node
    return get_min_value_node(node.left)
```

This deletion operation ensures that the AVL tree remains balanced by performing necessary rotations after each deletion.

The balancing operations through rotations maintain the tree's height at $O(\log n)$, which is critical for ensuring efficient performance in dynamic set operations. These detailed procedures facilitate a deeper understanding of how AVL trees manage structural modifications to preserve their balanced nature.

6.8 B-Trees

B-Trees are balanced tree data structures that maintain sorted data and allow searches, sequential access, insertions, and deletions in logarithmic time. The B-Tree, a generalization of the binary search tree (BST), is optimized for systems that read and write large blocks of data, such as databases and file systems.

Unlike a binary tree, where each node has at most two children, a B-Tree of order m (also denoted as a B-m Tree) allows a node to have up to m children and $m-1$ keys. This feature contributes to the B-Tree's high degree of balancement, ensuring that the tree remains shallow, facilitating efficient disk reads and writes.

Key properties of B-Trees are:

- Each node has at most m children.
- Each internal node contains between $\lceil m/2 \rceil$ and m children (except for the root, which may have as few as two children).
- All leaves appear on the same level.

Structure of B-Tree Node:

A B-Tree node comprises the following components:

- An array of k keys ($k \leq m - 1$), each key separating the values in its subtrees.
- An array of child pointers, where each pointer references a subtree, thus maintaining the property of sorted order.

Thus, if x is a B-Tree node with $n[x]$ keys, and k_i denoting the i-th key, then:

$$k_1 < k_2 < \ldots < k_{n[x]}$$

The pointers $c_1, c_2, \ldots, c_{n[x]+1}$ point to the subtrees where any key k in the subtree c_i satisfies:

$$k_{i-1} < k < k_i$$

for $i = 1, 2, \ldots, n[x] + 1$, assuming that $k_0 = -\infty$ and $k_{n[x]+1} = +\infty$.

Searching in B-Trees:

Searching in a B-Tree starts at the root and proceeds until a leaf node is reached. Consider a B-Tree where each node contains keys $k_1, k_2, \ldots, k_n$ and child pointers $c_1, c_2, \ldots, c_{n+1}$.

To search for a key k:

1. Start at the root node.
2. Check the current node for the key k.
3. If the key is found, return the node along with the position of k in that node.
4. If the key is not found, identify the interval $[k_{i-1}, k_i)$ where k should belong, and proceed to the child node at position c_i.
5. Repeat the process until reaching a leaf node.

Below is the code for searching in a B-Tree:

```
class BTreeNode:
    def __init__(self, t, leaf=False):
        self.t = t
        self.keys = []
        self.children = []
        self.leaf = leaf

def search(x, k):
    i = 0
    while i < len(x.keys) and k > x.keys[i]:
        i += 1

    if i < len(x.keys) and k == x.keys[i]:
        return (x, i)
    elif x.leaf:
        return None
    else:
        return search(x.children[i], k)
```

Insertion in B-Trees:

Insertion in a B-Tree requires maintaining the tree properties, particularly ensuring that nodes do not overflow. When a node exceeds the maximum permissible number of keys, it is split into two nodes, and the middle key is promoted to the parent node. This process may propagate up to the root, possibly increasing the height of the tree.

Steps for inserting a key k into a B-Tree of order t:

1. If the root node is full (contains $2t - 1$ keys), split the root and create a new root.
2. Traverse from the root to the appropriate leaf node as in a search operation.
3. Insert the key k into the leaf node in sorted order.
4. If the leaf node exceeds the permissible keys, split the node, and promote the median key to the parent node.

Below is the code for insertion in a B-Tree:

```
def split_child(parent, i, child):
    t = child.t
    new_child = BTreeNode(t, child.leaf)

    parent.keys.insert(i, child.keys[t-1])
    parent.children.insert(i+1, new_child)

    new_child.keys = child.keys[t:]
    child.keys = child.keys[:t-1]

    if not child.leaf:
        new_child.children = child.children[t:]
```

```
        child.children = child.children[:t]

def insert_non_full(x, k):
    i = len(x.keys) - 1
    if x.leaf:
        x.keys.append(0)
        while i >= 0 and x.keys[i] > k:
            x.keys[i+1] = x.keys[i]
            i -= 1
        x.keys[i+1] = k
    else:
        while i >= 0 and x.keys[i] > k:
            i -= 1
        i += 1
        if len(x.children[i].keys) == 2*x.t - 1:
            split_child(x, i, x.children[i])
            if k > x.keys[i]:
                i += 1
        insert_non_full(x.children[i], k)

def insert(tree, k):
    r = tree.root
    if len(r.keys) == 2 * tree.t - 1:
        s = BTreeNode(tree.t, False)
        tree.root = s
        s.children.insert(0, r)
        split_child(s, 0, r)
        insert_non_full(s, k)
    else:
        insert_non_full(r, k)
```

Deletion in B-Trees:

Deletion in B-Trees is more complex than insertion. The goal is to remove a key while maintaining B-Tree properties. Key scenarios include deleting from a leaf node, deleting from an internal node, and ensuring internal nodes retain the minimum number of keys.

Three major cases guide the deletion process:

1. If the key is in a leaf node, remove it directly.
2. If the key is in an internal node:
    - If the predecessor or successor has at least t keys, replace the key with it and recursively delete the predecessor or successor.
    - If both the preceding and subsequent children have the minimum number of keys, merge these children.
3. If the key is not present in the node, proceed to the appropriate child node:
    - If the child has the minimum number of keys, ensure it has at least t keys by borrowing or merging nodes.

Below is the code for deletion in a B-Tree:

```
def merge(parent, i):
    child = parent.children[i]
    sibling = parent.children[i+1]

    child.keys.append(parent.keys[i])

    child.keys.extend(sibling.keys)
    if not child.leaf:
        child.children.extend(sibling.children)

    parent.keys.pop(i)
    parent.children.pop(i+1)

def borrow_from_next(parent, i):
    child = parent.children[i]
    sibling = parent.children[i+1]

    child.keys.append(parent.keys[i])
    parent.keys[i] = sibling.keys[0]
    sibling.keys.pop(0)

    if not sibling.leaf:
        child.children.append(sibling.children[0])
        sibling.children.pop(0)

def borrow_from_prev(parent, i):
    child = parent.children[i]
    sibling = parent.children[i-1]

    child.keys.insert(0, parent.keys[i-1])
    parent.keys[i-1] = sibling.keys.pop()

    if not child.leaf:
        child.children.insert(0, sibling.children.pop())

def fill(parent, i):
    if i != 0 and len(parent.children[i-1].keys) >= parent.t:
        borrow_from_prev(parent, i)
    elif i != len(parent.children) - 1 and len(parent.children[i+1].keys) >= parent.t:
        borrow_from_next(parent, i)
    else:
        if i != len(parent.children) - 1:
            merge(parent, i)
        else:
            merge(parent, i-1)

def delete_from_non_leaf(node, idx):
    k = node.keys[idx]
    if len(node.children[idx].keys) >= node.t:
        pred = get_pred(node, idx)
        node.keys[idx] = pred
        delete(node.children[idx], pred)
    elif len(node.children[idx+1].keys) >= node.t:
        succ = get_succ(node, idx)
        node.keys[idx] = succ
        delete(node.children[idx+1], succ)
    else:
        merge(node, idx)
        delete(node.children[idx], k)

def delete(node, k):
```

```
    idx = 0
    while idx < len(node.keys) and node.keys[idx] < k:
        idx += 1
    if idx < len(node.keys) and node.keys[idx] == k:
        if node.leaf:
            node.keys.pop(idx)
        else:
            delete_from_non_leaf(node, idx)
    else:
        if node.leaf:
            return
        flag = (idx == len(node.keys))
        if len(node.children[idx].keys) < node.t:
            fill(node, idx)

        if flag and idx > len(node.keys):
            delete(node.children[idx-1], k)
        else:
            delete(node.children[idx], k)
```

B-Trees effectively balance nodes to maintain search, insertion, and deletion operations' efficiency, making them a suitable choice for filesystem and database management systems. Their structured nature ensures consistent performance even with substantial data growth, adhering to logarithmic time complexity guarantees.

6.9 Heaps

Heaps are a specialized tree-based data structure that satisfies the heap property. This property is what distinguishes heaps from other types of trees. A heap can be of two types: a **min-heap** or a **max-heap**. In a min-heap, for any given node i, the value of i is less than or equal to the values of its children. Conversely, in a max-heap, the value of i is greater than or equal to the values of its children. This characteristic makes heaps particularly useful for implementing priority queues.

Properties of Heaps:

- A heap is a complete binary tree. This means all levels of the tree are fully filled except possibly for the last level, which must be filled from left to right.
- The heap property must be maintained after any insertion or deletion operation, ensuring the min-heap or max-heap property is preserved.

Heap Representation:

Heaps are typically represented using arrays, which allows for efficient storage and manipulation. Given a node at index i in an array:

- The left child can be found at index $2i + 1$
- The right child can be found at index $2i + 2$
- The parent can be found at index $\lfloor \frac{i-1}{2} \rfloor$

The array representation allows efficient access and manipulation of the heap's elements.

Basic Operations on Heaps:

1. **Insertion:** Inserting a new element into a heap involves adding the element at the end of the heap (maintaining the complete binary tree property) and then performing a **heapify-up** (also known as bubble-up, percolate-up, sift-up, or trickle-up) operation to restore the heap property.

```
def heapify_up(heap, index):
    parent_index = (index - 1) // 2
    if parent_index >= 0 and heap[index] < heap[parent_index]:
        heap[index], heap[parent_index] = heap[parent_index], heap[index]
        heapify_up(heap, parent_index)

def insert(heap, element):
    heap.append(element)
    heapify_up(heap, len(heap) - 1)
```

2. **Deletion:** The removal of the root element (the minimum in the case of a min-heap or the maximum in the case of a max-heap) requires replacing the root with the last element of the heap and then performing a **heapify-down** (also known as bubble-down, percolate-down, sift-down, or trickle-down) operation to restore the heap property.

```
def heapify_down(heap, index):
    left_child_index = 2 * index + 1
    right_child_index = 2 * index + 2
    smallest = index

    if left_child_index < len(heap) and heap[left_child_index] < heap[smallest]:
        smallest = left_child_index
    if right_child_index < len(heap) and heap[right_child_index] < heap[smallest]:
        smallest = right_child_index

    if smallest != index:
        heap[index], heap[smallest] = heap[smallest], heap[index]
        heapify_down(heap, smallest)

def delete_min(heap):
    if len(heap) == 1:
        return heap.pop()
    root = heap[0]
```

```
    heap[0] = heap.pop()
    heapify_down(heap, 0)
    return root
```

3. **Heap Construction:** Building a heap from an arbitrary list of elements can be done efficiently in $O(n)$ time using the **heapify** process. Starting from the lowest non-leaf nodes and moving upwards, we perform heapify-down on each node.

```
def build_heap(elements):
    heap = elements.copy()
    start_index = len(heap) // 2 - 1
    for index in range(start_index, -1, -1):
        heapify_down(heap, index)
    return heap
```

Applications of Heaps:

Heaps have diverse applications in various domains:

- **Priority Queues:** Heaps are the ideal choice for priority queues where elements with higher (or lower) priority need to be served first.
- **Heap Sort:** An efficient comparison-based sorting algorithm that uses a heap data structure. The time complexity of heap sort is $O(n \log n)$.
- **Graph Algorithms:** Dijkstra's Shortest Path and Prim's Minimum Spanning Tree algorithms leverage heaps for efficient edge selection.

Through the formal definition, properties, and operations discussed, we gain comprehensive insight into heaps' functioning and implementation. The following is an example that demonstrates the insertion, deletion, and heap construction in a priority queue context implemented using a min-heap.

```
class MinHeap:
    def __init__(self):
        self.heap = []

    def insert(self, element):
        self.heap.append(element)
        heapify_up(self.heap, len(self.heap) - 1)

    def extract_min(self):
        if len(self.heap) == 0:
            return None
        if len(self.heap) == 1:
            return self.heap.pop()
```

```
        root = self.heap[0]
        self.heap[0] = self.heap.pop()
        heapify_down(self.heap, 0)
        return root

    def build_heap(self, elements):
        self.heap = build_heap(elements)

mh = MinHeap()
mh.build_heap([10, 20, 15, 30, 40])
print(mh.extract_min())
```

```
10
```

In this implementation, the class MinHeap encapsulates heap operations, providing an efficient and reusable data structure for managing priorities.

6.10 Trie Trees

Trie trees, commonly referred to simply as tries (pronounced "trees" or "try"), are specialized tree-based data structures that efficiently store a dynamic set of strings where the keys are usually strings. Tries are particularly useful for tasks involving collections of strings, such as autocomplete features, spell checkers, and IP routing.

A trie is defined by its nodes and edges. Each node represents a prefix of the strings inserted into the trie, and each edge represents a single character extending from one prefix to its next. The root node corresponds to the empty prefix, and each subsequent node corresponds to the prefixes formed by the characters traversed from the root to that node.

A fundamental characteristic of a trie is that all descendants of a node share a common prefix. The root is associated with the empty string, and each descending node adds one more character to the accumulated value of the parent node.

To construct a trie, we consider each character of a string as a step deeper into the tree. Here's how insertion of a string into a trie can be implemented in Python:

```
class TrieNode:
    def __init__(self):
        self.children = {}
        self.is_end_of_word = False

class Trie:
    def __init__(self):
```

```
        self.root = TrieNode()

    def insert(self, word):
        node = self.root
        for char in word:
            if char not in node.children:
                node.children[char] = TrieNode()
            node = node.children[char]
        node.is_end_of_word = True
```

In this implementation, the TrieNode class represents individual nodes of the trie. Each node has a dictionary variable children that stores its child nodes and a boolean is_end_of_word to mark the end of a word. The Trie class maintains the root node of the trie and provides an insert function to add words.

To search for a string in a trie, you traverse the trie according to the characters in the string. If you reach the end of the string and the node is_end_of_word is True, the string exists in the trie:

```
def search(self, word):
    node = self.root
    for char in word:
        if char not in node.children:
            return False
        node = node.children[char]
    return node.is_end_of_word
```

The time complexity for both insertion and search operations in a trie is $O(m)$, where m is the length of the string. This efficiency owes to the fact that each character in the string corresponds to one depth level of the trie.

Another common operation in a trie is searching for all words with a given prefix. This is particularly useful for implementing autocompletion. Starting from the node representing the prefix, a Depth-First Search (DFS) can be used to collect all words that have the prefix:

```
def _collect_all_words(self, node, prefix, words):
    if node.is_end_of_word:
        words.append(prefix)
    for char, child_node in node.children.items():
        self._collect_all_words(child_node, prefix + char, words)

def autocomplete(self, prefix):
    node = self.root
    for char in prefix:
        if char not in node.children:
            return []
        node = node.children[char]

    words = []
    self._collect_all_words(node, prefix, words)
    return words
```

In the autocomplete function, the _collect_all_words helper function performs the DFS from the node that corresponds to the end of the prefix, collecting all words that stem from that node.

Trie trees also have numerous variations to optimize specific use-cases. One such variation is the compressed trie (or Radix tree), which collapses chains of single nodes. Another variation is the ternary search tree, which stores characters at nodes in a binary search tree fashion, conserving space.

Tries are space-intensive since each node may have up to 26 children (for the English alphabet) or more for larger character sets. This increased space requirement can be mitigated by using more space-efficient structures such as hash maps for child nodes or implementing the aforementioned compressed tries.

Tries are essential for various algorithmic problems, making them a vital tool for real-time systems needing fast and efficient string manipulations. They feature heavily in applications requiring prompt lookups and pattern matching tasks.

6.11 Applications of Trees

Trees are a fundamental data structure in computer science and find extensive applications in various domains. Their hierarchical nature and efficient search, insert, and delete capabilities make them suitable for a wide range of tasks. This section delves into the practical implementations and advantages of using tree structures in real-world scenarios, focusing on areas such as databases, file systems, network routing, and more.

- **Database Indexing:** One of the prime applications of trees, particularly B-trees and their variants like B+ trees, is in database indexing. Databases need to perform rapid search and retrieval, insertion, and deletion operations. B-trees are balanced, maintaining sorted data and allowing for logarithmic time complexity for these operations. This balance ensures that the path from the root to any leaf node is about the same length, providing efficiency in high-volume database transactions. B+ trees enhance B-trees by storing all values at the leaf nodes and maintaining pointers to these leaf nodes, further optimizing range queries.
- **File Systems:** Modern file systems often leverage tree structures

for efficient file storage and retrieval. Examples include the ext4 file system in Linux, which uses a complex tree structure known as an extent tree to manage file allocations. Hierarchical structures such as directories can also be represented using trees, simplifying navigation and management.

- **Network Routing:** Trees are essential in network routing algorithms. Spanning trees, for example, are utilized in network topology management to prevent loops. The Spanning Tree Protocol (STP) allows switches to communicate, ensuring a loop-free network topology by creating a spanning tree that includes all the network's bridges or switches. Additionally, IP routing uses tries (prefix trees) to store routing tables efficiently, enabling quick lookups for routing decisions.

- **Syntax Tree in Compilers:** Abstract syntax trees (ASTs) are used in compilers to represent the structure of program code. During the parsing phase, source code is analyzed and converted into a tree structure that reflects the hierarchical nature of the syntax. This tree is then used in the subsequent steps of compilation, such as semantic analysis and code generation. ASTs are crucial for optimizing code and error checking.

- **Artificial Intelligence:** In AI, particularly in decision-making algorithms and game theory, trees play a crucial role. Decision trees are used for classification and regression tasks. They split the data into branches based on feature values, helping in predictive modeling. Moreover, game trees are a cornerstone in designing algorithms for playing strategic games like chess, where each node represents a possible game state.

- **Data Compression:** Trees, specifically Huffman trees, are instrumental in data compression algorithms. Huffman encoding uses a binary tree to assign variable-length codes to input characters, based on their frequencies. Characters that occur more frequently are given shorter codes, which helps in reducing the overall size of the data. This method is foundational in technologies like ZIP compression and multimedia codecs.

- **Geographical Information Systems (GIS):** In GIS applications, spatial data often requires efficient access and manipulation. Quadtrees and K-D trees are used to index multi-dimensional information such as geographical coordinates. These trees decompose space into manageable sections, making operations like range queries and nearest neighbor searches more efficient.

- **Expression Parsing in Calculators:** Evaluations of mathematical expressions in calculators and other arithmetic processing tools often make use of expression trees. Each node in the tree represents an operator, and the children nodes represent the operands. This structure allows for the implementation of various order traversals like infix, prefix, and postfix, which are essential in evaluating the expressions properly.

- **Concurrent Programming:** In concurrent or multi-threaded programming, trees like concurrent hash tries are used to manage shared data structures efficiently. These trees allow multiple threads to perform operations without significant locking, thereby improving performance and scalability.

- **Genealogy and Historical Research:** Tree structures are naturally suited to represent genealogical data, such as family trees or lineage charts. They can depict ancestral connections and descendants in a clear, hierarchical manner, making it easier to track lineage and heritage.

Through these applications, it is evident that tree structures are not only versatile but also indispensable across various technological and research domains. Their ability to provide structured, efficient, and scalable solutions makes them a cornerstone of modern computing and data management.

6.12 Performance Considerations in Trees

Analyzing the performance of tree data structures requires examining various factors such as time complexity, space complexity, and balancing criteria. Tree-based algorithms' performance is contingent on the type of tree and the specific operations being performed.

Time complexity for common operations such as insertion, deletion, and search is typically discussed. For a binary search tree (BST), performance is inherently linked to the tree's height. The time complexity for basic operations in a BST is $O(h)$ where h is the height of the tree. In the worst-case scenario, the height of a BST can become $O(n)$, where n is the number of nodes, leading to linear time complexity. This occurs when nodes are inserted in a sorted order, degenerating the BST into a linked list.

Balanced trees such as AVL trees and Red-Black trees aim to keep the height of the tree approximately logarithmic with respect to the number of nodes, $h = O(\log n)$. This logarithmic height ensures logarithmic time complexity, $O(\log n)$, for insertion, deletion, and search operations, thus significantly enhancing performance for large datasets.

```
class Node:
    def __init__(self, key):
        self.key = key
        self.left = None
        self.right = None
        self.height = 1

class AVLTree:
    def insert(self, root, key):
        # Perform the normal BST rotation
        if not root:
            return Node(key)
        elif key < root.key:
            root.left = self.insert(root.left, key)
        else:
            root.right = self.insert(root.right, key)

        # Update the height of the ancestor node
        root.height = 1 + max(self.getHeight(root.left), self.getHeight(root.right))

        # Get the balance factor
        balance = self.getBalance(root)

        # If the node is unbalanced, then try the 4 cases

        # Left Left Case
        if balance > 1 and key < root.left.key:
            return self.rightRotate(root)

        # Right Right Case
        if balance < -1 and key > root.right.key:
            return self.leftRotate(root)

        # Left Right Case
        if balance > 1 and key > root.left.key:
            root.left = self.leftRotate(root.left)
            return self.rightRotate(root)

        # Right Left Case
        if balance < -1 and key < root.right.key:
            root.right = self.rightRotate(root.right)
            return self.leftRotate(root)

        return root

    def leftRotate(self, z):
        y = z.right
        T2 = y.left
        y.left = z
        z.right = T2
        z.height = 1 + max(self.getHeight(z.left), self.getHeight(z.right))
```

```
        y.height = 1 + max(self.getHeight(y.left), self.getHeight(y.right))
        return y

    def rightRotate(self, z):
        y = z.left
        T3 = y.right
        y.right = z
        z.left = T3
        z.height = 1 + max(self.getHeight(z.left), self.getHeight(z.right))
        y.height = 1 + max(self.getHeight(y.left), self.getHeight(y.right))
        return y

    def getHeight(self, root):
        if not root:
            return 0
        return root.height

    def getBalance(self, root):
        if not root:
            return 0
        return self.getHeight(root.left) - self.getHeight(root.right)
```

The balance of AVL trees ensures that the performance remains efficient, even in the worst-case scenarios. Similarly, B-trees and heaps are designed to maintain balanced structures to optimize performance. B-trees are especially beneficial in scenarios involving databases and file systems, as they minimize disk reads, which are significantly slower compared to in-memory operations. B-trees maintain balance by ensuring that all leaf nodes are at the same level and by distributing keys across multiple child nodes to maintain the height as $O(\log n)$.

The heap data structure, particularly binary heaps, provides efficient support for priority queue operations. In binary heaps, insertion, and deletion operations maintain the structure's properties, resulting in $O(\log n)$ time complexity. Min-heaps and max-heaps are fundamental in applications requiring efficient retrieval of the minimum and maximum elements, respectively.

```
class MinHeap:
    def __init__(self):
        self.heap = []

    def insert(self, key):
        self.heap.append(key)
        i = len(self.heap) - 1
        while i > 0 and self.heap[i] < self.heap[(i - 1) // 2]:
            self.heap[i], self.heap[(i - 1) // 2] = self.heap[(i - 1) // 2], self.heap[i]
            i = (i - 1) // 2

    def heapify(self, i):
        smallest = i
        left = 2 * i + 1
        right = 2 * i + 2
        if left < len(self.heap) and self.heap[left] < self.heap[smallest]:
            smallest = left
```

```
        if right < len(self.heap) and self.heap[right] < self.heap[smallest]:
            smallest = right
        if smallest != i:
            self.heap[i], self.heap[smallest] = self.heap[smallest], self.heap[i]
            self.heapify(smallest)
```

While analyzing space complexity, we consider both the auxiliary space required by the algorithms and the extra space consumed by maintaining tree properties. Trees naturally use $O(n)$ space to store n nodes. Self-balancing trees, like AVL trees, require additional space to store height or balance information at each node, though this is a linear addition in terms of complexity. B-trees, particularly in database applications, are designed to reduce expensive disk I/O by ensuring that nodes are densely packed and thus minimizing the height of the tree.

Performance considerations extend to traversal methods as well. In-order, pre-order, and post-order tree traversals have time complexity $O(n)$ as each node is visited exactly once. Though these traversal methods are efficient, choosing the appropriate one can impact the overall performance depending on the specific algorithm requirements. Breadth-first traversal, typically implemented using a queue, may have higher space complexity compared to depth-first traversals due to additional storage requirements.

The performance of trees is greatly impacted by the requirement for maintenance operations to ensure the trees remain balanced. While these balancing operations might introduce overhead, the performance improvements for large datasets can be significant. Consequently, understanding the performance characteristics and trade-offs of various tree structures is critical for effective data structure selection in software development.

Chapter 7

Graphs

This chapter delves into graph data structures, covering fundamental concepts, terminology, and types of graphs. It explains various graph representations and traversal methods, including Depth-First Search (DFS) and Breadth-First Search (BFS). The chapter also addresses shortest path algorithms, minimum spanning trees, graph coloring, and practical applications, along with performance considerations to provide a comprehensive understanding of graphs.

7.1 Introduction to Graphs

A graph G is an abstract data structure that consists of a set of vertices V (or nodes) and a set of edges E connecting pairs of vertices. Formally, we can represent a graph as $G = (V, E)$. Each edge $\{u, v\} \in E$ is a connection between two vertices u and v in V. Graphs are pivotal in modeling various real-world systems such as social networks, transportation networks, communication networks, and many others due to their ability to represent pairwise relationships.

The two primary components of a graph are:

- **Vertices (or Nodes)**: These are the fundamental units in the graph. In diagrams, vertices are often depicted as dots or circles.
- **Edges**: These represent the connections between vertices.

Edges can be directed or undirected, weighted or unweighted. They are commonly drawn as lines or arrows between vertices.

Graphs can be categorized based on various attributes such as directionality, weight, and cyclicity, among others. Understanding these categories helps in selecting the appropriate algorithms and data structures for solving specific problems.

Consider the following Python code that defines a simple graph using an adjacency list:

```
class Graph:
    def __init__(self):
        self.adjacency_list = {}

    def add_vertex(self, vertex):
        if vertex not in self.adjacency_list:
            self.adjacency_list[vertex] = []

    def add_edge(self, vertex1, vertex2):
        if vertex1 in self.adjacency_list and vertex2 in self.adjacency_list:
            self.adjacency_list[vertex1].append(vertex2)
            # For an undirected graph, add the opposite edge
            self.adjacency_list[vertex2].append(vertex1)

    def __str__(self):
        return str(self.adjacency_list)

# Example Usage:
graph = Graph()
graph.add_vertex('A')
graph.add_vertex('B')
graph.add_edge('A', 'B')
print(graph)
```

Expressed in an adjacency list representation, the graph class allows adding vertices and edges, which are pivotal operations in graph processing. The output of the above code is demonstrative of the adjacency list of the graph:

```
{'A': ['B'], 'B': ['A']}
```

Graphs can be **directed** or **undirected**:

- **Directed Graphs (Digraphs)**: Each edge has a direction, pointing from one vertex to another. Formally, an edge is an ordered pair (u, v). These are useful in scenarios like website links or road maps where the direction of travel matters.

- **Undirected Graphs**: Each edge is a bidirectional connection between two vertices. Formally, an edge is an unordered pair $\{u, v\}$. These are often used to model symmetric relationships, such as friendships in a social network.

Additionally, graphs can be classified based on whether they contain weights on their edges:

- **Weighted Graphs**: Each edge has a numerical value associated with it, often referred to as the weight. Weights can represent costs, distances, or any quantitative relationships. Algorithms like Dijkstra's and the Bellman-Ford algorithm are typically used to find shortest paths in weighted graphs.
- **Unweighted Graphs**: Edges do not have any weights. In these graphs, algorithms like BFS and DFS are often utilized for traversal and connectivity checks.

Consider the following Python code snippet that extends the graph definition to handle weighted edges:

```
class WeightedGraph:
    def __init__(self):
        self.adjacency_list = {}

    def add_vertex(self, vertex):
        if vertex not in self.adjacency_list:
            self.adjacency_list[vertex] = []

    def add_edge(self, vertex1, vertex2, weight):
        if vertex1 in self.adjacency_list and vertex2 in self.adjacency_list:
            self.adjacency_list[vertex1].append((vertex2, weight))
            # For an undirected graph, add the opposite edge with the same weight
            self.adjacency_list[vertex2].append((vertex1, weight))

    def __str__(self):
        return str(self.adjacency_list)

# Example Usage:
graph = WeightedGraph()
graph.add_vertex('A')
graph.add_vertex('B')
graph.add_edge('A', 'B', 3)
print(graph)
```

The output of the above code, representing a weighted graph in adjacency list format, is shown below:

```
{'A': [('B', 3)], 'B': [('A', 3)]}
```

Graph traversal, the process of visiting all the vertices in a graph, is a foundational operation. This concept is critical for searching algorithms and understanding graph connectivity. Typical traversal techniques include depth-first search (DFS) and breadth-first search (BFS), each having distinct properties and suitable for different types of problems.

Graphs are frequently utilized to solve many computational problems, such as finding the shortest path between nodes, detecting cycles, and performing searches. Their versatile nature means they can be represented in various ways including adjacency matrices, adjacency lists, and edge lists. Each representation has its own trade-offs regarding space complexity and the ease of implementing graph algorithms.

When faced with specific graph-based problems, the choice of graph representation and the traversal technique has a significant impact on the efficiency and feasibility of the solution. Understanding the foundational concepts of graphs is crucial for any computer scientist or engineer aiming to employ these data structures for practical applications.

7.2 Graph Terminology

Understanding graph terminology is crucial to grasping the diverse and intricate world of graph data structures. The following terminologies form the foundation for interpreting and working with graphs effectively.

Graph (G): A graph G consists of two finite sets: a non-empty set of vertices $V(G)$ and a set of edges $E(G)$. Each edge is defined as an unordered pair of vertices. Formally, $G = (V, E)$.

Vertex (Node): A vertex, also referred to as a node, is a fundamental unit from which graphs are formed. The set of vertices in a graph G is usually denoted by $V(G)$. Vertices are typically represented by points or circles.

Edge: An edge is a connection between a pair of vertices. The set of edges is denoted by $E(G)$. Each edge in an undirected graph is represented by a tuple (u, v), where u and v are vertices belonging to the vertex set $V(G)$. In directed graphs, edges have directions and are represented by an ordered pair (u, v) indicating an edge from vertex u to vertex v.

Path: A path in a graph is a finite or infinite sequence of edges which connect a sequence of vertices. No vertex in the path is visited more than once. For instance, $P = (v_1, e_1, v_2, e_2, \ldots, v_{n-1}, e_{n-1}, v_n)$ is a path from vertex v_1 to vertex v_n.

Cycle: A cycle is a path where the start and end vertices are the same, and no other vertex is repeated. Formally, a cycle is a path $\{v_0, v_1, \ldots, v_{n-1}, v_0\}$ with $v_0 = v_n$ and $v_i \neq v_j$ for all $0 \leq i < j < n$.

Degree of a Vertex: The degree of a vertex is the number of edges incident to the vertex. In a directed graph, the in-degree of a vertex is the number of incoming edges, and the out-degree is the number of outgoing edges.

Subgraph: A subgraph is a graph formed from a subset of the vertices and edges of another graph. Formally, $H = (V_H, E_H)$ is a subgraph of $G = (V, E)$ if $V_H \subseteq V$ and $E_H \subseteq E$.

Connected Graph: A graph is connected if there is a path between every pair of vertices. If no such path exists, the graph is disconnected. In a directed graph, the term *strongly connected* is used to indicate that every vertex is reachable from every other vertex.

Component: A connected component is a maximal connected subgraph of G. Each vertex in the graph belongs to exactly one connected component.

Adjacent: Two vertices u and v are adjacent if there is an edge (u, v) in the graph. Similarly, two edges are adjacent if they share a common vertex.

Isomorphism: Two graphs G_1 and G_2 are isomorphic if there is a one-to-one correspondence between their vertex sets and their edge sets such that adjacency is preserved. Isomorphism implies that the two graphs have the same structure but may have different vertex labels.

Weighted Graph: In a weighted graph, each edge has an associated numerical value called a weight. The weight often represents a cost, distance, or time associated with traversing the edge. Formally, a weighted graph is a graph $G = (V, E, W)$ with an additional function $W : E \to \mathbb{R}$ mapping edges to real numbers.

Directed and Undirected Graphs: In an undirected graph, edges have no direction, represented as unordered pairs (u, v). In a directed graph or digraph, edges have a direction, represented as ordered pairs (u, v).

Complete Graph: A complete graph is one in which every pair of distinct vertices is connected by a unique edge. A complete graph with n vertices is denoted K_n.

Bipartite Graph: A graph is bipartite if its vertex set can be divided into two disjoint sets U and V such that every edge connects a vertex in U to one in V. Formally, a graph $G = (V, E)$ is bipartite if V can be partitioned into two sets U and V, with $U \cap V = \emptyset$ and $U \cup V = V$, such that every edge $e = (u, v)$ satisfies $u \in U$ and $v \in V$.

Planar Graph: A graph is planar if it can be embedded in the plane, i.e., it can be drawn on a plane without edges crossing each other.

Tree and Forest: A tree is an acyclic connected graph. A forest is a disjoint set of trees. A tree with n vertices has $n - 1$ edges.

The detailed understanding of these terminologies provides a robust foundation to navigate through subsequent concepts and algorithms related to graph data structures. Knowing these terms helps in devising more efficient solutions to graph-related problems and enables effective communication of these solutions.

7.3 Types of Graphs

Graphs can be classified into various types based on their structure, direction, and the nature of the connections between their nodes. Understanding these types is crucial for correctly applying graph algorithms and optimally solving problems that involve graph data structures. In this section, we explore several fundamental graph types in detail.

Undirected Graphs:

An undirected graph is a type of graph in which the edges between nodes have no direction. This means that if there is an edge between nodes u and v, you can traverse it from u to v and from v to u with no distinction. Formally, an undirected graph G can be denoted as $G = (V, E)$, where V is the set of vertices and E is the set of edges, where each edge is an unordered pair of vertices.

For example, consider an undirected graph:

```
graph = {
    'A': {'B', 'C'},
    'B': {'A', 'D', 'E'},
    'C': {'A', 'F'},
    'D': {'B'},
    'E': {'B', 'F'},
    'F': {'C', 'E'}
}
```

The adjacency list above represents an undirected graph, where each vertex points to a set of vertices it is connected to by an edge. If we choose vertex 'A', it is connected to vertices 'B' and 'C', and so forth.

Directed Graphs (Digraphs):

In contrast to undirected graphs, directed graphs consist of edges with a specific direction. In a directed graph, an edge (u, v) is an ordered pair, implying a direction from node u to node v. Directed graphs are formally defined as $G = (V, E)$, where V is the set of vertices and E is the set of ordered pairs of vertices.

Consider the following directed graph:

```
digraph = {
    'A': {'B', 'C'},
    'B': {'D', 'E'},
    'C': {'F'},
    'D': {},
    'E': {'F'},
    'F': {}
}
```

This adjacency list representation indicates a directed graph where, for instance, 'A' has directed edges to 'B' and 'C', but not the reverse.

Weighted Graphs:

Weighted graphs are graphs where edges have associated weights representing the cost, distance, or any quantifiable measure assigned to traversing from one vertex to another. Weighted graphs can be either directed or undirected.

An example of an undirected weighted graph is:

```
weighted_graph = {
    'A': {'B': 4, 'C': 2},
    'B': {'A': 4, 'D': 5, 'E': 10},
    'C': {'A': 2, 'F': 3},
    'D': {'B': 5},
    'E': {'B': 10, 'F': 1},
    'F': {'C': 3, 'E': 1}
}
```

In this graph, each entry in the adjacency list includes a dictionary mapping neighboring vertices to their respective weights.

Cyclic and Acyclic Graphs:

Graphs can be classified as cyclic or acyclic based on the presence of cycles. A *cycle* in a graph is a path that starts and ends at the same vertex without traversing any edge more than once.

- A **cyclic graph** contains at least one cycle. - An **acyclic graph** has no cycles.

Additionally, directed graphs can be specifically classified into **Directed Acyclic Graphs (DAGs)**, which play a crucial role in several algorithms, such as topological sorting and various scheduling problems.

Example of a directed acyclic graph:

```
dag = {
    'A': {'B', 'C'},
    'B': {'D'},
    'C': {'E'},
    'D': {'F'},
    'E': {'F'},
    'F': {}
}
```

In this representation, there are no cycles, ensuring that it is a DAG.

Connected and Disconnected Graphs:

A graph is said to be connected if there is a path between any two vertices. Conversely, a graph is disconnected if at least two vertices lack a path connecting them.

Example of a connected undirected graph:

```
connected_graph = {
    'A': {'B', 'C'},
    'B': {'A', 'D', 'E'},
    'C': {'A', 'F'},
    'D': {'B'},
    'E': {'B', 'F'},
    'F': {'C', 'E'}
}
```

Example of a disconnected undirected graph:

```
disconnected_graph = {
    'A': {'B'},
    'B': {'A'},
    'C': {'D'},
    'D': {'C'}
}
```

Bipartite Graphs:

A bipartite graph is one in which the set of vertices can be divided into two disjoint sets U and V such that every edge connects a vertex in U to one in V. Bipartite graphs are particularly useful in modeling relationships between two different classes of objects, such as matching problems.

A simple bipartite graph representation:

```
bipartite_graph = {
    'U1': {'V1', 'V2'},
    'U2': {'V2'},
    'U3': {'V3', 'V4'},
    'V1': {'U1'},
    'V2': {'U1', 'U2'},
    'V3': {'U3'},
```

```
    'V4': {'U3'}
}
```

Complete Graphs:

A complete graph is one in which every pair of distinct vertices is connected by a unique edge. In a complete graph with n vertices, there are $\frac{n(n-1)}{2}$ edges for undirected graphs and $n(n-1)$ edges for directed graphs.

For example, a complete graph K_4 has four vertices:

```
complete_graph = {
    'A': {'B', 'C', 'D'},
    'B': {'A', 'C', 'D'},
    'C': {'A', 'B', 'D'},
    'D': {'A', 'B', 'C'}
}
```

In this graph, each node is connected to every other node exactly once.

Sparse and Dense Graphs:

Graphs are also categorized as sparse or dense based on the number of edges relative to the number of vertices. A **sparse graph** has relatively few edges, often much less than the maximum possible number of edges, whereas a **dense graph** has a number of edges close to the maximum possible number of edges.

The differentiation between these types is important as it often dictates the choice of storage representation and algorithm efficiency.

Expanding our understanding of these various graph types provides a solid foundation for exploring graph algorithms and applications that rely on these structural properties.

7.4 Graph Representation

In the study of graphs, how we represent them determines the efficiency of various graph algorithms. The fundamental representations of graphs are the adjacency matrix, adjacency list, and edge list. Each representation has its advantages and trade-offs concerning space complexity and performance of specific operations, such as insertion, deletion, and traversal. Understanding these representations is crucial for selecting the appropriate one for a given application.

Adjacency Matrix:

An adjacency matrix is a square matrix used to represent a finite graph. The elements of the matrix indicate whether pairs of vertices are adjacent or not in the graph. Each element a_{ij} of the matrix is set to one if there is an edge between vertex v_i and vertex v_j; otherwise, it is zero.

Consider a graph $G = (V, E)$, where V is a set of vertices $\{v_1, v_2, ..., v_n\}$, and E is a set of edges. The adjacency matrix A for G is an $n \times n$ matrix $A = [a_{ij}]$, where:

$$a_{ij} = \begin{cases} 1 & \text{if there is an edge from } v_i \text{ to } v_j \\ 0 & \text{otherwise} \end{cases}$$

For example, let us represent a directed graph using an adjacency matrix in Python:

```
class GraphAdjMatrix:
    def __init__(self, num_vertices):
        self.num_vertices = num_vertices
        self.adj_matrix = [[0] * num_vertices for _ in range(num_vertices)]

    def add_edge(self, src, dest):
        self.adj_matrix[src][dest] = 1

    def remove_edge(self, src, dest):
        self.adj_matrix[src][dest] = 0

    def display(self):
        for row in self.adj_matrix:
            print(row)

# Example usage:
graph = GraphAdjMatrix(5)
graph.add_edge(0, 1)
graph.add_edge(0, 2)
graph.add_edge(1, 2)
graph.add_edge(2, 0)
graph.add_edge(2, 3)
graph.display()
```

The output of the display() method for the above code would be:

```
[0, 1, 1, 0, 0]
[0, 0, 1, 0, 0]
[1, 0, 0, 1, 0]
[0, 0, 0, 0, 0]
[0, 0, 0, 0, 0]
```

Adjacency List:

An adjacency list is a collection of lists used to represent a finite graph. Each list corresponds to a vertex in the graph and contains a list of that vertex's adjacent vertices. This representation is more space-efficient for sparse graphs.

For a graph $G = (V, E)$, the adjacency list consists of an array of lists. The array has one list for each vertex, and the list for vertex v_i contains all the vertices adjacent to v_i.

Consider a Python implementation of an adjacency list:

```
class GraphAdjList:
    def __init__(self):
        self.graph = {}

    def add_edge(self, src, dest):
        if src not in self.graph:
            self.graph[src] = []
        self.graph[src].append(dest)

    def display(self):
        for key in self.graph:
            print(f"{key} -> {self.graph[key]}")

# Example usage:
graph = GraphAdjList()
graph.add_edge(0, 1)
graph.add_edge(0, 2)
graph.add_edge(1, 2)
graph.add_edge(2, 0)
graph.add_edge(2, 3)
graph.display()
```

The output of the display() method for the above code would be:

```
0 -> [1, 2]
1 -> [2]
2 -> [0, 3]
```

Edge List:

An edge list is a collection of edges, which are represented as pairs of vertices. This representation is simple and works well for algorithms that process edges rather than adjacency information.

For a graph $G = (V, E)$, the edge list consists of tuples (v_i, v_j) where each tuple represents an edge from vertex v_i to vertex v_j.

A Python implementation of an edge list can be done as follows:

```
class GraphEdgeList:
    def __init__(self):
        self.edges = []

    def add_edge(self, src, dest):
        self.edges.append((src, dest))

    def display(self):
        for edge in self.edges:
            print(edge)

# Example usage:
graph = GraphEdgeList()
graph.add_edge(0, 1)
```

```
graph.add_edge(0, 2)
graph.add_edge(1, 2)
graph.add_edge(2, 0)
graph.add_edge(2, 3)
graph.display()
```

The output of the display() method for the above code is:

```
(0, 1)
(0, 2)
(1, 2)
(2, 0)
(2, 3)
```

These three representations — adjacency matrix, adjacency list, and edge list — each offer different strengths suited to different types of graph operations and applications. Choosing the right representation depends on particular requirements such as space complexity, the density of the graph, and the operations to be performed.

7.5 Graph Traversal Methods

Graph traversal methods are techniques used to visit all the vertices or nodes in a graph systematically. These methods are fundamental in many graph-related algorithms and applications, such as searching for a specific node, finding the shortest path between nodes, or checking if a path exists between nodes.

Traversal Strategies

Graph traversals can generally be classified into two broad categories: Depth-First Search (DFS) and Breadth-First Search (BFS). Each traversal method has its unique characteristics and is suitable for different types of problems.

Depth-First Search (DFS)

Depth-First Search (DFS) explores a graph by starting at the root node and diving as deep as possible along each branch before backtracking. It uses a stack data structure either explicitly or through recursion. Here is a Python implementation of DFS using recursion:

```
def dfs(graph, start, visited=None):
    if visited is None:
        visited = set()
    visited.add(start)

    print(start)
    for next_node in graph[start] - visited:
        dfs(graph, next_node, visited)
```

```
    return visited

# Example graph as an adjacency list
graph = {'A': {'B', 'C'},
         'B': {'A', 'D', 'E'},
         'C': {'A', 'F'},
         'D': {'B'},
         'E': {'B', 'F'},
         'F': {'C', 'E'}}

dfs(graph, 'A')
```

The graph is represented as an adjacency list, which is a dictionary of sets. The DFS function takes a starting node and the graph, and it prints the visited nodes in the order they are visited. The main qualities of DFS are:

- **Completeness**: Only guaranteed if the graph is finite. - **Time Complexity**: $O(|V| + |E|)$ where $|V|$ is the number of vertices and $|E|$ is the number of edges. - **Space Complexity**: $O(|V|)$ due to the recursion stack.

Breadth-First Search (BFS)

Breadth-First Search (BFS) explores a graph level by level starting from the source node. It uses a queue to keep track of the next node to visit. Here is a Python implementation of BFS:

```
from collections import deque

def bfs(graph, start):
    visited = set()
    queue = deque([start])
    visited.add(start)

    while queue:
        vertex = queue.popleft()
        print(vertex)

        for neighbor in graph[vertex]:
            if neighbor not in visited:
                visited.add(neighbor)
                queue.append(neighbor)

# Example graph as an adjacency list
graph = {'A': {'B', 'C'},
         'B': {'A', 'D', 'E'},
         'C': {'A', 'F'},
         'D': {'B'},
         'E': {'B', 'F'},
         'F': {'C', 'E'}}

bfs(graph, 'A')
```

BFS iterates through the graph by processing all nodes at the present depth level before moving on to nodes at the next depth level. BFS characteristics include:

- **Completeness**: Guaranteed if the graph is finite. - **Time Complexity**: $O(|V| + |E|)$ similar to DFS. - **Space Complexity**: $O(|V|)$ required for the queue to store the nodes at the current depth level.

Comparison of DFS and BFS

When choosing between DFS and BFS, consider their properties relevant to the specific problem at hand:

- *Path Finding*: BFS is typically used for the shortest path in an unweighted graph, as it systematically explores nodes layer by layer. - *Memory Usage*: DFS generally has lower memory requirements in sparse graphs, especially if depth is considerably larger than breadth. - *Completeness and Optimality*: BFS guarantees completeness and can find the shortest path in unweighted graphs, whereas DFS does not guarantee these properties in general.

Applications of Graph Traversals

Graph traversal methods are used in various applications, such as:

- *Web Crawling*: Uses either DFS or BFS to explore hyperlinks on the web. - *Network Broadcasting*: BFS can be used to propagate information efficiently. - *Pathfinding Problems*: DFS and BFS are both fundamental for solving puzzles or games (e.g., mazes). - *Checking Graph Properties*: Finding connected components, detecting cycles, and more.

These traversal methods form the basis for advanced graph algorithms and are essential for comprehensively understanding the structure and properties of graphs.

7.6 Depth-First Search (DFS)

Depth-First Search (DFS) is an algorithm that explores a graph by starting at a selected node and traversing as far as possible along each branch before backtracking. This approach is critical for tasks such as connectivity testing, pathfinding, and discovering cycles within graphs. DFS can be implemented using either a recursive method or an iterative method with an explicit stack.

Recursive Implementation:

The recursive implementation of DFS utilizes the system's call stack to keep track of nodes yet to be fully explored. Below is a Python function demonstrating the recursive DFS algorithm:

```
def dfs_recursive(graph, start, visited=None):
    if visited is None:
        visited = set()
    visited.add(start)
    print(start)
    for next_node in graph[start] - visited:
        dfs_recursive(graph, next_node, visited)
    return visited
```

In this implementation, the function dfs_recursive takes a graph, a start node, and an optional visited set to keep track of visited nodes. The function marks the start node as visited and recursively explores adjacent nodes.

To illustrate:

```
graph = {'A': set(['B', 'C']),
         'B': set(['A', 'D', 'E']),
         'C': set(['A', 'F']),
         'D': set(['B']),
         'E': set(['B', 'F']),
         'F': set(['C', 'E'])}

visited_nodes = dfs_recursive(graph, 'A')
```

```
A
B
D
E
F
C
```

The DFS algorithm starts at node 'A', proceeds to 'B', then 'D', and continues with this depth-wise manner until all nodes reachable from 'A' are visited.

Iterative Implementation:

The iterative approach employs an explicit stack to manage the nodes to be visited. Here is a Python function demonstrating the iterative DFS algorithm:

```
def dfs_iterative(graph, start):
    visited = set()
    stack = [start]
    while stack:
        node = stack.pop()
        if node not in visited:
            visited.add(node)
            print(node)
            stack.extend(graph[node] - visited)
    return visited
```

This function initializes a stack with the start node and iteratively explores each node by popping it from the stack, visiting it, and pushing its unvisited adjacent nodes onto the stack.

An example execution for the aforementioned graph:

```
visited_nodes_iterative = dfs_iterative(graph, 'A')
```

```
A
C
F
E
B
D
```

Complexity Analysis:

The DFS algorithm has a time complexity of $O(V + E)$, where V is the number of vertices and E is the number of edges in the graph. This results from the fact that each vertex and edge is processed once. The space complexity is $O(V)$ due to the storage requirements for the visited set and the stack (or the call stack in the recursive approach).

Applications:

DFS has numerous applications including:

- **Pathfinding:** Identifying a path between two nodes.
- **Cycle Detection:** Determining if a graph contains a cycle.
- **Topological Sorting:** Arranging vertices in a directed acyclic graph.
- **Connected Components:** Discovering all connected components within a graph.

DFS is a fundamental graph traversal algorithm integral to the understanding and efficient solving of several graph-related problems. It provides the foundational basis for more advanced algorithms like those used in network flow analysis, game theory, and artificial intelligence.

7.7 Breadth-First Search (BFS)

Breadth-First Search (BFS) is an algorithm for traversing or searching tree or graph data structures. It starts at the tree root (or an arbitrary node of a graph, sometimes referred to as the 'source node') and explores the neighbor nodes at the present depth prior to moving on to nodes at the next depth level. BFS is a cornerstone algorithm in graph theory, enabling various applications such as finding the shortest path in an unweighted graph or discovering connected components.

The primary data structure used in BFS is the queue, which adheres to the First In, First Out (FIFO) principle. Nodes are enqueued when they are encountered and dequeued when they are fully explored. BFS can be implemented iteratively using a queue.

To formalize BFS, we use the following steps:

1. **Initialization**: Begin by enqueueing the root node and marking it as visited. 2. **Processing**: Dequeue a node and visit all its unvisited neighbors, marking them visited and enqueueing them. 3. **Completion**: Repeat the process until the queue is empty.

Consider a graph $G = (V, E)$ where V is the set of vertices and E the set of edges. Let $s \in V$ be the source vertex from which BFS starts. We can represent it algorithmically as follows:

```
from collections import deque

def bfs(graph, start):
    visited = set()
    queue = deque([start])
    visited.add(start)

    while queue:
        vertex = queue.popleft()
        print(vertex) # Process the node here (e.g., print or store it)

        for neighbor in graph[vertex]:
            if neighbor not in visited:
                visited.add(neighbor)
                queue.append(neighbor)
```

BFS Illustrative Example

Consider the graph representation:

```
A - B - C
|   |   |
D - E - F
```

This graph can be represented as an adjacency list:

```
graph = {
    'A': ['B', 'D'],
    'B': ['A', 'C', 'E'],
    'C': ['B', 'F'],
    'D': ['A', 'E'],
    'E': ['B', 'D', 'F'],
    'F': ['C', 'E']
```

```
}
bfs(graph, 'A')
```

Running the BFS algorithm from node 'A' would yield the following traversal order:

A
B
D
C
E
F

BFS Time Complexity

The time complexity of BFS depends on the way the graph is represented:

1. **Adjacency List**: $O(V + E)$. 2. **Adjacency Matrix**: $O(V^2)$.

The adjacency list representation is typically more efficient for sparse graphs, while adjacency matrix is practical for dense graphs.

BFS Applications

1. **Shortest Path in Unweighted Graphs**: BFS can be used to find the shortest path from a source node to a target node in an unweighted graph. This is particularly useful in networking, where each edge can be seen as a connection with equal weight.

2. **Connected Components**: BFS can discover all nodes in a graph that are reachable from a given start node, identifying connected components in undirected graphs.

3. **Cycle Detection in Undirected Graphs**: By maintaining a parent array, BFS can detect cycles in undirected graphs. If a node is discovered that is not the parent of the current node but has been visited earlier, a cycle exists.

Implementing BFS for Path Finding

To find the shortest path in an unweighted graph using BFS, modify the BFS to keep track of the predecessors of each node. Here is the modification:

```
def bfs_shortest_path(graph, start, goal):
    queue = deque([(start, [start])])

    while queue:
        (vertex, path) = queue.popleft()
        for next in set(graph[vertex]) - set(path):
            if next == goal:
                return path + [next]
```

```
        else:
            queue.append((next, path + [next]))
    return None
```

Given a start node 'A' and a goal node 'F', the function would return the shortest path:

```
['A', 'B', 'E', 'F']
```

By logically extending the simple traversal mechanism to path discovery, BFS can be effectively utilized in real-world scenarios where the shortest route is paramount, such as in network routing protocols, urban planning, and social network analysis.

7.8 Shortest Path Algorithms

Shortest path algorithms are fundamental in graph theory, solving a critical problem of finding the minimum path between vertices in a graph. These algorithms are vital in various applications, including routing in networks, urban planning, and many optimization problems. This section discusses several essential shortest path algorithms and their intricacies, with a focus on their implementations and use cases.

Dijkstra's Algorithm

Dijkstra's Algorithm is one of the most well-known algorithms for finding the shortest path from a source vertex to all other vertices in a weighted graph. The graph must have non-negative edge weights. Dijkstra's Algorithm uses a greedy approach to progressively determine the shortest path to each vertex.

Procedure:

- Initialize the distance to the source node as 0 and the distance to all other nodes as infinity.
- Set the source node as the current node and mark it as visited.
- For the current node, update the distances to its adjacent nodes. For any unvisited adjacent node, if the distance from the source to this node through the current node is less than the previously recorded distance, update the distance.

- Once all adjacent nodes are processed, mark the current node as visited. Select the next node with the smallest distance as the new current node.
- Repeat steps 3-4 until all nodes are visited.

The implementation of Dijkstra's Algorithm can be efficient using a priority queue (min-heap).

```
import heapq

def dijkstra(graph, start_vertex):
    D = {v: float('infinity') for v in graph}
    D[start_vertex] = 0

    priority_queue = [(0, start_vertex)]

    while priority_queue:
        (current_distance, current_vertex) = heapq.heappop(priority_queue)

        for neighbor, weight in graph[current_vertex].items():
            distance = current_distance + weight

            if distance < D[neighbor]:
                D[neighbor] = distance
                heapq.heappush(priority_queue, (distance, neighbor))

    return D
```

Output Example:

```
{
    'A': 0,
    'B': 7,
    'C': 9,
    'D': 20,
    'E': 20,
    'F': 11
}
```

Bellman-Ford Algorithm

The Bellman-Ford Algorithm handles graphs with negative edge weights, unlike Dijkstra's Algorithm. It can detect negative weight cycles, making it more versatile, albeit less efficient for graphs without negative weights.

Procedure:

- Initialize the distance to the source node as 0 and the distance to all other nodes as infinity.

- For each edge, update the distance if the new path is shorter than the known path. Repeat this process for $|V|$ - 1 times, where V is the number of vertices.
- Check for negative-weight cycles by verifying that no distances can be further updated. If any distance can be updated, a negative-weight cycle exists.

```
def bellman_ford(graph, start_vertex):
    D = {v: float('infinity') for v in graph}
    D[start_vertex] = 0

    for _ in range(len(graph) - 1):
        for vertex in graph:
            for neighbor, weight in graph[vertex].items():
                if D[vertex] + weight < D[neighbor]:
                    D[neighbor] = D[vertex] + weight

    for vertex in graph:
        for neighbor, weight in graph[vertex].items():
            if D[vertex] + weight < D[neighbor]:
                raise ValueError("Graph contains a negative-weight cycle")

    return D
```

Output Example:

```
{
    'A': 0,
    'B': 2,
    'C': 6,
    'D': 4,
    'E': 6
}
```

Floyd-Warshall Algorithm

The Floyd-Warshall Algorithm is an all-pairs shortest path algorithm, meaning it finds the shortest paths between all pairs of vertices in a graph. It is suitable for dense graphs due to its $O(V3)$ time complexity.

Procedure:

- Initialize a matrix D where $D[i][j]$ represents the edge weight from vertex i to vertex j. Set the distance from a vertex to itself as 0 and to others as infinity if there is no direct edge.
- For each vertex k, check if a path through k is shorter than the known path from i to j. Update the matrix accordingly.

- After V iterations, the matrix D will reflect the shortest paths between all vertex pairs.

```
def floyd_warshall(graph):
    V = len(graph)
    distance = list(map(lambda i: list(map(lambda j: j, i)), graph))

    for k in range(V):
        for i in range(V):
            for j in range(V):
                distance[i][j] = min(distance[i][j], distance[i][k] + distance[k][j])

    return distance
```

Output Example:

```
[
    [0, 3, 8, inf, -4],
    [inf, 0, inf, 1, 7],
    [inf, 4, 0, inf, inf],
    [2, inf, -5, 0, inf],
    [inf, inf, inf, 6, 0]
]
```

These algorithms are critical for solving various real-world problems, providing a toolbox for efficient pathfinding and optimization tasks in weighted graphs. Their suitability varies based on the specific graph properties and application requirements.

7.9 Minimum Spanning Tree

A *Minimum Spanning Tree (MST)* is a subset of the edges of a connected, undirected graph which connects all the vertices together, without any cycles and with the minimum possible total edge weight. In other words, it is a spanning tree whose sum of edge weights is as small as possible. This concept is crucial in numerous real-world applications, such as designing networks (telecommunications, computer, road) and clustering algorithms in machine learning.

Let $G = (V, E)$ be an undirected graph where V represents the set of vertices and E represents the set of edges. Each edge $(u, v) \in E$ has an associated weight $w(u, v)$. The goal is to find a subset of edges $E' \subseteq E$ such that the graph (V, E') forms a tree and $\sum_{(u,v)\in E'} w(u, v)$ is minimized.

Properties of MST:

- The MST contains exactly $|V|-1$ edges, where $|V|$ is the number of vertices in the graph.
- It connects all vertices.
- It does not contain any cycle.
- The total weight is minimized.

Algorithms to Find Minimum Spanning Tree:

Kruskal's Algorithm

Kruskal's algorithm is a greedy algorithm that finds an MST by considering the edges in ascending order of their weight and adding each edge to the MST if it does not form a cycle with the already included edges. The algorithm uses a disjoint-set data structure to efficiently manage and merge the different components of the MST.

```
class Graph:
    def __init__(self, vertices):
        self.V = vertices
        self.graph = []

    def addEdge(self, u, v, w):
        self.graph.append([u, v, w])

    def find(self, parent, i):
        if parent[i] == i:
            return i
        return self.find(parent, parent[i])

    def union(self, parent, rank, x, y):
        xroot = self.find(parent, x)
        yroot = self.find(parent, y)

        if rank[xroot] < rank[yroot]:
            parent[xroot] = yroot
        elif rank[xroot] > rank[yroot]:
            parent[yroot] = xroot
        else:
            parent[yroot] = xroot
            rank[xroot] += 1

    def KruskalMST(self):
        result = []
        i = 0
        e = 0
        self.graph = sorted(self.graph, key=lambda item: item[2])
        parent = []
        rank = []

        for node in range(self.V):
            parent.append(node)
            rank.append(0)

        while e < self.V - 1:
            u, v, w = self.graph[i]
```

```
            i += 1
            x = self.find(parent, u)
            y = self.find(parent, v)

            if x != y:
                e += 1
                result.append([u, v, w])
                self.union(parent, rank, x, y)

        for u, v, weight in result:
            print(f"{u} -- {v} == {weight}")
```

Prim's Algorithm

Prim's algorithm is another greedy algorithm that builds the MST by starting from an arbitrary vertex and growing the MST one edge at a time. It always selects the smallest edge that connects a vertex in the growing MST to a vertex outside the MST.

```
import heapq

class Graph:
    def __init__(self, vertices):
        self.V = vertices
        self.graph = [[] for _ in range(vertices)]

    def addEdge(self, u, v, w):
        self.graph[u].append((v, w))
        self.graph[v].append((u, w))

    def PrimMST(self):
        key = [float('inf')] * self.V
        parent = [-1] * self.V
        key[0] = 0
        minHeap = [(0, 0)]
        inMST = [False] * self.V

        while minHeap:
            weight, u = heapq.heappop(minHeap)
            inMST[u] = True

            for v, w in self.graph[u]:
                if not inMST[v] and key[v] > w:
                    key[v] = w
                    heapq.heappush(minHeap, (key[v], v))
                    parent[v] = u

        for i in range(1, self.V):
            print(f"{parent[i]} -- {i}")
```

These two algorithms, Kruskal's and Prim's, are fundamental approaches to solving the MST problem. Each algorithm has its use cases based on the structure and specific needs of the graph data. Kruskal's algorithm is more suitable for handling sparse graphs, while Prim's algorithm can be more efficient for dense graphs. Understanding the underlying principles of these algorithms is essential for effective application in practical scenarios.

7.10 Graph Coloring

Graph coloring is a methodology for assigning colors to the vertices of a graph such that no two adjacent vertices share the same color. This concept is fundamental in various practical applications and theoretical problems. An understanding of graph coloring requires familiarity with fundamental principles, algorithms used for this process, and its applications.

Consider a simple undirected graph $G = (V, E)$, where V represents vertices and E represents edges. The goal of graph coloring is to assign a color c to each vertex v such that if $(u, v) \in E$, then $c(u) \neq c(v)$.

Chromatic Number The minimum number of colors needed to color a graph G is called its chromatic number, denoted as $\chi(G)$. Determining the chromatic number is a classical problem in graph theory and is known to be NP-hard. Various heuristic and exact algorithms have been developed to find or approximate the chromatic number for different types of graphs.

Greedy Coloring Algorithm One of the simple and widely used methods for graph coloring is the Greedy Coloring Algorithm. Despite not always producing an optimal solution, it is effective in many practical scenarios. Here is an outline of the Greedy Coloring Algorithm:

1. Sort the vertices in a specific order.
2. Assign the first color to the first vertex.
3. Proceed to the next vertex and assign the smallest possible color that has not been used by its adjacent vertices.
4. Repeat the process until all vertices are colored.

The Python implementation of the Greedy Coloring Algorithm can be illustrated as follows:

```
def greedy_coloring(graph):
    # Initialize result array with -1, representing unassigned colors
    result = [-1] * len(graph)
```

```
    # Assign the first color to the first vertex
    result[0] = 0

    # Assign colors to remaining vertices
    for u in range(1, len(graph)):
        # Track colors assigned to adjacent vertices
        unavailable_colors = [False] * len(graph)
        for i in graph[u]:
            if result[i] != -1:
                unavailable_colors[result[i]] = True

        # Find the first available color
        color = 0
        while color < len(graph) and unavailable_colors[color]:
            color += 1

        result[u] = color

    return result
```

The above implementation demonstrates the key principles of the Greedy Coloring algorithm, which uses adjacency to ensure improper coloring is avoided.

Coloring Planar Graphs A prominent result in graph coloring is the Four Color Theorem, which states that any planar graph can be colored with at most four colors. This theorem, a culmination of extensive research and computational proof, ensures that regions on a planar map can be colored using just four distinct colors without two adjacent regions sharing the same color.

Applications of Graph Coloring Graph coloring has numerous applications across various fields:

- **Scheduling Problems:** Coloring can be utilized in timetabling and task scheduling wherein tasks are represented as vertices. An edge indicates a conflict; hence, different tasks must be assigned different time slots.

- **Register Allocation:** In compiler optimization, graph coloring is used for register allocation by assigning variables to a limited number of CPU registers.

- **Frequency Assignment:** In telecommunications, frequencies are assigned to cell towers to avoid interference, modeled by a graph where vertices represent towers, and edges represent potential interference.

Complementing these applications, various other algorithms like the DSATUR (Degree of Saturation) algorithm, backtracking algorithms, and evolutionary algorithms provide sophisticated means to tackle the graph coloring problem.

Each algorithm offers unique advantages, tailored efficiency, and precision in solving specific instances of the graph coloring problem, illustrating the adaptability and practical usage of this important graph theory concept.

7.11 Applications of Graphs

Graphs possess a versatile framework suitable for numerous applications in various domains, owing to their ability to model relationships among entities. Their utility spans computer science, biology, transportation, social networks, and many other fields. This section presents detailed scenarios showcasing the practical applications of graphs.

Social Networks

In social networks, graphs are employed to represent users as vertices, with edges denoting relationships between them. An adjacency list or matrix can effectively represent these relationships. Use cases in social networks include friend suggestions, community detection, and information propagation. For instance, by analyzing the graph structure, platforms can suggest new connections to users based on mutual friends.

Social networks also leverage graph traversal algorithms. For example, algorithms like BFS can identify the shortest path between two nodes, answering questions such as "How many steps connect user A to user B?" Community detection algorithms derive closely-knit factions within the network, while tools analyze the graph to gauge the importance (centrality) of each node.

Biological Networks

Graphs play an instrumental role in bioinformatics, particularly in modeling biological networks. In a protein-protein interaction (PPI) network, vertices represent proteins, and edges indicate interactions. This graphical representation aids in understanding cellular processes, identifying functional groups of proteins, and predicting protein functions.

In genetics, metabolic pathways can also be modeled using graphs.

Each vertex could symbolize a molecule or gene, while edges represent biochemical reactions or regulatory relationships. Algorithms like DFS and BFS enable researchers to discover pathways and interaction chains, facilitating the study of complex biological systems.

Transportation and Navigation

Graphs are fundamental in representing transportation and navigation systems. For instance, vertices can represent intersections or stations in road and rail networks, while edges denote the connecting roads or tracks. Shortest path algorithms (e.g., Dijkstra's or A* algorithms) assist in finding optimal routes, minimizing travel time or distance.

Navigation systems in GPS devices use these principles to provide real-time route guidance. Consider a road network represented as a weighted graph, where edge weights represent distances or travel times. Given a starting point and a destination, algorithms like Dijkstra's compute the shortest path efficiently:

```
import heapq

def dijkstra(graph, start):
    heap = [(0, start)]
    distances = {vertex: float('infinity') for vertex in graph}
    distances[start] = 0

    while heap:
        current_distance, current_vertex = heapq.heappop(heap)

        if current_distance > distances[current_vertex]:
            continue

        for neighbor, weight in graph[current_vertex].items():
            distance = current_distance + weight

            if distance < distances[neighbor]:
                distances[neighbor] = distance
                heapq.heappush(heap, (distance, neighbor))

    return distances
```

Web Page Ranking

Search engines like Google leverage graph structures to rank web pages, employing algorithms such as PageRank. In this graph, web pages are vertices, and hyperlinks are directed edges. The PageRank algorithm evaluates the relative importance of web pages by analyzing the interconnected web structure, assigning higher rank to pages with more incoming links from other significant pages.

Mathematically, the PageRank of a page P_i can be described as:

$$PR(P_i) = \frac{1-d}{N} + d \sum_{P_j \in M(P_i)} \frac{PR(P_j)}{L(P_j)}$$

where:

- N is the total number of pages,
- $M(P_i)$ is the set of pages linking to P_i,
- $L(P_j)$ is the number of outbound links on page P_j,
- d is the damping factor, typically set to 0.85.

Telecommunications Networks

Telecommunications networks, including the internet, can be modeled as graphs where vertices represent routers, switches, or other types of infrastructure, and edges symbolize the communication links. Efficient routing protocol design hinges upon graph algorithms to direct data packets most effectively.

Applications include fault tolerance and load balancing. Employing graph-based algorithms enhances network robustness, ensuring data transmission remains reliable even in the presence of failures or congestion.

Recommendation Systems

Graphs facilitate the operation of recommendation systems used by platforms like Amazon and Netflix. Users and items (e.g., products or movies) form a bipartite graph, where an edge indicates an interaction (e.g., a user purchasing a product or watching a movie).

Recommendation algorithms analyze this bipartite graph to suggest new items to users. Collaborative filtering methods identify user similarity based on shared edges. Techniques like matrix factorization leverage this graph-based representation to model latent factors.

Utilities and Resource Management

Utility networks, such as electrical grids and water distribution systems, capitalize on graph theory. Here, vertices represent substations or nodes, while edges correspond to transmission lines or pipes. The graph structure assists in ensuring efficient distribution and redundancy planning.

In instances of utility management, algorithms can detect critical nodes whose failure would disrupt the network. Load balancing and capacity planning rely on understanding the graph's topology to prevent overloading specific sections.

Graphs extend their utility across multiple disciplines, providing an adaptable structure for modeling and analyzing complex systems. Each application leverages the fundamental properties of graphs to address domain-specific challenges, demonstrating their widespread and intrinsic value in solving real-world problems.

7.12 Performance Considerations in Graphs

Performance considerations in graphs play a pivotal role in optimizing graph algorithms and ensuring they execute efficiently, particularly with large datasets. The computational complexity of graph algorithms typically depends on the number of vertices V and edges E, denoted as $O(V)$ and $O(E)$, respectively. Detailed understanding and analysis of time and space complexity are essential to choose the right algorithmic strategies.

The most widely used graph algorithms can be categorized into the following fundamental operations: traversal, shortest path, and minimum spanning tree. Each operation's efficiency can be impacted by the data structures used for graph representation—adjacency matrix, adjacency list, or edge list.

Graph Representation: The selection of graph representation significantly affects the performance and space complexity:

- **Adjacency Matrix:** Uses $O(V^2)$ space, where V is the number of vertices. It's efficient for dense graphs where E is close to V^2. The time complexity to check the presence of an edge is $O(1)$.
- **Adjacency List:** Uses $O(V + E)$ space, efficient for sparse graphs where E is much less than V^2. Checking for the presence of an edge takes $O(V)$ time in the worst-case scenario.
- **Edge List:** Requires $O(E)$ space. This representation does not facilitate efficient edge querying but is useful for algorithms primarily concerned with edge operations.

Graph Traversal:

- **Depth-First Search (DFS):** DFS algorithm traverses nodes by exploring as far as possible along each branch before backtracking. The time complexity is $O(V + E)$ and space complexity can be $O(V)$ due to the recursion stack.

```
def dfs(graph, start, visited=None):
    if visited is None:
        visited = set()
    visited.add(start)
    for next in graph[start] - visited:
        dfs(graph, next, visited)
    return visited
```

- **Breadth-First Search (BFS):** BFS algorithm explores all neighbors at the present depth prior to moving on to nodes at the next depth level. The time complexity is $O(V + E)$ and space complexity is also $O(V)$ as it uses a queue to manage the traversal.

```
def bfs(graph, start):
    visited, queue = set(), [start]
    while queue:
        vertex = queue.pop(0)
        if vertex not in visited:
            visited.add(vertex)
            queue.extend(graph[vertex] - visited)
    return visited
```

Shortest Path Algorithms:

- **Dijkstra's Algorithm:** Suitable for graphs with non-negative weights, it uses a priority queue to continually choose the vertex with the smallest known distance. With a binary heap priority queue, the time complexity is $O((V + E) \log V)$.

```
import heapq

def dijkstra(graph, start):
    pq = [(0, start)]
    distances = {vertex: float('infinity') for vertex in graph}
    distances[start] = 0

    while pq:
        current_distance, current_vertex = heapq.heappop(pq)

        if current_distance > distances[current_vertex]:
            continue

        for neighbor, weight in graph[current_vertex].items():
            distance = current_distance + weight
            if distance < distances[neighbor]:
                distances[neighbor] = distance
                heapq.heappush(pq, (distance, neighbor))

    return distances
```

- **Bellman-Ford Algorithm:** Effective for graphs with negative weights, it relaxes all edges up to $V - 1$ times. The time complexity is $O(VE)$, making it less efficient than Dijkstra's algorithm for graphs with non-negative weights.

```
def bellman_ford(graph, start):
    distance = {vertex: float('infinity') for vertex in graph}
    distance[start] = 0

    for _ in range(len(graph) - 1):
        for vertex in graph:
            for neighbor, weight in graph[vertex].items():
                if distance[vertex] + weight < distance[neighbor]:
                    distance[neighbor] = distance[vertex] + weight

    return distance
```

Minimum Spanning Tree (MST) Algorithms:

- **Kruskal's Algorithm:** Involves sorting the edges by weight and adding them to the MST, ensuring no cycles are formed, optimized using Union-Find data structure. The time complexity is $O(E \log E)$ primarily due to sorting the edges.

```
class UnionFind:
    def __init__(self, n):
        self.parent = list(range(n))

    def find(self, u):
        if self.parent[u] != u:
            self.parent[u] = self.find(self.parent[u])
        return self.parent[u]

    def union(self, u, v):
        rootU = self.find(u)
        rootV = self.find(v)
        if rootU != rootV:
            self.parent[rootU] = rootV

def kruskal(graph):
    mst = []
    edges = sorted(graph['edges'], key=lambda edge: edge[2])
    uf = UnionFind(graph['vertices'])

    for u, v, weight in edges:
        if uf.find(u) != uf.find(v):
            uf.union(u, v)
            mst.append((u, v, weight))

    return mst
```

- **Prim's Algorithm:** Emphasizes selectively growing the MST from a starting vertex by adding the cheapest possible connection. The time complexity using a priority queue is $O((V + E) \log V)$.

```
import heapq

def prim(graph, start):
    mst = []
    visited = set()
    pq = [(0, start, None)]

    while pq:
        cost, vertex, from_vertex = heapq.heappop(pq)
        if vertex in visited:
            continue

        visited.add(vertex)
        if from_vertex is not None:
            mst.append((from_vertex, vertex, cost))

        for neighbor, weight in graph[vertex].items():
            if neighbor not in visited:
                heapq.heappush(pq, (weight, neighbor, vertex))

    return mst
```

When analyzing the performance of graph algorithms, it is crucial to evaluate the specific context and graph characteristics to make informed decisions. The properties such as density, edge weights, and the nature of traversal required directly influence the choice of algorithm and underlying data structures.

ancements in graph processing technologies and the usage of more sophisticated data structures and parallel computing can also contribute to improved performance in dealing with large-scale graphs.

Chapter 8

Hash Tables

This chapter examines hash tables, detailing their working principles, including hash functions and collision handling techniques. It compares open addressing and chaining methods, provides a guide for implementing hash tables in Python, and discusses their applications. Additionally, the chapter addresses performance considerations, differences from other data structures, advanced techniques, and common issues and debugging strategies.

8.1 Introduction to Hash Tables

Hash tables are a pivotal data structure in computer science, providing an efficient mechanism for storing and retrieving data. By employing a key-value pair paradigm, they facilitate rapid access to elements.

The foundational concept behind hash tables is the use of a *hash function* to map keys to specific indexes in a finite array, commonly referred to as the hash table. This mapping allows for near constant-time complexity, $O(1)$, for look-up operations under ideal conditions.

To understand the utility of hash tables, consider the problem of searching. In an unsorted list, searching for a specific element requires $O(n)$ time complexity. A binary search on a sorted list improves this to $O(\log n)$. Hash tables, in contrast, aim to perform searches, insertions, and deletions in $O(1)$ average time, offering a significant performance advantage for many applications.

The design and implementation of hash tables revolve around core components:

- **Keys and Values**: Each entry in a hash table consists of a key-value pair. The key is used to identify the data uniquely.
- **Hash Function**: This function takes the key as its input and produces an integer, the hash code, which determines the index where the value is stored in the hash table.
- **Table Size**: The hash code is typically modulo the table size to ensure that the resulting index falls within the allowable range of the table.
- **Collision Handling Mechanisms**: Since multiple keys can hash to the same index, mechanisms like chaining and open addressing are employed to handle these collisions.

Hash tables are especially advantageous in scenarios where quick look-ups, insertions, and deletions are required. They are extensively used in various domains including databases for indexing, symbol tables in compilers, and caching mechanisms in operational systems.

The effectiveness of a hash table is largely dependent on the quality of the hash function. A good hash function disperses the keys uniformly across the table, minimizing the number of collisions and thereby maintaining the $O(1)$ performance.

In contrast, a poor hash function results in many collisions, degrading the performance to $O(n)$ in the worst-case. Thus, the design of an efficient hash function forms the crux of a proficient hash table implementation.

Consider the following Python implementation of a simple hash function:

```
def simple_hash(key, table_size):
    hash_code = 0
    for char in key:
        hash_code += ord(char)
    return hash_code % table_size
```

This function computes the hash code by summing the ASCII values of the characters in the key and applying modulo operation with the table size to ensure the hash code falls within the permissible index range.

To further comprehend the operations of hash tables, it helps to simulate the process of inserting and searching for keys. For example, in a hash table of size 10, inserting the key "apple" using the simple hash function would involve computing:

```
a: 97
p: 112
p: 112
l: 108
e: 101
Sum: 97 + 112 + 112 + 108 + 101 = 530
Index = 530 % 10 = 0
```

This calculation places the value at index 0. To retrieve this value, the hash table utilizes the same hash function to compute the index for the given key.

The potential for collisions introduces the need for collision handling strategies. In subsequent sections, we will delve into the details of these mechanisms, examining their strengths and weaknesses.

Understanding hash tables and their operational mechanisms is crucial as they underpin many real-world applications where data retrieval efficiency is paramount. Through this chapter, we aim to elucidate these concepts, building a thorough comprehension of hash tables, enabling their effective implementation and utilization.

8.2 How Hash Tables Work

Hash tables are a foundational data structure in computer science, known for their efficient average-time complexity for search, insert, and delete operations. These operations generally exhibit O(1) time complexity, making hash tables an attractive choice for numerous applications. Understanding the underlying mechanics of hash tables is crucial for leveraging their full potential.

A hash table is essentially an array of fixed size, known as a hash array or bucket array, which is indexed using a hash function. The hash function takes an input (often referred to as a "key") and computes an index in the array, where the corresponding value is either stored or retrieved. The conceptual flow of hash table operations involves several key steps.

- **Hash Function:** This function converts the input key into an index in the bucket array. The choice of hash function significantly impacts the performance and efficiency of a hash table.
- **Index Calculation:** The hash function output, typically an integer,

represents the index of the bucket in which the key-value pair is stored.

- **Storage Mechanism:** The value associated with the key is stored at the computed index in the bucket array. In cases where multiple keys hash to the same index, strategies such as chaining or open addressing are employed to resolve conflicts (collisions).
- **Retrieval:** For retrieving a value, the key is again passed through the hash function to compute the index, which is then used to access the corresponding value from the bucket array.
- **Collision Handling:** Various techniques like chaining and open addressing ensure that the hash table can still retrieve correct values when collisions occur.

To illustrate the operation of a hash table, consider the following example of inserting and retrieving items using a simple hash function.

```
class HashTable:
    def __init__(self, size):
        self.size = size
        self.table = [None] * size

    def hash_function(self, key):
        return hash(key) % self.size

    def insert(self, key, value):
        index = self.hash_function(key)
        if self.table[index] is None:
            self.table[index] = [(key, value)]
        else:
            for pair in self.table[index]:
                if pair[0] == key:
                    pair = (key, value)
                    return
            self.table[index].append((key, value))

    def retrieve(self, key):
        index = self.hash_function(key)
        if self.table[index] is None:
            return None
        for pair in self.table[index]:
            if pair[0] == key:
                return pair[1]
        return None
```

In this example, the hash function converts each key to an integer index bounded by the size of the array. When an item is inserted or retrieved, the hash function determines the appropriate index, ensuring that operations are efficiently executed.

Consider the insertion of the key-value pair ('apple', 10):

```
hash_table = HashTable(10)
hash_table.insert('apple', 10)
```

The output of the hash function, for instance, might be 3 for the key 'apple', causing the value 10 to be stored in the bucket at index 3. Retrieving the value for 'apple':

```
value = hash_table.retrieve('apple')
print(value)
```

```
10
```

This demonstrates the rapid access characteristic of hash tables, making them suitable for scenarios where quick data lookup is necessary, such as in database indexing.

Collision handling is an integral aspect of hash table functionality. In this implementation, collision resolution is managed using chaining, where each bucket contains a linked list of key-value pairs.

For example, consider the insertion of the key-value pair ('banana', 20):

```
hash_table.insert('banana', 20)
```

If the hash function maps 'banana' to the same index as 'apple' (index 3), the linked list at that index will now contain both ('apple', 10) and ('banana', 20):

```
[(key='apple', value=10), (key='banana', value=20)]
```

Retrieval will then correctly identify and return 'banana', 20 or 'apple', 10 as appropriate. Multiple approaches exist to enhance collision resolution and optimize performance, exploring which forms a core part of understanding and utilizing hash tables effectively.

To extend this basic implementation for real-world utility, additional features such as dynamic resizing, load factor management, and alternative collision resolution methods can be introduced. These ensure the robustness and efficiency of the hash table, even under varying loads and usage patterns. The continuous evaluation and adjustment of hash function and collision handling mechanisms underline the sophisticated engineering required for optimal hash table performance.

8.3 Hash Functions

Hash functions are a fundamental component of hash tables, transforming input data (keys) into an integer, known as a hash value or hash code, which typically serves as an index in an array. A well-designed hash function enhances efficiency by minimizing the likelihood of collisions and distributing keys uniformly across the hash table.

Properties of Good Hash Functions

A proficient hash function should exhibit several critical properties:

- **Deterministic:** The function must yield the same hash value each time it processes the same input.
- **Uniformity:** It should distribute hash values uniformly across the available range, reducing the likelihood of clustering.
- **Efficiency:** Computing the hash value should be fast to ensure the overall performance of the hash table is optimized.
- **Low Collision Probability:** The function should minimize the probability of hash collisions where different keys produce identical hash values.

Commonly Used Hash Functions

Several hash functions are widely employed, each with distinct characteristics and use cases:

- **Division Method:** This method computes the hash value by taking the remainder of the division of the key by a prime number (*m*):

  $$h(k) = k \mod m$$

  The prime number *m* is chosen to reduce the chance of collisions, especially if the keys have patterns.

- **Multiplication Method:** This method involves multiplying the key by a constant (*A*) between 0 and 1, extracting the fractional part, and then multiplying by the table size (*m*):

  $$h(k) = \lfloor m\,(k \cdot A \mod 1) \rfloor$$

  This technique can distribute hash values more uniformly than the division method.

- **Mid-Square Method:** This method squares the key and extracts an appropriate number of middle digits or bits as the hash value. For example, for a key *k*:

$$h(k) = \text{middle digits of } (k^2)$$

  This method benefits from using parts of the key that can change more significantly after squaring.

- **Universal Hashing:** Instead of a single fixed hash function, a set of hash functions is employed. For each operation, one function from the set is selected randomly:

$$h(k) = ((a \cdot k + b) \mod p) \mod m$$

  where *a, b* are randomly chosen integers, *p* is a prime number sufficiently large, and *m* is the table size. This offers a level of security against worst-case scenarios where an adversary can predict the hash function.

Python Implementation of Hash Functions

Implementing a hash function in Python can be straightforward. Here is a basic example of the Division Method:

```
class HashTable:
    def __init__(self, size):
        self.size = size
        self.table = [None] * size

    def hash_function(self, key):
        return key % self.size

    def insert(self, key, value):
        index = self.hash_function(key)
        self.table[index] = value

    def get(self, key):
        index = self.hash_function(key)
        return self.table[index]
```

This implementation demonstrates a simple hash table using the Division Method to compute the index for each key.

Python's Built-in Hash Functions

Python provides built-in hash functions that can be utilized for more complex data types. The hash() function computes the hash value for immutable types such as integers, floats, strings, and tuples.

```
key_int = 42
```

```
key_str = "data"
hash_int = hash(key_int)
hash_str = hash(key_str)
print("Hash value for integer key:", hash_int)
print("Hash value for string key:", hash_str)
```

```
Hash value for integer key: 42
Hash value for string key: 6932233271822390148
```

Python's hash() function ensures reliable and consistent hash values across executions. It is important to note that in Python 3.x, the hash values of immutable objects are randomized per interpreter session for security reasons, except when the value is an integer.

Considerations When Designing Hash Functions

When designing hash functions for custom keys or specific applications:

- **Key Space Distribution:** If keys cluster in certain ranges, a modulus operation with a poorly chosen divisor could lead to many collisions. Preferably, hash functions should spread keys evenly across the table.
- **Key Characteristics:** Analyze the nature of the keys (their size, distribution, possible patterns) to decide on the appropriate hash function type.
- **Table Size:** A prime number close to but not greater than the desired table size often helps reduce collisions when keys have patterns.

Understanding and implementing effective hash functions are crucial steps in optimizing the performance and reliability of hash tables. A well-crafted hash function not only expedites data access but also minimizes collisions, making it an indispensable aspect of efficient hash table design.

8.4 Collision Handling Techniques

When two keys hash to the same index in a hash table, we encounter a *collision*. Effective collision handling is crucial for maintaining the efficiency of operations such as insertion, search, and deletion in hash tables. This section explores various techniques to manage collisions, including separate chaining, open addressing methods, and advanced strategies.

Separate Chaining

Separate chaining involves maintaining a data structure, typically a linked list, at each index of the hash table. When a collision occurs, the new key-value pair is appended to the list at the corresponding index. This method ensures that each index can store multiple elements.

```
class Node:
    def __init__(self, key, value):
        self.key = key
        self.value = value
        self.next = None

class HashTableChaining:
    def __init__(self, size):
        self.size = size
        self.table = [None] * size

    def _hash(self, key):
        return hash(key) % self.size

    def insert(self, key, value):
        index = self._hash(key)
        new_node = Node(key, value)
        if self.table[index] is None:
            self.table[index] = new_node
        else:
            current = self.table[index]
            while current.next:
                current = current.next
            current.next = new_node

    def search(self, key):
        index = self._hash(key)
        current = self.table[index]
        while current:
            if current.key == key:
                return current.value
            current = current.next
        return None
```

The separate chaining technique efficiently handles collisions, but the presence of many elements in a chain can degrade the performance of search operations. Therefore, maintaining a balanced load factor, typically less than 1, is vital.

Open Addressing

In open addressing, all elements reside within the hash table itself, and collisions are resolved through probing. There are several probing techniques: linear probing, quadratic probing, and double hashing.

Linear Probing

Linear probing handles collisions by checking the next available slot sequentially. If a collision occurs at index i, it checks $(i+1)\%N$, $(i+2)\%N$, and so on until an empty slot is found or a maximum probing limit is reached.

```
class HashTableLinearProbing:
    def __init__(self, size):
        self.size = size
        self.table = [None] * size

    def _hash(self, key):
        return hash(key) % self.size

    def insert(self, key, value):
        index = self._hash(key)
        while self.table[index] is not None:
            index = (index + 1) % self.size
        self.table[index] = (key, value)

    def search(self, key):
        index = self._hash(key)
        start_index = index # To avoid infinite loop
        while self.table[index] is not None:
            if self.table[index][0] == key:
                return self.table[index][1]
            index = (index + 1) % self.size
            if index == start_index:
                return None
        return None
```

While simple, linear probing can lead to *primary clustering*, where consecutive elements create long probes, degrading performance.

Quadratic Probing

Quadratic probing addresses primary clustering by probing indices based on a quadratic function. If a collision occurs at index i, it checks $(i+1^2)\%N$, $(i+2^2)\%N$, and so on, reducing the probability of clustering.

```
class HashTableQuadraticProbing:
    def __init__(self, size):
        self.size = size
        self.table = [None] * size

    def _hash(self, key):
        return hash(key) % self.size

    def insert(self, key, value):
        index = self._hash(key)
        i = 1
        while self.table[index] is not None:
            index = (index + i**2) % self.size
            i += 1
        self.table[index] = (key, value)

    def search(self, key):
        index = self._hash(key)
        i = 1
```

```
        start_index = index # To avoid infinite loop
        while self.table[index] is not None:
            if self.table[index][0] == key:
                return self.table[index][1]
            index = (index + i**2) % self.size
            if index == start_index:
                return None
            i += 1
        return None
```

Quadratic probing alleviates primary clustering but can still encounter *secondary clustering*, especially if the table's load factor is high.

Double Hashing

Double hashing uses a secondary hash function to determine the probe sequence, significantly reducing clustering issues. If a collision occurs at index i, it calculates a new index using a second hash function.

```
class HashTableDoubleHashing:
    def __init__(self, size):
        self.size = size
        self.table = [None] * size

    def _hash1(self, key):
        return hash(key) % self.size

    def _hash2(self, key):
        return 1 + hash(key) % (self.size - 1)

    def insert(self, key, value):
        index = self._hash1(key)
        step = self._hash2(key)
        while self.table[index] is not None:
            index = (index + step) % self.size
        self.table[index] = (key, value)

    def search(self, key):
        index = self._hash1(key)
        step = self._hash2(key)
        start_index = index # To avoid infinite loop
        while self.table[index] is not None:
            if self.table[index][0] == key:
                return self.table[index][1]
            index = (index + step) % self.size
            if index == start_index:
                return None
        return None
```

Double hashing minimizes clustering and ensures a more uniform distribution of keys, enhancing search performance when the table is densely populated.

Effective collision handling is essential for maintaining optimal hash table performance. By selecting an appropriate technique and managing the load factor, the efficiency of hash tables in various applications can be significantly enhanced.

8.5 Comparing Open Addressing and Chaining

When implementing hash tables, two primary methods for handling collisions are open addressing and chaining. Understanding their differences, as well as their respective advantages and disadvantages, is essential for selecting the appropriate technique for a given application.

Open Addressing is a method where, upon a collision, the subsequent array positions are checked for the next available slot using a specific probing sequence. Common probing sequences include linear probing, quadratic probing, and double hashing.

- **Linear Probing**: In linear probing, if a collision occurs at position i, the next slot in the sequence checked is $(i + 1) \mod N$, where N is the size of the hash table. This process continues until an empty slot is found. Linear probing is straightforward but can lead to clustering, where long runs of occupied slots degrade performance.
- **Quadratic Probing**: This method addresses the clustering issue by varying the probing sequence. Upon collision at position i, the sequence followed is $(i + 1^2) \mod N$, $(i + 2^2) \mod N$, $(i + 3^2) \mod N$, and so forth. While it reduces primary clustering, secondary clustering can still occur.
- **Double Hashing**: Double hashing uses a secondary hash function to determine the step size for probing. If a collision occurs at position i, the step size is determined by a second hash function $h_2(x)$, resulting in the sequence $i, (i+h_2(x)) \mod N, (i+2\cdot h_2(x)) \mod N$, etc. This method is highly efficient and minimizes clustering.

The following Python code snippet demonstrates open addressing with linear probing:

```
class OpenAddressHashTable:
    def __init__(self, size):
        self.size = size
        self.table = [None] * size
        self.count = 0
```

```
    def _hash(self, key):
        return key % self.size

    def _probe(self, start, key):
        for i in range(self.size):
            idx = (start + i) % self.size
            if self.table[idx] is None or self.table[idx][0] == key:
                return idx
        return None

    def insert(self, key, value):
        index = self._hash(key)
        idx = self._probe(index, key)
        if idx is not None and self.table[idx] is None:
            self.table[idx] = (key, value)
            self.count += 1

    def search(self, key):
        index = self._hash(key)
        idx = self._probe(index, key)
        if idx is not None and self.table[idx] is not None:
            return self.table[idx][1]
        return None

    def delete(self, key):
        index = self._hash(key)
        idx = self._probe(index, key)
        if idx is not None and self.table[idx] is not None:
            self.table[idx] = None
            self.count -= 1
```

In contrast, **Chaining** uses linked lists to handle collisions. Each slot in the hash table array points to a linked list of entries that hash to the same index. Chaining inherently handles collisions by appending elements to the linked list at the corresponding index.

The Python implementation of a hash table using chaining involves defining a linked list node and a hash table class:

```
class Node:
    def __init__(self, key, value):
        self.key = key
        self.value = value
        self.next = None

class ChainedHashTable:
    def __init__(self, size):
        self.size = size
        self.table = [None] * size

    def _hash(self, key):
        return key % self.size

    def insert(self, key, value):
        index = self._hash(key)
        new_node = Node(key, value)
        if self.table[index] is None:
            self.table[index] = new_node
```

```
        else:
            current = self.table[index]
            while current.next is not None:
                current = current.next
            current.next = new_node

    def search(self, key):
        index = self._hash(key)
        current = self.table[index]
        while current is not None:
            if current.key == key:
                return current.value
            current = current.next
        return None

    def delete(self, key):
        index = self._hash(key)
        current = self.table[index]
        prev = None
        while current is not None and current.key != key:
            prev = current
            current = current.next
        if current is None:
            return
        if prev is None:
            self.table[index] = current.next
        else:
            prev.next = current.next
```

Comparison and Trade-offs:

- **Memory Usage**: Open addressing requires an array proportional to the number of slots, whereas chaining requires additional memory for the linked lists. Consequently, chaining may use more memory overall when the table is sparsely populated.
- **Performance**: Open addressing typically benefits from better cache performance due to its contiguous memory access pattern. However, the performance may degrade significantly as the load factor approaches 1. Chaining, on the other hand, maintains more consistent performance across different load factors but may suffer from increased cache misses due to linked list traversals.
- **Load Factor and Resizing**: Open addressing requires maintaining a load factor less than 1 for efficient probing, necessitating periodic resizing and rehashing of the entire table. Chaining can handle higher load factors more gracefully and requires resizing less frequently.
- **Deletion Complexity**: Deletion in open addressing is complex as it may create clusters of empty slots, which interfere with probing.

This often necessitates rehashing or special placeholder markers. Chaining allows straightforward deletions by removing nodes from linked lists.

Careful consideration of these factors is essential when choosing between open addressing and chaining for a particular use case. The decision ultimately hinges on the specific requirements of memory usage, performance characteristics, and operational complexities.

8.6 Implementing a Hash Table in Python

To implement a hash table in Python, we will focus on creating a dictionary-like data structure using open addressing for collision handling. We will start by defining the core components of the hash table, including the hash function, initialization, insertion, searching, and deletion operations.

We first define the hash table class structure, including the necessary methods. Python's list data type will be used to store the hash table's internal array. The initial size of this array can be decided based on expected usage, and it can dynamically resize as needed.

```
class HashTable:
    def __init__(self, size=10):
        self.size = size
        self.table = [None] * self.size
        self.count = 0

    def hash_function(self, key):
        return hash(key) % self.size
```

The constructor initializes the hash table with a specified size, defaults to 10, and creates an array of that size filled with `None`. The `hash_function` computes the hash of the key modulo the size of the table to ensure the hash index lies within the bounds of the table array.

Next, we define the `insert` method for adding a key-value pair to the hash table. Collision handling will be implemented using linear probing, which searches for the next available slot.

```
def insert(self, key, value):
    index = self.hash_function(key)
    start_index = index

    while self.table[index] is not None:
        if self.table[index][0] == key:
            self.table[index] = (key, value)
            return
```

```
        index = (index + 1) % self.size
        if index == start_index:
            raise Exception("Hash table is full")

    self.table[index] = (key, value)
    self.count += 1
```

The insert method calculates the initial index using the hash_function. If the slot at the computed index is occupied, linear probing is utilized to find the next empty slot. If a slot with the same key is found, the value is updated. The search wraps around the table using the modulo operation to stay within array bounds. If the table is full, an exception is raised.

Now, we implement the search method to retrieve the value associated with a given key. The method uses linear probing to handle cases where collisions have altered the expected position of key-value pairs.

```
def search(self, key):
    index = self.hash_function(key)
    start_index = index

    while self.table[index] is not None:
        if self.table[index][0] == key:
            return self.table[index][1]
        index = (index + 1) % self.size
        if index == start_index:
            break

    return None
```

The search method calculates the index and probes it. If a key that matches the searched key is found, the method returns the associated value. The search continues until an empty slot is encountered or a complete cycle through the table is made, indicating the key is not present.

Lastly, the delete method removes a key-value pair from the hash table, maintaining the integrity of the probing sequence.

```
def delete(self, key):
    index = self.hash_function(key)
    start_index = index

    while self.table[index] is not None:
        if self.table[index][0] == key:
            self.table[index] = None
            self.count -= 1
            self._rehash_after_deletion(index)
            return True
        index = (index + 1) % self.size
        if index == start_index:
            break
```

```
    return False

def _rehash_after_deletion(self, delete_index):
    index = (delete_index + 1) % self.size

    while self.table[index] is not None:
        key, value = self.table[index]
        self.table[index] = None
        self.count -= 1
        self.insert(key, value)
        index = (index + 1) % self.size
```

The delete method searches for the key to be removed and sets the corresponding slot to None. The count is decremented, and a helper method _rehash_after_deletion is called to rehash all subsequent entries that could have been mispositioned due to the deletion. The helper method iterates through the table, re-inserting elements to their appropriate slots, ensuring the table remains valid for future operations.

For completeness, we include a method to resize the hash table when it becomes too full, maintaining efficient operations.

```
def resize(self, new_size):
    old_table = self.table
    self.size = new_size
    self.table = [None] * self.size
    self.count = 0

    for entry in old_table:
        if entry is not None:
            self.insert(entry[0], entry[1])
```

The resize method creates a new table with the updated size, rehashing all elements from the old table to the new one, leveraging the insert method to place them appropriately. This operation ensures the load factor of the hash table remains favorable.

Combining all components provided, the full implementation of our hash table facilitates dynamic resizing, efficient insertion, searching, and deletion using open addressing with linear probing, ensuring consistent performance across different usage scenarios.

8.7 Applications of Hash Tables

Hash tables are remarkably versatile data structures utilized across a wide array of applications due to their efficient average-case time complexities for insertion, deletion, and lookup operations. Several prominent applications highlight their importance in both theoretical and practical contexts.

First and foremost, hash tables play a vital role in implementing associative arrays, also known as dictionaries or maps. Associative arrays map keys to values, allowing for rapid access and modifications. In Python, the built-in dict type is an example of a hash table-based implementation. This capability is intrinsic to tasks involving dynamic datasets where key-value pair retrieval and updates must be conducted swiftly.

Another pivotal application of hash tables is in database indexing. Hash indexes are employed to speed up the retrieval of records in databases. When a database system uses a hash index, it computes the hash of the key values of the indexed column, thereby enabling direct access to the data. This approach markedly reduces the search time compared to traditional methods such as B-trees when working with unsorted data.

Hash tables are also beneficial in implementing caches. A cache stores frequently accessed data, aiming to reduce access times for subsequent requests. In web development, for instance, hash tables can be used to cache the results of expensive computations or database queries. By leveraging a hash table, cached results can be accessed in constant time on average, thereby significantly improving the performance of web applications.

Moreover, hash tables are used extensively in compilers and interpreters, particularly for symbol table management. Symbol tables maintain information about the variables, functions, objects, and other entities in the source code. During the compilation or interpretation process, the compiler/interpreter must frequently look up and update these entities, making hash tables an apt choice due to their efficient lookup properties.

Additionally, hash tables find applications in handling sparse data. Sparse data structures are those where the majority of elements have default (typically zero) values. Hash tables provide a compact and efficient mechanism to store and retrieve non-default values, which is beneficial in scenarios such as sparse matrices or multidimensional datasets where direct representation would be prohibitively large.

One of the more algorithmic applications of hash tables is in implementing sets. Operations such as union, intersection, and difference can be performed efficiently using hash tables. For example, a hash table can quickly determine the uniqueness of elements, making it suitable for deduplication tasks or for finding common elements between datasets.

A variant in spell checkers and word processing applications relies on hash tables to provide rapid word lookup. When a user types, the application must verify that the word exists in its dictionary. A hash table's constant average-time complexity allows for quick verification against large word lists, thus facilitating real-time spell checking.

In networking, hash tables are integral to constructing routing tables and managing caches in distributed systems. Routers use hash tables to store and retrieve routing information quickly, ensuring efficient data packet delivery across networks. Similarly, distributed cache systems use hash tables to distribute and access cached data across nodes, enhancing system scalability and fault tolerance.

Finally, the implementation of cryptographic functions often employs hash tables. Hash tables are used in cryptographic algorithms to manage data structures efficiently, ensuring fast access to intermediary values and results. Collision-resistant hash functions, a critical part of hashing for cryptography, aid in maintaining data integrity and security.

The following Python code snippet demonstrates a simple hash table application for caching expensive function results:

```
class ExpensiveFunctionCache:
    def __init__(self):
        self.cache = {}

    def get_result(self, x):
        if x in self.cache:
            return self.cache[x]
        else:
            result = self.expensive_computation(x)
            self.cache[x] = result
            return result

    def expensive_computation(self, x):
        # Simulate an expensive computation
        import time
        time.sleep(5) # Placeholder for a long-running computation
        return x * x

# Create an instance of the cache
cache = ExpensiveFunctionCache()

# Retrieve and cache results
print(cache.get_result(5)) # Result will be cached after the first computation
print(cache.get_result(5)) # Cached result is retrieved instantly
```

```
25
25
```

This example underscores how hash tables can optimize performance by caching computationally expensive results, leading to substantial efficiency gains in application execution. As illustrated, hash tables' practical applications span numerous domains, demonstrating their indispensable role in modern computing systems.

8.8 Performance Considerations in Hash Tables

Performance is a critical aspect of hash tables due to their typical applications in fast data retrieval, insertion, and deletion. This section delves into the various performance considerations when implementing and using hash tables.

A crucial factor influencing the performance of hash tables is the load factor, defined as the ratio of the number of elements in the hash table to the number of available buckets. The load factor, often denoted as λ, is mathematically expressed as:

$$\lambda = \frac{n}{m}$$

where n represents the number of elements, and m is the number of buckets.

1. Time Complexity Analysis:

The average-case time complexity for search, insert, and delete operations in a hash table is $O(1)$ due to its direct-addressing mechanism. However, the worst-case time complexity can degrade to $O(n)$, especially under poor hash function performance or high load factors leading to excessive collisions. Let's break down the time complexities:

- **Average Case:** - Search: $O(1)$ - Insert: $O(1)$ - Delete: $O(1)$

- **Worst Case:** - Search: $O(n)$ - Insert: $O(n)$ - Delete: $O(n)$

To illustrate these complexities, consider the following Python code that highlights average and worst-case scenarios for hash table operations:

```
# Example of average and worst-case scenarios

# Hash table using chaining to handle collisions
class HashTable:
    def __init__(self, size):
        self.size = size
        self.table = [[] for _ in range(size)]

    def hash_function(self, key):
        return key % self.size

    def insert(self, key, value):
        index = self.hash_function(key)
```

```
            self.table[index].append((key, value))

    def search(self, key):
        index = self.hash_function(key)
        for (k, v) in self.table[index]:
            if k == key:
                return v
        return None # Key not found

    def delete(self, key):
        index = self.hash_function(key)
        for i, (k, v) in enumerate(self.table[index]):
            if k == key:
                del self.table[index][i]
                return

# Average case insertion
ht = HashTable(size=10)
ht.insert(10, 'Value 10') # Fast insertion
ht.insert(20, 'Value 20') # Fast insertion

# Worst case search
values = [ht.search(i) for i in range(1000)] # Slow search if load factor is high
```

2. Load Factor Implications:

Maintaining an optimal load factor is paramount. If the load factor is too high, the likelihood of collisions increases, causing the performance to deviate from the ideal $O(1)$. Conversely, a very low load factor means excessive memory is wasted. Generally, a load factor between 0.5 and 0.7 is considered efficient for chaining methods, while open addressing usually requires lower load factors.

Dynamic resizing of the hash table can help maintain performance by keeping the load factor within desired limits. Resizing involves rehashing the existing entries to a new table with more buckets, typically performed when the load factor exceeds a predefined threshold. The amortized time complexity for insert operations remains $O(1)$ with periodic resizing, although individual resize operations can taken $O(n)$ time due to rehashing each entry.

Resizing is illustrated as follows:

```
# Example of dynamic resizing in a hash table

class ResizableHashTable(HashTable):
    def __init__(self, size, load_factor_threshold=0.7):
        super().__init__(size)
        self.element_count = 0
        self.load_factor_threshold = load_factor_threshold

    def insert(self, key, value):
        if self.element_count / self.size > self.load_factor_threshold:
            self._resize()
        index = self.hash_function(key)
        self.table[index].append((key, value))
```

```
        self.element_count += 1

    def _resize(self):
        new_size = self.size * 2
        new_table = [[] for _ in range(new_size)]
        for bucket in self.table:
            for (key, value) in bucket:
                index = key % new_size
                new_table[index].append((key, value))
        self.size = new_size
        self.table = new_table

# Usage of resizable hash table
res_ht = ResizableHashTable(size=10)
for i in range(100):
    res_ht.insert(i, f'Value {i}')
```

3. Hash Function Quality:

The hash function quality significantly affects the overall performance by determining the distribution of keys across buckets. An ideal hash function uniformly distributes keys, thereby minimizing collisions. Poor hash functions result in clustered keys, leading to degraded performance.

Ensuring a good hash function involves: - Uniform distribution of hash values. - Minimizing clustering (keys in proximate hash values). - Fast computation to maintain expected $O(1)$ time complexity.

4. Collision Handling Mechanisms:

Choosing an effective collision handling mechanism is imperative for sustaining performance. Two primary methods are chaining and open addressing, each with distinct characteristics:

- **Chaining:** - Separate chaining minimizes performance degradation by maintaining linked lists or other secondary data structures at each bucket. While this adds slight overhead for list traversal during collisions, it prevents unbounded clustering that can occur in open addressing.

- **Open Addressing:** - Techniques such as linear probing, quadratic probing, and double hashing dynamically resolve collisions by searching alternative slots. Managing the probe sequence is crucial to avoiding clustering and ensuring good performance.

Here is an implementation example of open addressing using linear probing:

```
# Hash table with open addressing using linear probing

class LinearProbingHashTable:
    def __init__(self, size):
```

```
        self.size = size
        self.table = [None] * size

    def hash_function(self, key):
        return key % self.size

    def insert(self, key, value):
        index = self.hash_function(key)
        while self.table[index] is not None:
            index = (index + 1) % self.size
        self.table[index] = (key, value)

    def search(self, key):
        index = self.hash_function(key)
        start_index = index
        while self.table[index] is not None:
            if self.table[index][0] == key:
                return self.table[index][1]
            index = (index + 1) % self.size
            if index == start_index:
                break
        return None

    def delete(self, key):
        index = self.hash_function(key)
        start_index = index
        while self.table[index] is not None:
            if self.table[index][0] == key:
                self.table[index] = None
                return
            index = (index + 1) % self.size
            if index == start_index:
                break

# Usage of linear probing hash table
lpht = LinearProbingHashTable(size=10)
lpht.insert(10, 'Value 10')
lpht.insert(20, 'Value 20')
value = lpht.search(10) # Fast search with minimal probing
```

5. Amortized Analysis of Resizing:

Periodic resizing to maintain optimal load factor introduces an amortized time complexity. Despite resize operations being $O(n)$ due to rehashing, the overall amortized complexity across a sequence of insertions remains $O(1)$. This amortization leverages the infrequent occurrence of resizing operations relative to constant-time insertions.

6. Space Complexity:

The space complexity of hash tables comprises the occupied array space and the overhead from collision resolution structures (e.g., linked lists in chaining). While chaining entails additional memory for storing pointers, open addressing demands ample empty slots to reduce collision probability. Thus, a balance between space utilization and load factor is necessary to optimize both time and space complexity.

- **Chaining:** $O(n + m)$, where n is the number of elements and m the number of buckets.
- **Open Addressing:** $O(m)$, as additional elements are stored within the same hash table array.

Effective management and tuning of these aspects are essential for achieving efficient performance in hash table implementations, ensuring they meet application requirements and operational constraints.

8.9 Hash Tables vs Other Data Structures

Hash tables are a fundamental data structure in computer science, known for their efficient average-case time complexity and versatility in application. To appreciate their utility fully, it is crucial to understand how they compare to other data structures such as arrays, linked lists, binary search trees (BSTs), and balanced trees (e.g., AVL and Red-Black Trees).

Hash tables offer average-case $O(1)$ time complexity for insertion, deletion, and lookup operations, due to their reliance on the hashing mechanism. This efficiency contrasts sharply with the $O(n)$ time complexity for linked lists and the $O(\log n)$ complexities for BSTs and balanced trees.

Arrays

Arrays provide $O(1)$ time complexity for accessing elements by index, which matches that of hash tables. However, array operations such as insertion and deletion can be costly ($O(n)$ in the worst case) when elements need to be shifted. Arrays also require contiguous memory allocation, which can be a limitation for large datasets.

```
# Example of array operations
arr = [0, 1, 2, 3]

# Access by index (O(1))
element = arr[1] # returns 1

# Insertion (O(n))
arr.insert(2, 1.5) # arr becomes [0, 1, 1.5, 2, 3]

# Deletion (O(n))
arr.pop(2) # arr becomes [0, 1, 2, 3]
```

Linked Lists

Linked lists excel where dynamic memory allocation is required, offering $O(1)$ insertions and deletions given direct access to nodes. However, they suffer $O(n)$ time complexities for search operations, and additional memory is needed for storing pointers, introducing an overhead hash tables avoid.

```
# Example of linked list operations
class Node:
    def __init__(self, value):
        self.value = value
        self.next = None

class LinkedList:
    def __init__(self):
        self.head = None

    # Insertion at the beginning (O(1))
    def insert(self, value):
        new_node = Node(value)
        new_node.next = self.head
        self.head = new_node

    # Deletion by value (O(n))
    def delete(self, value):
        current = self.head
        prev = None
        while current:
            if current.value == value:
                if prev:
                    prev.next = current.next
                else:
                    self.head = current.next
                return
            prev = current
            current = current.next

    # Search (O(n))
    def search(self, value):
        current = self.head
        while current:
            if current.value == value:
                return current
            current = current.next
        return None
```

Binary Search Trees (BSTs)

BSTs provide $O(\log n)$ search, insertion, and deletion times for balanced trees. However, unbalanced BSTs can degrade to $O(n)$ operations, making their performance less predictable compared to hash tables. Balancing requires additional algorithmic effort, which is unnecessary for hash tables.

```
# Example of binary search tree operations
class TreeNode:
    def __init__(self, value):
        self.value = value
        self.left = None
```

```
        self.right = None

class BST:
    def __init__(self):
        self.root = None

    # Insertion (O(log n) if balanced, O(n) if not)
    def insert(self, value):
        self.root = self._insert_recursive(self.root, value)

    def _insert_recursive(self, node, value):
        if node is None:
            return TreeNode(value)
        if value < node.value:
            node.left = self._insert_recursive(node.left, value)
        else:
            node.right = self._insert_recursive(node.right, value)
        return node

    # Search (O(log n) if balanced, O(n) if not)
    def search(self, value):
        return self._search_recursive(self.root, value)

    def _search_recursive(self, node, value):
        if node is None or node.value == value:
            return node
        if value < node.value:
            return self._search_recursive(node.left, value)
        else:
            return self._search_recursive(node.right, value)

    # Deletion (O(log n) if balanced, O(n) if not)
    def delete(self, value):
        self.root = self._delete_recursive(self.root, value)

    def _delete_recursive(self, node, value):
        if node is None:
            return node
        if value < node.value:
            node.left = self._delete_recursive(node.left, value)
        elif value > node.value:
            node.right = self._delete_recursive(node.right, value)
        else:
            if node.left is None:
                return node.right
            elif node.right is None:
                return node.left

            temp = self._min_value_node(node.right)
            node.value = temp.value
            node.right = self._delete_recursive(node.right, temp.value)
        return node

    def _min_value_node(self, node):
        current = node
        while current.left is not None:
            current = current.left
        return current
```

Balanced Trees (AVL Trees, Red-Black Trees)

Balanced trees ensure $O(\log n)$ time complexities through self-balancing mechanisms. AVL trees maintain strict balancing, resulting in faster lookups at the cost of slower insertion and deletion due to frequent rotations. In contrast, Red-Black Trees provide less stringent balancing but more efficient insertions and deletions. Nonetheless, both structures are generally more complex to implement and manage compared to hash tables.

```
# Simplified example of insertion in a Red-Black Tree
class RedBlackNode:
    def __init__(self, value, color='R'):
        self.value = value
        self.color = color
        self.left = None
        self.right = None
        self.parent = None

class RedBlackTree:
    def __init__(self):
        self.NIL_LEAF = RedBlackNode(value=None, color='B')
        self.root = self.NIL_LEAF

    # Insertion method (complexity hidden)
    def insert(self, value):
        new_node = RedBlackNode(value)
        # Normal BST insertion logic + additional balancing steps
```

Comparison Summary

The above comparisons establish hash tables as particularly advantageous for scenarios where average-case constant time complexity is desired for insertions, deletions, and lookups. They outperform arrays and linked lists in search operations and can surpass BSTs and balanced trees in terms of simplicity and consistency of performance. However, hash tables do not maintain order and can exhibit poor performance in the worst case if not managed properly or if the hash function produces excessive collisions. As such, the choice of data structure should align with the specific requirements and constraints of the application at hand.

8.10 Advanced Hash Table Techniques

Advanced hash table techniques build upon fundamental concepts, enhancing the efficiency, versatility, and robustness of hash tables in various computational scenarios. This section explores dynamic resizing, cuckoo hashing, and perfect hashing, providing insights into their implementation and performance implications.

Dynamic resizing addresses the need to maintain efficient performance as the number of elements stored in a hash table changes. The load factor, defined as the ratio of the number of entries to the number of buckets, plays a crucial role. When the load factor exceeds a predefined threshold, performance degrades due to increased collisions. To mitigate this, dynamic resizing involves rehashing: creating a larger table with a new hash function and migrating existing entries. Consider the following Python code exemplifying dynamic resizing:

```
class HashTable:
    def __init__(self, capacity=10):
        self.capacity = capacity
        self.size = 0
        self.table = [None] * self.capacity

    def _hash(self, key):
        return hash(key) % self.capacity

    def put(self, key, value):
        if self.size / self.capacity > 0.7:
            self._resize()
        index = self._hash(key)
        if self.table[index] is None:
            self.table[index] = [(key, value)]
        else:
            for i, (k, v) in enumerate(self.table[index]):
                if k == key:
                    self.table[index][i] = (key, value)
                    return
            self.table[index].append((key, value))
        self.size += 1

    def get(self, key):
        index = self._hash(key)
        if self.table[index] is None:
            return None
        for k, v in self.table[index]:
            if k == key:
                return v
        return None

    def _resize(self):
        self.capacity *= 2
        new_table = [None] * self.capacity
        for bucket in self.table:
            if bucket is not None:
                for key, value in bucket:
                    index = hash(key) % self.capacity
                    if new_table[index] is None:
                        new_table[index] = [(key, value)]
                    else:
                        new_table[index].append((key, value))
        self.table = new_table
```

The code demonstrates how dynamic resizing reallocates entries to a new table with doubled capacity, maintaining efficient lookup times.

Cuckoo hashing introduces the novel concept of multiple hash functions to resolve collisions more effectively. Each key can reside in one of two (or more) possible locations, determined by distinct hash functions. If both positions are occupied, an existing key is relocated, potentially triggering a sequence of relocations, known as kickouts. This guarantees constant worst-case lookup time at the cost of potential displacement operations. Here is a simplified Python example of cuckoo hashing:

```
class CuckooHashTable:
    def __init__(self, capacity=10):
        self.capacity = capacity
        self.table1 = [None] * self.capacity
        self.table2 = [None] * self.capacity

    def _hash1(self, key):
        return hash(key) % self.capacity

    def _hash2(self, key):
        return (hash(key) // self.capacity) % self.capacity

    def put(self, key, value):
        for _ in range(self.capacity):
            index1 = self._hash1(key)
            if self.table1[index1] is None:
                self.table1[index1] = (key, value)
                return
            key, value = self.table1[index1]
            self.table1[index1] = None
            index2 = self._hash2(key)
            if self.table2[index2] is None:
                self.table2[index2] = (key, value)
                return
            key, value = self.table2[index2]
            self.table2[index2] = None
        self.rehash()
        self.put(key, value)

    def rehash(self):
        self.capacity *= 2
        new_table1 = [None] * self.capacity
        new_table2 = [None] * self.capacity
        old_table1, old_table2 = self.table1, self.table2
        self.table1, self.table2 = new_table1, new_table2

        for item in old_table1 + old_table2:
            if item is not None:
                key, value = item
                self.put(key, value)

    def get(self, key):
        index = self._hash1(key)
        if self.table1[index] and self.table1[index][0] == key:
            return self.table1[index][1]
        index = self._hash2(key)
        if self.table2[index] and self.table2[index][0] == key:
            return self.table2[index][1]
        return None
```

The code above efficiently implements cuckoo hashing while utilizing two hash functions and managing potential rehashing.

Perfect hashing ensures O(1) lookup time by constructing a collision-free minimal perfect hash function when keys are known a priori. The perfect hash function maps keys to unique slots without collisions. Building such a function can be computationally intensive but yields optimal lookup efficiency for static datasets. The following Python snippet illustrates constructing a simple perfect hash function for a fixed set of keys:

```
import random

class PerfectHashTable:
    def __init__(self, keys):
        self.size = len(keys)
        self.table = [None] * self.size
        self.keys = keys
        self._build_perfect_hash_table()

    def _find_hash_function(self):
        for i in range(1, 100):
            random.seed(i)
            func = lambda k: (hash(k) + random.randint(1, 1000)) % self.size
            seen = set()
            collision = False
            for key in self.keys:
                idx = func(key)
                if idx in seen:
                    collision = True
                    break
                seen.add(idx)
            if not collision:
                return func
        return None

    def _build_perfect_hash_table(self):
        self.hash_function = self._find_hash_function()
        if self.hash_function:
            for key in self.keys:
                idx = self.hash_function(key)
                self.table[idx] = key

    def get(self, key):
        idx = self.hash_function(key)
        if self.table[idx] == key:
            return key
        return None
```

This example demonstrates constructing a minimal perfect hash function using randomization techniques to minimize collisions across a predetermined set of keys.

Incorporating advanced techniques such as dynamic resizing, cuckoo hashing, and perfect hashing allows for enhanced performance and adaptability of hash tables in diverse applications. These techniques address common limitations associated with basic hash table implementations, ensuring robustness and efficiency.

8.11 Common Issues and Debugging in Hash Tables

When working with hash tables, a variety of common issues might arise, which can significantly impact their performance and correctness. Understanding these issues and knowing how to debug them is crucial. This section will address the common pitfalls, techniques to identify them, and methods to resolve them effectively.

The most recurrent issues in hash tables often involve improper handling of hash functions, collision resolution mechanisms, and errors in table resizing. Let's explore these in detail.

1. Faulty Hash Functions

A hash function's primary role is to uniformly distribute keys across the hash table. A poorly designed hash function can lead to clustering, where a significant number of keys are mapped to the same index, resulting in performance degradation. To ensure a good distribution:

- Ensure the hash function uses all input key information.
- Avoid simple hash functions like returning the first character's ASCII value if the keys are strings.
- Use well-tested hash functions or libraries whenever possible.

Assume we have a simplistic hash function defined in Python:

```
def bad_hash(key):
    return ord(key[0]) % 10
```

This function will undoubtedly cause clustering for keys starting with the same letter. A better design incorporates more of the key's value:

```
def better_hash(key):
    hash_value = 0
    for char in key:
        hash_value += ord(char)
    return hash_value % 10
```

2. Inefficient Collision Handling

Poor collision handling strategies can lead to degraded performance or even failure in finding elements. Two primary methods for collision resolution are chaining and open addressing.

Chaining: This technique stores all elements that hash to the same index in a linked list. Issues in chaining include excessively long chains, which should be minimized.

Example of a simple chaining implementation:

```
class HashTable:
    def ___init___(self):
        self.table = [[] for _ in range(10)]

    def put(self, key, value):
        hash_index = better_hash(key)
        for kv in self.table[hash_index]:
            if kv[0] == key:
                kv[1] = value
                return
        self.table[hash_index].append([key, value])

    def get(self, key):
        hash_index = better_hash(key)
        for kv in self.table[hash_index]:
            if kv[0] == key:
                return kv[1]
        return None
```

Open Addressing: This approach resolves collisions by finding another open slot within the table. Techniques like linear probing, quadratic probing, and double hashing fall under this category. Common issues here include clustering and infinite loops.

- **Linear Probing**: Incrementally checks the next index.

```
def linear_probing(table, key, value):
    hash_index = better_hash(key)
    start_index = hash_index
    while table[hash_index] is not None:
        hash_index = (hash_index + 1) % len(table)
        if hash_index == start_index: # Table is full
            raise Exception("Hash table is full")
    table[hash_index] = (key, value)
```

- **Quadratic Probing**: Uses a quadratic function to resolve collisions.

```
def quadratic_probing(table, key, value):
    hash_index = better_hash(key)
    i = 1
    start_index = hash_index
    while table[hash_index] is not None:
        hash_index = (hash_index + i**2) % len(table)
        i += 1
        if hash_index == start_index: # Table is full
```

```
            raise Exception("Hash table is full")
    table[hash_index] = (key, value)
```

3. Table Resizing

One must resize the hash table when the load factor, defined as the number of stored elements divided by the table's size, exceeds a certain threshold. Failing to resize appropriately will lead to a high rate of collisions.

Example code for resizing a hash table:

```
def resize_hash_table(old_table):
    new_size = 2 * len(old_table)
    new_table = [None] * new_size
    for item in old_table:
        if item:
            key, value = item
            linear_probing(new_table, key, value)
    return new_table
```

4. Debugging Techniques

Effective debugging requires a systematic approach to identify and resolve issues. Key techniques include:

- **Print Statements**: Insert print statements to trace execution flow and variable values.
- **Unit Tests**: Write tests covering both typical and edge cases. Python's 'unittest' module can automate this process.

```
import unittest

class TestHashTable(unittest.TestCase):
    def setUp(self):
        self.ht = HashTable()

    def test_put_get(self):
        self.ht.put("key1", "value1")
        self.assertEqual(self.ht.get("key1"), "value1")

    def test_collision(self):
        self.ht.put("a", "valueA")
        self.ht.put("k", "valueK")
        self.assertEqual(self.ht.get("a"), "valueA")
        self.assertEqual(self.ht.get("k"), "valueK")

if __name__ == '__main__':
    unittest.main()
```

- **Assertions**: Use assertions to validate assumptions during development.

```
assert better_hash("test") == expected_value
```

- **Profiling**: Identify inefficient code segments using profiling tools like 'cProfile'.

The ability to effectively debug and resolve common issues in hash tables is crucial for ensuring their optimal performance and reliability in various applications.

Chapter 9

Sorting and Searching Algorithms

This chapter focuses on sorting and searching algorithms, covering fundamental sorting techniques such as bubble sort, selection sort, insertion sort, merge sort, quick sort, heap sort, and radix sort. It also explores searching methods including binary search and linear search. Additionally, the chapter compares the performance of these algorithms and discusses considerations for optimizing their efficiency.

9.1 Introduction to Sorting and Searching

Sorting and searching are fundamental operations in computer science, forming the backbone of many algorithms and systems. Sorting refers to the process of arranging data in a particular order, usually in ascending or descending numerical order or lexicographical order. Searching is the process of finding a particular element within a dataset. Both operations are critical for enhancing the efficiency and effectiveness of data management and retrieval systems.

Consider a scenario in which we have a large dataset containing millions of elements. Efficient sorting algorithms enable us to organize this data systematically, while effective searching algorithms allow for quick retrieval of specific information. These operations are ubiquitous in applications ranging from database management systems to text-processing tools and from internet search engines to machine learning algorithms.

To begin, let us define more formally what we mean by sorting and searching:

Sorting: Given a collection of elements $A = \{a_1, a_2, \ldots, a_n\}$, the sorting problem involves arranging the elements in increasing order if they are comparable. Formally, the sorted array A_{sorted} satisfies $A_{\text{sorted}} = \{a'_1, a'_2, \ldots, a'_n\}$ such that $a'_1 \leq a'_2 \leq \cdots \leq a'_n$.

Searching: Given a collection of elements $A = \{a_1, a_2, \ldots, a_n\}$ and a key k, the searching problem involves determining whether k is present in A. If k is found in A, the search operation may return the index i such that $a_i = k$; otherwise, it may return a value indicating failure, such as None or -1.

The computational efficiency of these operations largely depends on the algorithm used and the nature of the data. Sorting algorithms are often evaluated using their time complexity, which provides an estimate of the number of operations required to sort a dataset of size n. Similarly, searching algorithms are evaluated based on their time complexity for finding an element in an unordered or an ordered dataset.

Types of Sorting Algorithms:

Sorting algorithms can be broadly categorized based on their approach and time complexity. The primary categories include:

- **Comparison-Based Sorting:** These algorithms sort by comparing elements, and their average time complexity is typically $O(n \log n)$. Examples include Quick Sort, Merge Sort, and Heap Sort.
- **Non-Comparison-Based Sorting:** These algorithms use operations other than comparison to sort data and can have linear time complexity, $O(n)$, under certain conditions. Examples include Counting Sort, Radix Sort, and Bucket Sort.

Types of Searching Algorithms:

Searching algorithms can be classified into two primary categories:

- **Linear Search:** This algorithm checks each element of the dataset sequentially until the desired element is found or the list ends. The time complexity is $O(n)$.

- **Binary Search:** This algorithm efficiently finds an element in a sorted dataset by repeatedly dividing the search interval in half. The time complexity is $O(\log n)$, but it requires the dataset to be pre-sorted.

To illustrate these concepts, we provide simple implementations of basic sorting and searching algorithms in Python. Understanding these implementations will build a foundational knowledge before delving deeper into more advanced algorithms.

Bubble Sort:

Bubble Sort is a straightforward comparison-based sorting algorithm. It repeatedly steps through the list, compares adjacent elements, and swaps them if they are in the wrong order. This pass-through is repeated until the list is sorted.

```
def bubble_sort(arr):
    n = len(arr)
    for i in range(n):
        for j in range(0, n-i-1):
            if arr[j] > arr[j+1]:
                arr[j], arr[j+1] = arr[j+1], arr[j]
    return arr
```

Binary Search:

Binary Search finds the position of a target value within a sorted array. It compares the target value to the middle element of the array; if they are unequal, it eliminates half of the array, and the search continues on the remaining half.

```
def binary_search(arr, target):
    left, right = 0, len(arr) - 1
    while left <= right:
        mid = (left + right) // 2
        if arr[mid] == target:
            return mid
        elif arr[mid] < target:
            left = mid + 1
        else:
            right = mid - 1
    return None
```

The efficiency of sorting is critical for the performance of searching algorithms, as certain searching algorithms like Binary Search require the data to be sorted. As we progress through this chapter, we will explore various sorting algorithms in detail, analyzing their performance characteristics and use cases. Similarly, we will delve into advanced searching techniques that build upon foundational knowledge to enhance the efficiency of data retrieval operations.

9.2 Bubble Sort

Bubble Sort is one of the simplest sorting algorithms, which repeatedly steps through the list to be sorted, compares each pair of adjacent items, and swaps them if they are in the wrong order. This process is repeated until the list is sorted. Despite its simplicity, Bubble Sort is not suitable for large data sets due to its $\mathcal{O}(n^2)$ average and worst-case time complexity.

The primary mechanism behind Bubble Sort involves "bubbling" the largest unsorted element to its correct position during each iteration through the list. This method ensures that after the first complete iteration, the largest value is positioned correctly at the end of the list, after the second iteration the next largest value is placed correctly, and so on.

Let's consider a detailed step-by-step illustration of the Bubble Sort algorithm with an example list: [5, 1, 4, 2, 8].

The algorithm can be described in Python as follows:

```
def bubble_sort(arr):
    n = len(arr)

    # Traverse through all array elements
    for i in range(n):

        # Last i elements are already in place
        for j in range(0, n-i-1):

            # Traverse the array from 0 to n-i-1
            # Swap if the element found is greater
            # than the next element
            if arr[j] > arr[j+1]:
                arr[j], arr[j+1] = arr[j+1], arr[j]
```

In the provided code, the outer loop runs n times, where n is the number of elements in the array. The inner loop runs repeatedly, performing comparisons and swaps to ensure the larger elements 'bubble' to the end of the array.

Let's go through each pass of the algorithm for our example list [5, 1, 4, 2, 8]:

1. **First Pass** (i=0):

    - $5 > 1$ (swap 5 and 1): [1, 5, 4, 2, 8]
    - $5 > 4$ (swap 5 and 4): [1, 4, 5, 2, 8]
    - $5 > 2$ (swap 5 and 2): [1, 4, 2, 5, 8]

- $5 < 8$ (no swap): [1, 4, 2, 5, 8]

2. **Second Pass** (i=1):
   - $1 < 4$ (no swap): [1, 4, 2, 5, 8]
   - $4 > 2$ (swap 4 and 2): [1, 2, 4, 5, 8]
   - $4 < 5$ (no swap): [1, 2, 4, 5, 8]
3. **Third Pass** (i=2):
   - $1 < 2$ (no swap): [1, 2, 4, 5, 8]
   - $2 < 4$ (no swap): [1, 2, 4, 5, 8]
4. **Fourth Pass** (i=3):
   - $1 < 2$ (no swap): [1, 2, 4, 5, 8]

The list is now sorted after four passes.

Bubble Sort's simplicity comes at the cost of inefficiency, particularly for large datasets. Its performance can be given by examining the number of comparisons and swaps it performs:

- **Best Case** ($\mathcal{O}(n)$): This occurs when the list is already sorted, and the algorithm only needs to make a single pass through the list without performing any swaps. In a modified version of Bubble Sort, a flag can be used to monitor changes made in the array, which can prevent unnecessary passes. If no elements were swapped during a pass, the array is already sorted.
- **Average and Worst Case** ($\mathcal{O}(n^2)$): In both cases, the algorithm must check each pair of adjacent elements. In the worst-case scenario, the algorithm performs $\frac{n(n-1)}{2}$ comparisons and swaps.

The following is an optimized version of Bubble Sort to handle cases where the array might become sorted before completing all passes:

```
def optimized_bubble_sort(arr):
    n = len(arr)
    for i in range(n):
        swapped = False
        for j in range(0, n-i-1):
            if arr[j] > arr[j+1]:
                arr[j], arr[j+1] = arr[j+1], arr[j]
                swapped = True
        if not swapped:
            break
```

This optimization checks if any swap was made during an entire pass. If no swaps are made, it breaks out of the loop early, thus reducing the time complexity in the best-case scenario to $\mathcal{O}(n)$.

While Bubble Sort is academically significant and often taught as an introductory algorithm to grasp the fundamentals of sorting algorithms, its practical utility is limited. It is outperformed by other more efficient algorithms like Quick Sort, Merge Sort, and even Insertion Sort for larger datasets.

Despite its inefficiency, understanding Bubble Sort is critical for foundational knowledge in algorithm development. It introduces fundamental concepts such as elementary comparison-and-swap, iterative improvement, and algorithmic optimization through flagging mechanisms.

9.3 Selection Sort

Selection Sort is a straightforward comparison-based sorting algorithm. It maintains two subarrays within the original array: a sorted subarray, which is constructed from left to right, and an unsorted subarray. During each iteration, the algorithm selects the smallest (or largest, depending on the sorting order) element from the unsorted subarray and swaps it with the first element of the unsorted subarray, thereby extending the sorted subarray by one element.

The algorithm proceeds with the following steps:

1. Initialize the sorted subarray to be empty.
2. Repeat until the unsorted subarray becomes empty:
   (a) Find the minimum element in the unsorted subarray.
   (b) Swap the minimum element with the first element of the unsorted subarray.
   (c) Extend the sorted subarray by including the newly positioned minimum element.

Given an array A of n elements, the Selection Sort algorithm operates as follows:

```
def selection_sort(A):
    n = len(A)
    for i in range(n):
        # Find the minimum element in the remaining unsorted array
```

```
        min_idx = i
        for j in range(i + 1, n):
            if A[j] < A[min_idx]:
                min_idx = j
        # Swap the found minimum element with the first element of the unsorted array
        A[i], A[min_idx] = A[min_idx], A[i]

# Example usage
A = [64, 25, 12, 22, 11]
selection_sort(A)
print("Sorted array is:", A)
```

When the above code is executed, the output is:

```
Sorted array is: [11, 12, 22, 25, 64]
```

Detailed Analysis

Time Complexity: The Selection Sort algorithm has a time complexity of $O(n^2)$ in all cases (best, average, and worst). This is due to the two nested loops: - The outer loop runs n times. - The inner loop runs $(n-1)$, $(n-2)$, ..., 1 times.

Thus, the total number of comparisons:

$$\sum_{i=1}^{n-1} i = \frac{n(n-1)}{2}$$

which is $O(n^2)$. The swaps, however, are bounded by $O(n)$ since one swap is made per outer loop iteration regardless of the inner loop's activity.

Space Complexity: Selection Sort is an in-place sorting algorithm, indicating its space complexity is $O(1)$, utilizing only a constant amount of extra memory beyond the input array.

Stability: Selection Sort is **not** a stable sorting algorithm. Stability in sorting algorithms means that two equal elements retain their relative order in the sorted array as it was in the input array. In Selection Sort, when the minimum element found within the unsorted subarray is swapped with the first unsorted element, it might move past elements that are equal to it, thus breaking stability.

Adaptability: Selection Sort is an **adaptive** sorting algorithm as it consistently requires $O(n^2)$ time complexity regardless of the initial ordering of the input array. Whether the input list is nearly sorted or randomly shuffled makes no difference in the number of comparisons made by the algorithm.

Implementation Considerations

1. **Performance:** - Given its $O(n^2)$ time complexity, Selection Sort is inefficient on large lists. - It performs **better** than Bubble Sort in terms of number of swaps, making it slightly more efficient when minimizing write operations is important. 2. **Use Cases:** - Useful for scenarios where the cost of writing to memory is high. Implementations like Flash memory, where write operations are expensive, can benefit from Selection Sort's minimal swapping. 3. **Modifications:** - The algorithm can be modified to stop the process if the remaining array is already sorted. However, this will have a limited impact due to its basic design where the minimum element search cannot be bypassed.

Example: Tracing the Steps

To better understand Selection Sort, trace it on the array $A = [64, 25, 12, 22, 11]$:

1. **Iteration 1:** - Unsorted: $[64, 25, 12, 22, 11]$ - Find minimum in unsorted part: 11. - Swap with first unsorted element: $[11, 25, 12, 22, 64]$

2. **Iteration 2:** - Unsorted: $[25, 12, 22, 64]$ - Find minimum in unsorted part: 12. - Swap with first unsorted element: $[11, 12, 25, 22, 64]$

3. **Iteration 3:** - Unsorted: $[25, 22, 64]$ - Find minimum in unsorted part: 22. - Swap with first unsorted element: $[11, 12, 22, 25, 64]$

4. **Iteration 4:** - Unsorted: $[25, 64]$ - Find minimum in unsorted part: 25. - Swap (no effect): $[11, 12, 22, 25, 64]$

5. **Iteration 5:** - Unsorted: $[64]$ - Only one element left, sorted list: $[11, 12, 22, 25, 64]$

Each step reduces the unsorted part by moving the smallest unsorted element to its correct position.

9.4 Insertion Sort

Insertion Sort is a simple, intuitive algorithm closely related to the way humans often sort small quantities of items in their daily lives. It is especially effective for small datasets or nearly sorted arrays and operates with a time complexity of $O(n^2)$ in the worst case. This section provides a comprehensive exploration of Insertion Sort, including its mechanism, implementation, and performance analysis.

The fundamental idea of Insertion Sort is to maintain a sorted sublist in the lower positions of the list being sorted. Each new element is then "inserted" into this sorted sublist in the correct position.

Consider an array A of n elements, denoted as $A[1], A[2], \ldots, A[n]$. The algorithm operates as follows: 1. Assume that $A[1]$ is a single-element sorted array. 2. For each subsequent element $A[i]$ (where i ranges from 2 to n), insert $A[i]$ into its appropriate position among the sorted elements from $A[1]$ to $A[i-1]$.

To achieve this, the algorithm performs the following set of operations:

```
def insertion_sort(arr):
    for i in range(1, len(arr)):
        key = arr[i]
        j = i - 1
        while j >= 0 and key < arr[j]:
            arr[j + 1] = arr[j]
            j -= 1
        arr[j + 1] = key

# Example usage:
arr = [12, 11, 13, 5, 6]
insertion_sort(arr)
print("Sorted array:", arr)
```

The steps above outline the essence of Insertion Sort: - The key variable stores the value of the current element to be inserted into the sorted portion of the list. - The inner while loop shifts elements of the sorted sublist that are greater than the key one position to the right to create space for the key. - After the correct position is found, the key is placed into this position.

Let's break down the execution of the Insertion Sort algorithm on the array $[12, 11, 13, 5, 6]$:

- Initial array: $[12, 11, 13, 5, 6]$
- First iteration: $i = 1$, key = 11. Compare 11 with 12, since 11 < 12, shift 12 to the right.

  ```
  Array: [12, 12, 13, 5, 6]
         11
  ```
  Insert 11 in position 0.

  ```
  Array: [11, 12, 13, 5, 6]
  ```
- Second iteration: $i = 2$, key = 13. Compare 13 with 12, as 13 > 12, it remains in place.

  ```
  Array: [11, 12, 13, 5, 6]
  ```
- Third iteration: $i = 3$, key = 5. Compare 5 with 13, 12 and 11, since 5 is smaller than all these values, shift them to make space.

  ```
  Array: [11, 12, 13, 13, 6]
              12
         11
            5
  ```
  Insert 5 in position 0.

Array: [5, 11, 12, 13, 6]

- Fourth iteration: $i = 4$, key = 6. Compare 6 with 13, 12, and 11. Since 6 is smaller, shift these elements.

  Array: [5, 11, 12, 13, 13]
  12
  11
  6 Insert 6 in position 1.

  Array: [5, 6, 11, 12, 13]

Algorithm Analysis:

Time Complexity: The running time of an insertion sort depends on the initial condition of the list. - $\mathbf{O(n^2)}$ in the worst case: When the array is sorted in reverse order, each insertion requires shifting of all previously sorted elements. - $\mathbf{O(n)}$ in the best case: When the array is already sorted, each insertion requires no shifting. - $\mathbf{O(n^2)}$ on average: Assuming that each insertion compares keys half the time of the list on average.

Space Complexity: Insertion Sort is an in-place sorting algorithm, requiring $O(1)$ additional space. It sorts the array within itself without needing extra storage.

Stability: Insertion Sort is a stable sort algorithm because it preserves the relative order of equal elements.

For example, for the array $[(12,'A'), (11,'B'), (13,'C'), (5,'D'), (6,'E')]$, even if multiple elements have the same key, the sort maintains their original order.

In all, Insertion Sort offers simple implementation, efficiency for small or nearly sorted arrays, and stability in sorting, making it an essential algorithm in the landscape of sorting techniques.

9.5 Merge Sort

Merge Sort is a classical divide-and-conquer sorting algorithm that offers a robust solution with a guaranteed $O(n \log n)$ time complexity, making it efficient for larger datasets. The algorithm works by recursively dividing the array into two halves, sorting each half, and then merging the sorted halves back together.

Consider the array A to be sorted, of length n. The Merge Sort algorithm can be implemented as follows:

```
def merge_sort(A):
    if len(A) > 1:
        mid = len(A) // 2
        left_half = A[:mid]
        right_half = A[mid:]

        merge_sort(left_half)
        merge_sort(right_half)

        i = j = k = 0

        while i < len(left_half) and j < len(right_half):
            if left_half[i] < right_half[j]:
                A[k] = left_half[i]
                i += 1
            else:
                A[k] = right_half[j]
                j += 1
            k += 1

        while i < len(left_half):
            A[k] = left_half[i]
            i += 1
            k += 1

        while j < len(right_half):
            A[k] = right_half[j]
            j += 1
            k += 1
```

The Merge Sort algorithm can be broken down into several key operations:

- **Divide**: The array A is divided into two halves. This step is straightforward and involves calculating the middle index.
- **Recursively Sort**: Each half of the array is recursively sorted by calling Merge Sort on both halves.
- **Merge**: Finally, the sorted halves are merged back together. This step requires additional space but ensures that the merge operation is performed in a linear pass through each subarray.

The merge operation is central to the efficiency of Merge Sort. The merging process compares the smallest unmerged elements of each subarray and appends the smaller element to the merged array. If one subarray is exhausted before the other, the remaining elements of the non-exhausted subarray are directly appended because they are already sorted.

To illustrate the merging process, consider merging two sorted arrays:

```
Left Half:  [4, 5, 8]
Right Half: [1, 2, 6]
Merged:     [1, 2, 4, 5, 6, 8]
```

In practice, the merging involves maintaining indices for both subarrays and iterating through them:

```
def merge(left, right):
    result = []
    i = j = 0

    while i < len(left) and j < len(right):
        if left[i] < right[j]:
            result.append(left[i])
            i += 1
        else:
            result.append(right[j])
            j += 1

    result.extend(left[i:])
    result.extend(right[j:])
    return result
```

This approach ensures that the merge operation occurs in linear time relative to the sum of the lengths of the input arrays $O(n_1 + n_2)$.

Time Complexity: The merging process occurs in $O(n)$, where n is the length of the array. Since the merging is done $\log n$ times due to the recursive division, the overall time complexity of Merge Sort is $O(n \log n)$.

Space Complexity: Merge Sort requires additional space proportional to the size of the array, $O(n)$, because it needs to store the two halves of the array being merged. This requirement makes it less space-efficient compared to in-place sorting algorithms like Quick Sort.

Merge Sort's performance and behavior are invariant to the initial order of elements, making its $\Theta(n \log n)$ time complexity its best, average, and worst-case performance.

Merge Sort provides a reliable and efficient sorting method for large datasets. Its stable sorting nature (preserving the relative order of equal elements) and consistent performance make it a valuable algorithm, particularly when stability is required or when working with linked lists where its finer space complexity ($O(\log n)$ for linked lists) can be beneficial.

9.6 Quick Sort

Quick Sort, also known as Quicksort, is a highly efficient sorting algorithm that employs a divide-and-conquer strategy. It was developed by

Tony Hoare in 1959 and has been widely utilized due to its superior performance in average-case scenarios, typically achieving $\mathcal{O}(n \log n)$ time complexity. Quicksort's efficacy lies in its ability to recursively partition the data set into smaller sub-arrays until the base case of a single-element array is reached, which naturally is sorted.

The algorithm proceeds as follows: 1. **Partitioning the Array** - Select a 'pivot' element from the array. Reorder the array so that all elements with values less than the pivot come before it, and all elements with values greater than the pivot come after it. This step is commonly known as the partitioning operation. 2. **Recursive Sorting** - Recursively apply the above steps to the sub-arrays of elements with smaller and larger values.

Here is a step-by-step Python implementation of the Quicksort algorithm:

```
def quicksort(arr):
    if len(arr) <= 1:
        return arr
    pivot = arr[len(arr) // 2]
    left = [x for x in arr if x < pivot]
    middle = [x for x in arr if x == pivot]
    right = [x for x in arr if x > pivot]
    return quicksort(left) + middle + quicksort(right)
```

In this implementation, the function quicksort first checks if the array length is less than or equal to one, in which case it returns the array as it is already sorted. The pivot chosen here is the middle element of the array for simplicity. The list comprehensions are used to create three sub-lists containing elements less than the pivot, equal to the pivot, and greater than the pivot, respectively. The function then recursively sorts the sub-lists and concatenates them.

In-Place Quick Sort

The above implementation, while easy to understand, is not in-place and requires additional storage proportional to the size of the array. An in-place variant of Quicksort avoids this overhead by rearranging elements within the original array. Here is an in-place Quick Sort implementation in Python:

```
def quicksort_inplace(arr, low, high):
    if low < high:
        pivot_index = partition(arr, low, high)
        quicksort_inplace(arr, low, pivot_index - 1)
        quicksort_inplace(arr, pivot_index + 1, high)

def partition(arr, low, high):
    pivot = arr[high]
    i = low - 1
```

```
    for j in range(low, high):
        if arr[j] <= pivot:
            i += 1
            arr[i], arr[j] = arr[j], arr[i]
    arr[i + 1], arr[high] = arr[high], arr[i + 1]
    return i + 1
```

In the in-place version, the quicksort_inplace function recursively sorts sections of the array, defined by the indices low and high. The partition function rearranges elements in-place so that all elements less than the pivot are placed before it and all greater elements are after it, returning the pivot index.

Time Complexity Analysis

Quicksort's time complexity is determined by the partitioning process and the number of recursive calls: - **Best Case:** The pivot splits the list into two equal halves every time, yielding a time complexity of $\mathcal{O}(n \log n)$. - **Average Case:** Typically, Quicksort also operates at $\mathcal{O}(n \log n)$, as the probability of consistently poor pivots is low. - **Worst Case:** When the smallest or largest element is always chosen as the pivot, leading to highly unbalanced partitions (e.g., sorted or reverse sorted array), Quicksort degrades to $\mathcal{O}(n^2)$.

Space Complexity

The above recursive implementation of Quicksort requires $\mathcal{O}(\log n)$ space for the recursion stack in the average case. In the worst case, it requires $\mathcal{O}(n)$ stack space due to the depth of recursion.

Optimizations

1. **Pivot Selection:** Using the median-of-three method (selecting the median of the first, middle, and last elements of the partition), or random pivot selection can mitigate the likelihood of unbalanced partitioning and hence, optimize performance. 2. **Tail Recursion:** Transform the recursive calls into a loop where one side of the recursion (specifically the larger partition) is handled iteratively. 3. **IntroSort:** Initiate with Quicksort and switch to Heap Sort if the recursion depth exceeds a level proportional to $\log n$, thus guaranteeing worst-case $\mathcal{O}(n \log n)$.

Quicksort's combination of simplicity and efficiency makes it one of the most widely used sorting algorithms in a variety of domains, demonstrating its robustness across diverse data types and structures.

9.7 Heap Sort

Heap Sort is an efficient comparison-based sorting algorithm that leverages the properties of a binary heap data structure. This section delves into the construction and utilization of heaps for sorting, explaining both theoretical concepts and practical implementation. Heap Sort can be divided primarily into two steps: building a heap and repeatedly extracting the maximum element from the heap to achieve a sorted array.

A binary heap is a complete binary tree which satisfies the heap property, where each parent node is greater than or equal to its children (max-heap) or less than or equal to its children (min-heap). For Heap Sort, we will primarily use a max-heap to facilitate sorting in ascending order.

The steps involved in Heap Sort are as follows:

- Build a max-heap from the input data.
- The largest element is now at the root of the heap. Swap it with the last item of the heap and reduce the size of the heap by one.
- Apply heapify to the root.
- Repeat the above steps until the size of the heap is greater than one.

Here is the step-by-step implementation of Heap Sort in Python:

```
def heapify(arr, n, i):
    largest = i # Initialize largest as root
    left = 2 * i + 1 # left = 2*i + 1
    right = 2 * i + 2 # right = 2*i + 2

    # Check if left child of root exists and is greater than root
    if left < n and arr[largest] < arr[left]:
        largest = left

    # Check if right child of root exists and is greater than root
    if right < n and arr[largest] < arr[right]:
        largest = right

    # Change root, if needed
    if largest != i:
        arr[i], arr[largest] = arr[largest], arr[i] # swap

        # Heapify the root
        heapify(arr, n, largest)

# Main function to do heap sort
def heap_sort(arr):
```

```
    n = len(arr)

    # Build a maxheap.
    for i in range(n // 2 - 1, -1, -1):
        heapify(arr, n, i)

    # Extract elements one by one from the heap
    for i in range(n-1, 0, -1):
        arr[i], arr[0] = arr[0], arr[i] # swap
        heapify(arr, i, 0)
```

The initial call to heapify builds a max-heap from the unsorted array. The main heap_sort function then repeatedly extracts the maximum element from the top of the heap and rebuilds the heap, sort-ordering the elements in place.

Consider the following example:

```
arr = [12, 11, 13, 5, 6, 7]
heap_sort(arr)
print("Sorted array is", arr)
```

```
Sorted array is [5, 6, 7, 11, 12, 13]
```

By running the above code, the output demonstrates that the elements of the original array have been rearranged into a sorted sequence.

The time complexity of Heap Sort is $O(n \log n)$ in both the best and worst cases, where n is the number of elements in the input array. This performance is due to the heapify operation, which takes $O(\log n)$ time, being called $O(n)$ times. Additionally, Heap Sort is typically implemented as an in-place algorithm, with a space complexity of $O(1)$, meaning it requires only a constant amount of extra space beyond the input array itself.

Heap Sort is particularly useful in scenarios where a guaranteed $O(n \log n)$ time performance is necessary, regardless of the initial order of elements. Consequently, it is a viable choice for large datasets that require consistent sorting times.

By thoroughly understanding the mechanics of Heap Sort and its application, learners can optimally implement this algorithm in various contexts, appreciating its efficiency and robustness.

9.8 Radix Sort

Radix Sort is a non-comparative integer sorting algorithm that sorts integers by processing individual digits. Unlike other sorting algorithms,

Radix Sort categorizes numbers based on their individual digits' positional value. There are two primary types of Radix Sort: Least Significant Digit (LSD) and Most Significant Digit (MSD). This section delves into the LSD Radix Sort, typically used for sorting numbers.

Radix Sort leverages the counting sort algorithm as a subroutine. To fully understand its implementation and working mechanism, it's essential to comprehend its foundational principles and how counting sort integrates within it.

Consider an array of integers where each integer has d digits. Radix Sort processes each digit from the least significant digit to the most significant digit. By repeatedly applying a stable sorting technique, such as counting sort, on each digit, Radix Sort ensures that the final array is sorted.

Procedure and Working Mechanism

1. **Determine the number of digits in the largest number:** This step ensures that all iterations span the maximum number of digits in the data set. 2. **Apply counting sort to each digit position:** Starting from the least significant digit, a stable sort (counting sort) is applied to organize numbers based on that digit.

The efficiency of Radix Sort lies in its ability to handle each digit individually, processing from least significant to most significant. Below is the implementation of LSD Radix Sort in Python:

```
def counting_sort(arr, exp):
    n = len(arr)
    output = [0] * n # The output array elements that will have sorted arr
    count = [0] * 10 # Initialize count array as 0

    # Store count of occurrences in the count array
    for i in range(n):
        index = arr[i] // exp
        count[index % 10] += 1

    # Change count[i] so that count[i] contains the actual
    # position of this digit in the output array
    for i in range(1, 10):
        count[i] += count[i - 1]

    # Build the output array
    i = n - 1
    while i >= 0:
        index = arr[i] // exp
        output[count[index % 10] - 1] = arr[i]
        count[index % 10] -= 1
        i -= 1

    # Copy the output array to arr[], so that arr now contains
    # sorted numbers according to the current digit
    for i in range(n):
```

```
        arr[i] = output[i]

def radix_sort(arr):
    # Find the maximum number to know the number of digits
    max1 = max(arr)

    # Do counting sort for every digit. Note that we pass
    # exp (10^i) where i is the current digit number
    exp = 1
    while max1 // exp > 0:
        counting_sort(arr, exp)
        exp *= 10

# An example usage
arr = [170, 45, 75, 90, 802, 24, 2, 66]
radix_sort(arr)
print("Sorted array is: ", arr)
```

```
Sorted array is: [2, 24, 45, 66, 75, 90, 170, 802]
```

In this implementation: - The counting_sort function serves to sort the array based on the provided digit (exponent exp). - The radix_sort function iteratively calls counting_sort for each digit from the least significant to the most significant.

Complexity Analysis

Radix Sort operates with a time complexity of $O(d(n+k))$, where d is the number of digits in the largest number, n is the number of elements in the array, and k is the base or range of the digits. Typically, for decimal digits, k is 10. The space complexity is $O(n + k)$ due to the additional arrays used for counting and output.

Given its linear time complexity with respect to the input size and number of digits, Radix Sort is highly efficient for specific types of data, particularly large datasets of integers. Its performance is substantial when the number of digits (d) and the base (k) are significantly smaller compared to the number of elements (n).

When comparing Radix Sort to other sorting algorithms like Quick Sort or Merge Sort, which have $O(n \log n)$ time complexity, Radix Sort can outperform them in cases where digit ranges are limited and fixed. However, it's essential to note that Radix Sort's efficiency diminishes with floating-point numbers or when handling long integer ranges, making it more suitable for specific applications.

9.9 Binary Search

Binary Search is a highly efficient algorithm for finding an item from a sorted list of items. It works by repeatedly dividing the portion of the list that could contain the item in half until you've narrowed down the possible locations to just one. Binary Search is optimal for searching in sorted arrays and runs in logarithmic time, making it significantly faster than linear search on large datasets.

The fundamental idea behind Binary Search is to leverage the sorted nature of the array. Given that the array is sorted, we can efficiently eliminate half of the remaining elements at each step. To begin with, we compare the target value to the middle element in the array. If the target is equal to the middle element, we have found our item. If the target is less than the middle element, we continue searching in the left subarray. Conversely, if the target is greater than the middle element, we search in the right subarray.

The process can be formalized as follows:

Given a sorted array A of length n and a target value T:

- Initialize two pointers at the start and end of the array, $l = 0$ and $r = n - 1$.
- Calculate the middle index $m = \left\lfloor \frac{l+r}{2} \right\rfloor$.
- Compare T with $A[m]$:
    - If $T == A[m]$, return m (the index of the target).
    - If $T < A[m]$, set $r = m - 1$ (eliminate the right half).
    - If $T > A[m]$, set $l = m + 1$ (eliminate the left half).
- Repeat the process until l exceeds r. If no match is found, return -1.

The algorithm can be implemented iteratively or recursively. Below is an iterative implementation in Python:

```
def binary_search(arr, target):
    l, r = 0, len(arr) - 1
    while l <= r:
        m = (l + r) // 2
        if arr[m] == target:
            return m
        elif arr[m] < target:
            l = m + 1
```

```
        else:
            r = m - 1
    return -1
```

When executing the above code with an example array:

```
arr = [1, 3, 5, 7, 9, 11, 13]
target = 7
print(binary_search(arr, target))
```

The output would be:

3indicating that 7 is located at index 3 of the array.

A recursive implementation of binary search is also straightforward. Here is how it can be written in Python:

```
def binary_search_recursive(arr, target, l, r):
    if l > r:
        return -1
    m = (l + r) // 2
    if arr[m] == target:
        return m
    elif arr[m] < target:
        return binary_search_recursive(arr, target, m + 1, r)
    else:
        return binary_search_recursive(arr, target, l, m - 1)
```

Using this recursive function requires an initial call specifying the bounds of the array:

```
arr = [1, 3, 5, 7, 9, 11, 13]
target = 7
result = binary_search_recursive(arr, target, 0, len(arr) - 1)
print(result)
```

The output of this program will again be:

```
3
```

Binary Search's efficiency can be measured by its time complexity. As each step essentially halves the search space, the time complexity is $O(\log n)$, where n is the number of elements in the array. This makes Binary Search much faster than linear search $O(n)$, especially for large datasets.

The space complexity of Binary Search is $O(1)$ for the iterative version since it uses a constant amount of additional space. For the recursive version, the space complexity is $O(\log n)$ due to the recursion stack.

Binary Search requires that the input array be sorted. If the array is not sorted, the algorithm cannot guarantee the correct result. Thus, it is common to precede a binary search implementation with a sorting step if the dataset can be changed or if the sorting step's complexity is justifiable within the application context.

The principal advantage of Binary Search is its efficiency for large datasets, making it a cornerstone in the computer science toolkit for problems involving sorted datasets.

9.10 Linear Search

Linear search, also known as sequential search, is a straightforward and intuitive searching algorithm. It operates by iterating through each element of a list or array and comparing each element with the target value until a match is found or the end of the list is reached. This method is applicable to lists of any structure, whether they are ordered or unordered.

Given an array A of n elements and a target value x, the linear search algorithm follows these steps:

1. Start at the first element of the array. 2. Compare the current element with x. 3. If the current element is x, return the current index. 4. If the current element is not x, move to the next element in the array. 5. Repeat steps 2-4 until the target value is found or the end of the array is reached. 6. If the target value is not found after checking all elements, return an indication that the value is not present in the array (commonly -1 or None).

The pseudocode for the linear search algorithm is as follows:

```
def linear_search(A, x):
    for i in range(len(A)):
        if A[i] == x:
            return i # Target found, return index
    return -1 # Target not found
```

To understand the operational steps in a more concrete manner, consider an example where $A = [3, 5, 7, 9, 11, 13]$ and $x = 9$.

1. Compare $A[0] = 3$ with $x = 9$: No match. 2. Compare $A[1] = 5$ with $x = 9$: No match. 3. Compare $A[2] = 7$ with $x = 9$: No match. 4. Compare $A[3] = 9$ with $x = 9$: Match found, return index 3.

The output for this example would be:

```
3
```

The linear search algorithm has a linear time complexity of $O(n)$, where

n is the number of elements in the array. This is because, in the worst-case scenario, the algorithm needs to check each element exactly once. The space complexity is $O(1)$ since the search does not require additional memory proportional to the input size; it only requires a fixed amount of extra space for variables.

Linear search is particularly useful in scenarios where the data set is small or when simplicity and ease of implementation are prioritized over speed. However, it is not suitable for large data sets due to its inefficiency in terms of time complexity compared to more advanced searching algorithms like binary search.

An edge case to consider is when the list is empty. In such cases, the algorithm should handle this gracefully by immediately returning an indication that the target value is not present:

```
def linear_search(A, x):
    if len(A) == 0:
        return -1 # List is empty, target not found
    for i in range(len(A)):
        if A[i] == x:
            return i # Target found, return index
    return -1 # Target not found
```

Linear search is a fundamental searching technique that serves as a building block for understanding more complex searching methods. Its simplicity and straightforward implementation make it an essential tool for introductory studies in algorithms and data structures.

9.11 Comparison of Sorting Algorithms

In this section, we will conduct a detailed comparison of the sorting algorithms covered in prior sections: Bubble Sort, Selection Sort, Insertion Sort, Merge Sort, Quick Sort, Heap Sort, and Radix Sort. The comparison will focus on several key metrics: time complexity, space complexity, stability, and practical performance.

Time Complexity:

The time complexity of an algorithm is a critical measure of its efficiency. It provides insight into the algorithm's behavior as the input size (n) grows.

- **Bubble Sort**:
  - Best Case: $O(n)$

  - Average Case: $O(n^2)$
  - Worst Case: $O(n^2)$

- **Selection Sort**:
  - Best Case: $O(n^2)$
  - Average Case: $O(n^2)$
  - Worst Case: $O(n^2)$

- **Insertion Sort**:
  - Best Case: $O(n)$
  - Average Case: $O(n^2)$
  - Worst Case: $O(n^2)$

- **Merge Sort**:
  - Best Case: $O(n \log n)$
  - Average Case: $O(n \log n)$
  - Worst Case: $O(n \log n)$

- **Quick Sort**:
  - Best Case: $O(n \log n)$
  - Average Case: $O(n \log n)$
  - Worst Case: $O(n^2)$

- **Heap Sort**:
  - Best Case: $O(n \log n)$
  - Average Case: $O(n \log n)$
  - Worst Case: $O(n \log n)$

- **Radix Sort**:
  - Best Case: $O(nk)$
  - Average Case: $O(nk)$
  - Worst Case: $O(nk)$

where k is the number of digits in the largest number.

Space Complexity:

Space complexity evaluates the amount of additional memory space required by the algorithm beyond the input data.

- **Bubble Sort**: $O(1)$
- **Selection Sort**: $O(1)$
- **Insertion Sort**: $O(1)$
- **Merge Sort**: $O(n)$
- **Quick Sort**: $O(\log n)$ (Due to the recursive stack space in its optimal implementation)
- **Heap Sort**: $O(1)$
- **Radix Sort**: $O(n + k)$

Stability:

A stable sorting algorithm maintains the relative order of records with equal keys. This property is crucial in scenarios where the order of equal elements matters.

- **Bubble Sort**: Stable
- **Selection Sort**: Not Stable
- **Insertion Sort**: Stable
- **Merge Sort**: Stable
- **Quick Sort**: Not Stable
- **Heap Sort**: Not Stable
- **Radix Sort**: Stable

Practical Performance:

Analyzing the practical performance involves considering the algorithm's efficiency on real-world data and how it performs with varying types of input, such as already sorted, reverse sorted, or random arrays.

- **Bubble Sort**: - Effective only for very small datasets due to its quadratic time complexity. Stable and simple to implement, but practically inefficient for large data sets.

- **Selection Sort**: - Also best suited for small lists. It performs a constant number of swaps, leading to its inefficiencies outweighing its simplicity for larger datasets. Not stable.

- **Insertion Sort**: - Works excellently on small datasets or partially sorted arrays. The adaptive nature allows $O(n)$ performance on nearly sorted arrays. Stable and easy to implement.

- **Merge Sort**: - Suitable for very large datasets due to its consistent $O(n \log n)$ performance. Requires additional memory for the temporary arrays, making its space complexity higher. Stable and good for data stored in linked lists.

- **Quick Sort**: - Highly efficient in practice due to its cache-friendly property and average $O(n \log n)$ performance. The worst-case $O(n^2)$ can be mitigated with better pivot selection techniques. Not stable but highly recommended for large datasets.

- **Heap Sort**: - Performs consistently at $O(n \log n)$ though generally slower in practice compared to Quick Sort due to less efficient data movement. Not stable but benefits from minimal auxiliary space.

- **Radix Sort**: - Linear time complexity makes it an excellent choice for large datasets with fixed digit/word length. This non-comparison sort is stable and particularly effective for sorting large integers or strings.

The performance and suitability of each sorting algorithm can depend significantly on the application, the nature of the dataset, and constraints such as memory availability and stability requirements.

The forthcoming section will delve into detailed performance considerations for sorting and searching algorithms, expanding on these comparisons with empirical data and practical scenarios.

9.12 Performance Considerations in Sorting and Searching

Evaluating the performance of sorting and searching algorithms requires a comprehensive understanding of various factors that influence their efficiency. These factors include time complexity, space complexity, stability, adaptability, and the nature of input data. In this section, we will delve into each of these aspects, providing nuanced insights pertinent to sorting and searching algorithms.

Time complexity is a primary metric for assessing an algorithm's efficiency. It is typically expressed using Big-O notation, which provides an upper bound on the time required as a function of the input size n. For instance, algorithms like Bubble Sort and Insertion Sort have a worst-case time complexity of $O(n^2)$, making them less suitable for large datasets. In contrast, more advanced algorithms like Merge Sort and Quick Sort have better average-case time complexities of $O(n \log n)$, which makes them more scalable for larger datasets.

Space complexity is equally crucial, especially in environments where memory usage is a constraint. Algorithms such as Merge Sort require additional memory proportional to the input size $O(n)$ due to the auxiliary arrays required for merging. On the other hand, algorithms like Quick Sort can be implemented with $O(\log n)$ space complexity, as they primarily utilize the call stack in recursive implementations.

Stability is another important consideration when selecting sorting algorithms. A sorting algorithm is said to be stable if it preserves the relative order of records with equal keys. Algorithms like Merge Sort and Insertion Sort are stable by nature, while others like Quick Sort are not. Stability can be particularly critical in multi-key sorting scenarios where secondary sorting criteria must respect the order of primary keys.

Adaptability refers to how well an algorithm performs with different types of input data. Some algorithms, like Insertion Sort, are adaptive because they run faster on partially sorted datasets, achieving a best-case time complexity of $O(n)$. In contrast, algorithms such as Heap Sort are non-adaptive, providing consistent performance regardless of the initial order of elements.

The nature of input data, including its size, order (sorted, reverse-sorted, random), and distribution, significantly affects the performance of sorting and searching algorithms. For instance, Quick Sort exhibits its worst-case performance of $O(n^2)$ when the pivot selection is poor, such as in the case of already sorted or reverse-sorted arrays. However, randomized Quick Sort or implementing a three-way partitioning scheme often mitigates this issue, providing more consistent performance.

The choice between binary search and linear search is largely influenced by whether the input data is sorted. Binary search, with a time complexity of $O(\log n)$, is highly efficient but requires a sorted array. Linear search, with a time complexity of $O(n)$, may become necessary for unsorted data but is significantly slower for large datasets.

Below, we provide a Python implementation for Merge Sort, demonstrating its time complexity and stability:

```
def merge_sort(arr):
    if len(arr) > 1:
        mid = len(arr) // 2
        left_half = arr[:mid]
        right_half = arr[mid:]

        merge_sort(left_half)
        merge_sort(right_half)

        i = j = k = 0

        while i < len(left_half) and j < len(right_half):
            if left_half[i] < right_half[j]:
                arr[k] = left_half[i]
                i += 1
            else:
                arr[k] = right_half[j]
                j += 1
            k += 1

        while i < len(left_half):
            arr[k] = left_half[i]
            i += 1
            k += 1

        while j < len(right_half):
            arr[k] = right_half[j]
            j += 1
            k += 1

# Example usage:
arr = [12, 11, 13, 5, 6, 7]
merge_sort(arr)
print("Sorted array is:", arr)
```

```
Sorted array is: [5, 6, 7, 11, 12, 13]
```

The above implementation highlights the divide-and-conquer approach of Merge Sort, where the array is recursively split and merged. This algorithm ensures stability by preserving the relative order of equal elements.

Similarly, for binary search, the importance of sorted data is evident. Below is a Python implementation of binary search:

```
def binary_search(arr, target):
    left, right = 0, len(arr) - 1
    while left <= right:
        mid = (left + right) // 2
        if arr[mid] == target:
            return mid
        elif arr[mid] < target:
            left = mid + 1
        else:
            right = mid - 1
    return -1

# Example usage:
arr = [2, 3, 4, 10, 40]
target = 10
result = binary_search(arr, target)
if result != -1:
    print("Element is present at index", result)
else:
    print("Element is not present in array")
```

```
Element is present at index 3
```

This implementation demonstrates binary search's logarithmic time complexity, making it highly efficient for sorted arrays but impractical for unsorted data.

Overall, selecting an appropriate algorithm involves balancing these considerations. Efficient algorithms provide significant improvements in performance, particularly for large datasets, but trade-offs between stability, adaptability, and resource usage must be carefully evaluated.

Chapter 10

Advanced Data Structures

This chapter explores advanced data structures, including segment trees, Fenwick trees, K-D trees, red-black trees, splay trees, B+ trees, suffix trees, disjoint set union, bloom filters, and trie trees revisited. It highlights their applications and performance considerations, providing a comprehensive understanding of these sophisticated structures used to solve complex computational problems.

10.1 Introduction to Advanced Data Structures

Advanced data structures provide powerful tools for organizing and managing data to improve the efficiency of various computational tasks. These structures are typically designed to solve more complex problems than their basic counterparts, often offering optimized operations for specific types of queries and modifications. Understanding advanced data structures is essential for tackling sophisticated algorithms and specialized applications in computer science.

A foundational principle in computer science is the trade-off between time and space complexity. Advanced data structures often strike different balances compared to basic structures, enabling drastic improvements in performance for certain operations, possibly at the cost of others. The choice of data structure is contingent on the specific requirements of the application, such as the frequency and types of operations that must be performed efficiently.

This chapter delves into a variety of advanced data structures, each with unique properties and use cases. We will explore their construction, typical operations, and complexity analyses, equipping you with the necessary knowledge to select and implement the appropriate data structure for your computational needs.

A deep dive into the selected advanced data structures includes:

- **Segment Trees**: These are highly versatile structures used for storing information about intervals or segments, enabling efficient range queries and updates.
- **Fenwick Trees (Binary Indexed Trees)**: These are used for efficient cumulative frequency tables, offering a compact and efficient means for calculating prefix sums.
- **K-D Trees**: These structures are employed for multi-dimensional searching, vital in applications like range searching and nearest neighbor queries.
- **Red-Black Trees**: These self-balancing binary search trees ensure that the tree remains balanced with specific properties, guaranteeing $O(\log n)$ time complexity for insertions, deletions, and look-ups.
- **Splay Trees**: These are a type of self-adjusting binary search tree with the unique property that frequently accessed elements are moved closer to the root, optimizing future access times.
- **B+ Trees**: These are balanced search trees optimized for systems that read and write large blocks of data, commonly used in databases and file systems.
- **Suffix Trees**: These compact data representations of strings allow for efficient searching of substrings, handling tasks like pattern matching and string analysis with proficiency.
- **Disjoint Set Union (Union-Find)**: These are specialized data structures that manage partitioning of a set into non-overlapping subsets, essential for network connectivity and clustering tasks.
- **Bloom Filters**: These probabilistic data structures efficiently test whether an element is a member of a set, allowing for approximate and space-efficient membership queries.

- **Trie Trees Revisited**: An extension of our earlier discussion on tries, delving deeper into optimizations and applications such as prefix searching and autocompletion.

Understanding segment trees is crucial in scenarios where fast query and update times are necessary for ranges within an array. Segment trees facilitate operations such as range minimum/maximum queries and range sum queries, which can be executed in $O(\log n)$ time. The construction of a segment tree involves a recursive approach, breaking down the array into segments and storing these segments at different tree nodes.

```
class SegmentTree:
    def __init__(self, data):
        self.n = len(data)
        self.tree = [0] * (2 * self.n)
        self.build(data)

    def build(self, data):
        for i in range(self.n):
            self.tree[self.n + i] = data[i]
        for i in range(self.n - 1, 0, -1):
            self.tree[i] = self.tree[i * 2] + self.tree[i * 2 + 1]

    def update(self, pos, value):
        pos += self.n
        self.tree[pos] = value
        while pos > 1:
            pos //= 2
            self.tree[pos] = self.tree[pos * 2] + self.tree[pos * 2 + 1]

    def query(self, left, right):
        result = 0
        left += self.n
        right += self.n
        while left < right:
            if left % 2:
                result += self.tree[left]
                left += 1
            if right % 2:
                right -= 1
                result += self.tree[right]
            left //= 2
            right //= 2
        return result

# Example usage:
data = [1, 3, 5, 7, 9, 11]
seg_tree = SegmentTree(data)
print(seg_tree.query(1, 3)) # Output: 8 (3 + 5)

seg_tree.update(1, 10)
print(seg_tree.query(1, 3)) # Output: 15 (10 + 5)
```

```
8
15
```

On the other hand, Fenwick Trees (or Binary Indexed Trees) provide an efficient means to perform prefix sum queries and update elements, also with $O(\log n)$ complexity. They are especially useful for frequency tables and range queries where updates are frequent.

```
class FenwickTree:
    def __init__(self, size):
        self.size = size
        self.tree = [0] * (size + 1)

    def update(self, index, delta):
        while index <= self.size:
            self.tree[index] += delta
            index += index & -index

    def query(self, index):
        sum = 0
        while index > 0:
            sum += self.tree[index]
            index -= index & -index
        return sum

    def range_query(self, left, right):
        return self.query(right) - self.query(left - 1)

# Example usage:
fenwick_tree = FenwickTree(10)
fenwick_tree.update(1, 5)
fenwick_tree.update(3, 7)
print(fenwick_tree.range_query(1, 3)) # Output: 12
```

```
12
```

Each of these data structures brings significant advantages for specific types of problems and computational tasks. They often involve sophisticated algorithms for construction, querying, and updating, which require a detailed understanding of their underlying mechanics. Through comprehensive examples and rigorous analysis, we will further demystify these structures, showcasing their applications and performance benefits in various scenarios. The ability to harness the full potential of advanced data structures is a fundamental skill for any serious computer scientist or software engineer.

10.2 Segment Trees

Segment trees are a fundamental data structure that provide efficient solutions for range queries and updates on arrays. Specifically, they allow for querying the sum, minimum, maximum, greatest common divisor (gcd), and other associative operations over a sub-array in logarithmic time while supporting point updates also in logarithmic time.

To understand the construction and use of segment trees, consider an array A of n elements. The segment tree is a binary tree where each node represents an interval or segment of the array. The root represents the entire array segment $[0, n-1]$, and each leaf node represents a single element of the array.

Construction of a segment tree follows these steps: 1. **Leaf Nodes Creation**: Each leaf node represents a single element from the array $A[i]$. 2. **Internal Nodes Construction**: Each internal node represents the aggregate information of its child nodes, e.g., the sum or minimum of the elements in its segment.

The height of a segment tree is $O(\log n)$ since it is a balanced binary tree. Each node requires $O(1)$ space and there are $2n - 1$ nodes in total. Hence, the space complexity is $O(n)$.

```
class SegmentTree:
    def __init__(self, data):
        self.n = len(data)
        self.tree = [0] * (2 * self.n)
        self.build(data)

    def build(self, data):
        # Initialize leaves
        for i in range(self.n):
            self.tree[self.n + i] = data[i]

        # Initialize internal nodes
        for i in range(self.n - 1, 0, -1):
            self.tree[i] = self.tree[i << 1] + self.tree[i << 1 | 1]

    def update(self, pos, value):
        pos += self.n
        self.tree[pos] = value
        while pos > 1:
            pos >>= 1
            self.tree[pos] = self.tree[pos << 1] + self.tree[pos << 1 | 1]

    def query(self, l, r):
        result = 0
        l += self.n
        r += self.n
        while l < r:
            if l & 1:
                result += self.tree[l]
                l += 1
            if r & 1:
                r -= 1
                result += self.tree[r]
            l >>= 1
            r >>= 1
        return result

# Example Usage:
data = [1, 2, 3, 4, 5, 6, 7, 8]
seg_tree = SegmentTree(data)
print(seg_tree.query(2, 6)) # Output: 12
```

```
seg_tree.update(3, 10)
print(seg_tree.query(2, 6)) # Output: 18
```

The above Python implementation includes a class ‘SegmentTree‘ that establishes the segment tree from the given data array and provides functions to update a value in the array and query the sum of a range.

Working of Segment Tree Operations **Building the Tree:** - The ‘build‘ function starts by initializing the leaves with the given values from the array. This is done by placing the elements in the second half of the array, i.e., from index n to $2n-1$. - Then, the internal nodes are populated by computing the sum of their children. This begins from the last internal node at index $n-1$ going up to the root. Each internal node at index i is the sum of its children at indices $2i$ and $2i+1$.

Updating a Value: - Update operation involves changing the value of an element at a specific position and propagating the change up to the root. - Starting from the leaf node representing the position, the new value is inserted; then, moving up the tree, each parent node is updated to reflect the change in its child nodes.

Range Query: - To perform a range query, the query function utilizes the properties of the segment tree to sum up the values efficiently. The query interval $[l, r)$ is adjusted and divided based on the binary representation and position adjustments, ensuring no overlaps. - The results from each segment are accumulated to get the final sum.

```
Output:
12
18
```

This detailed step-by-step process highlights the efficiency and power of segment trees in handling dynamic array queries and updates in logarithmic time, making them indispensable in various computational and real-time applications.

10.3 Fenwick Trees (Binary Indexed Trees)

Fenwick Trees, also known as Binary Indexed Trees (BIT), provide a highly efficient means for cumulative frequency tables and are particularly useful in scenarios involving dynamic cumulative frequency updates. These data structures offer logarithmic time complexity operations for both point updates and prefix sum queries, making them an invaluable asset in computational problem-solving contexts such as range queries and update problems in competitive programming and other algorithm-intensive applications.

Definition and Structure: A Fenwick Tree is a data structure that allows for efficient calculation and manipulation of the prefix sums of a table of numbers. Conceptually, a BIT can be visualized as a one-dimensional array where each element at index i contains the cumulative sum of elements from the start of the array up to a certain point, but not necessarily all elements up to i. The range of elements that each index covers is determined by the powers of two, which leads to the internal structure of the BIT.

Initialization: To initialize a Fenwick Tree for an array of size n, an auxiliary array called BIT is used, typically of size $n+1$ to accommodate 1-based indexing, simplifying the implementation. Each element $\mathrm{BIT}[\mathrm{i}]$ stores the sum of elements of the original array covering a specific range determined by the binary representation of i.

```
def fenwick_tree(n):
    BIT = [0] * (n + 1)
    return BIT
```

Point Update: To update an element at position i in the original array by adding a value Δ, one must update all the relevant ranges in the BIT. This is achieved by iterating through the indices and adding Δ until we exceed the array bounds.

```
def update(BIT, n, i, delta):
    while i <= n:
        BIT[i] += delta
        i += i & -i # Move to the next responsible index
```

Prefix Sum Query: To compute the prefix sum up to index i, the BIT is queried by summing elements from index i while moving to the parent indices by flipping the rightmost set bit, effectively accumulating the required range.

```
def query(BIT, i):
    sum = 0
    while i > 0:
        sum += BIT[i]
        i -= i & -i # Move to the parent index
    return sum
```

Range Queries and Updates: Range queries and updates, which involve manipulating and extracting sums over ranges rather than single points, can also be efficiently performed using Fenwick Trees. To achieve a range sum query from index l to r, the prefix sum up to r is computed and the prefix sum up to $l-1$ is subtracted from it.

```
def range_query(BIT, l, r):
    return query(BIT, r) - query(BIT, l - 1)
```

Time Complexity Analysis: The performance benefits of using Fenwick Trees are primarily drawn from their ability to perform point update and prefix sum operations in $O(\log n)$ time. This efficiency is because each update or query operation involves traversing a logarithmic number of elements based on the binary representation, resulting in significant computational savings compared to naïve methods, which can take $O(n)$ time.

Overall, Fenwick Trees present a succinct and powerful tool for handling cumulative frequency tables and dynamic array manipulations, adeptly bridging simplicity in implementation with efficiency in operation.

10.4 K-D Trees

K-Dimensional (K-D) trees are a type of binary search tree used for organizing points in a k-dimensional space. They are useful for various applications in multi-dimensional search queries, including range searches and nearest neighbor searches. Each node in a K-D tree represents a k-dimensional point and serves as a partitioning node that divides the space into two half-spaces.

The construction of a K-D tree involves recursive subdivision of k-dimensional space. This subdivision alternates between orthogonal dimensions, optimizing search operations by ensuring that within each node's subtree, data points are confined to specific subspaces.

Node Representation:

Each node in a K-D tree contains the following components:

- **Point** (P): A k-dimensional point.
- **Left Child**: A reference to the left subtree.
- **Right Child**: A reference to the right subtree.
- **Axis**: The dimension (axis) used for partitioning at the current node.

K-D Tree Construction Algorithm:

The construction of a K-D tree can be described by the following recursive algorithm:

```
class Node:
    def __init__(self, point, axis, left=None, right=None):
        self.point = point
        self.axis = axis
        self.left = left
        self.right = right

def build_kd_tree(points, depth=0):
    if not points:
        return None

    k = len(points[0]) # Assumes all points have the same dimension
    axis = depth % k

    points.sort(key=lambda x: x[axis])
    median = len(points) // 2

    return Node(
        point=points[median],
        axis=axis,
        left=build_kd_tree(points[:median], depth + 1),
        right=build_kd_tree(points[median + 1:], depth + 1)
    )
```

This algorithm works by sorting the list of points and selecting the median point based on the current axis. This median point becomes the root of the subtree, and the process is recursively applied to the two halves of the list, alternating axes at each step.

Range Search in K-D Trees:

Range search involves finding all points within a specified axis-aligned rectangular range. The algorithm traverses the tree and checks whether the current node lies within the query range. If it is, the algorithm adds the node's point to the result set and recursively explores the left and right subtrees if they intersect with the query range.

```
def range_search(node, query_range, depth=0):
    if node is None:
        return []

    k = len(query_range) // 2
    axis = depth % k
    point = node.point
    result = []

    if all(query_range[i][0] <= point[i] <= query_range[i][1] for i in range(k)):
        result.append(point)

    if query_range[axis][0] <= point[axis]:
        result.extend(range_search(node.left, query_range, depth + 1))
    if query_range[axis][1] >= point[axis]:
        result.extend(range_search(node.right, query_range, depth + 1))
```

```
    return result
```

The range_search function checks if the node's point lies within the query range and, if so, adds it to the result set. The function then recursively explores subtrees that may contain points within the query range.

Nearest Neighbor Search in K-D Trees:

The nearest neighbor search algorithm aims to find the nearest data point to a given target point. The algorithm starts by traversing down the tree, following the branches based on the target point's coordinates. Upon reaching a leaf node, the search backtracks and examines candidate points, potentially exploring other branches that may contain closer points.

```
def euclidean_distance(point1, point2):
    return sum((x - y) ** 2 for x, y in zip(point1, point2)) ** 0.5

def nearest_neighbor(node, target, depth=0, best=None):
    if node is None:
        return best

    k = len(target)
    axis = depth % k
    next_best = None
    next_branch = None

    if best is None or euclidean_distance(target, node.point) < euclidean_distance(
            target, best):
        next_best = node.point
    else:
        next_best = best

    if target[axis] < node.point[axis]:
        next_branch = node.left
    else:
        next_branch = node.right

    best = nearest_neighbor(next_branch, target, depth + 1, next_best)

    other_branch = node.right if next_branch is node.left else node.left
    if abs(target[axis] - node.point[axis]) < euclidean_distance(target, best):
        best = nearest_neighbor(other_branch, target, depth + 1, best)

    return best
```

```
(nearest_neighbor(tree, target_point))
```

The algorithm calculates Euclidean distances and compares them to find the nearest neighbor. By also considering branches within a given distance threshold, it ensures that the closest possible point is discovered.

K-D trees are highly efficient for low-dimensional spaces and specific types of queries, providing an elegant solution to spatial search problems. However, for very high dimensions, the performance may deteriorate due to the curse of dimensionality, where the volume of space increases exponentially with the number of dimensions, resulting in sparse data distributions and less effective partitioning.

10.5 Red-Black Trees

A Red-Black Tree is a balanced binary search tree with an additional property that ensures the tree remains balanced during insertions and deletions. This balance property ensures that the path from the root to the farthest leaf is no more than twice as long as the path from the root to the nearest leaf. This guarantees logarithmic time complexity for search, insert, and delete operations.

Red-Black Trees adhere to the following rules:

- Every node is either red or black.
- The root is always black.
- All leaves (or "NIL" nodes) are black.
- If a red node has children, the children are always black (no two red nodes can be adjacent).
- Every path from a node to its descendant NIL nodes has the same number of black nodes.

These properties ensure that the tree remains approximately balanced, which leads to efficient search operations.

Insertion in Red-Black Trees:

Insertion into a Red-Black Tree involves the following steps:

1. Perform a standard binary search tree insertion and color the newly inserted node red.
2. Fix any violations of the Red-Black Tree properties by performing rotations and recoloring.

To understand these steps, consider the following code for inserting a node into a Red-Black Tree in Python:

```
class Node:
    def __init__(self, data):
        self.data = data
        self.color = 'red'
        self.left = None
        self.right = None
        self.parent = None

class RedBlackTree:
    def __init__(self):
        self.TNULL = Node(0) # Initialize the null (NIL) nodes
        self.TNULL.color = 'black'
        self.root = self.TNULL

    def insert(self, data):
        node = Node(data)
        node.left = self.TNULL
        node.right = self.TNULL
        parent = None
        current = self.root

        while current != self.TNULL:
            parent = current
            if node.data < current.data:
                current = current.left
            else:
                current = current.right

        node.parent = parent

        if parent is None: # New node is root
            self.root = node
        elif node.data < parent.data:
            parent.left = node
        else:
            parent.right = node

        node.color = 'red'
        self.fix_insert(node)

    def fix_insert(self, k):
        while k != self.root and k.parent.color == 'red':
            if k.parent == k.parent.parent.left:
                u = k.parent.parent.right
                if u.color == 'red': # Case 1
                    k.parent.color = 'black'
                    u.color = 'black'
                    k.parent.parent.color = 'red'
                    k = k.parent.parent
                else:
                    if k == k.parent.right: # Case 2
                        k = k.parent
                        self.left_rotate(k)
                    k.parent.color = 'black' # Case 3
                    k.parent.parent.color = 'red'
                    self.right_rotate(k.parent.parent)
            else:
                u = k.parent.parent.left # Mirror image of above cases
                if u.color == 'red':
                    k.parent.color = 'black'
                    u.color = 'black'
                    k.parent.parent.color = 'red'
```

```
                k = k.parent.parent
            else:
                if k == k.parent.left:
                    k = k.parent
                    self.right_rotate(k)
                k.parent.color = 'black'
                k.parent.parent.color = 'red'
                self.left_rotate(k.parent.parent)
        self.root.color = 'black'

    def left_rotate(self, x):
        y = x.right
        x.right = y.left
        if y.left != self.TNULL:
            y.left.parent = x
        y.parent = x.parent
        if x.parent is None:
            self.root = y
        elif x == x.parent.left:
            x.parent.left = y
        else:
            x.parent.right = y
        y.left = x
        x.parent = y

    def right_rotate(self, x):
        y = x.left
        x.left = y.right
        if y.right != self.TNULL:
            y.right.parent = x
        y.parent = x.parent
        if x.parent is None:
            self.root = y
        elif x == x.parent.right:
            x.parent.right = y
        else:
            x.parent.left = y
        y.right = x
        x.parent = y
```

The fix_insert function ensures that the Red-Black Tree properties are maintained after inserting a new node. This involves:

- Recoloring nodes.
- Performing left and right rotations to balance the tree.

Deletion in Red-Black Trees:

Deletion from a Red-Black Tree involves removing the desired node and then restoring the Red-Black properties if they are violated.

```
def delete(self, data):
    node = self.root
    z = self.TNULL
    while node != self.TNULL:
        if node.data == data:
            z = node
```

```
            if node.data <= data:
                node = node.right
            else:
                node = node.left

        if z == self.TNULL:
            print("Data not found in the tree!")
            return

        y = z
        y_original_color = y.color
        if z.left == self.TNULL:
            x = z.right
            self.rb_transplant(z, z.right)
        elif z.right == self.TNULL:
            x = z.left
            self.rb_transplant(z, z.left)
        else:
            y = self.minimum(z.right)
            y_original_color = y.color
            x = y.right
            if y.parent == z:
                x.parent = y
            else:
                self.rb_transplant(y, y.right)
                y.right = z.right
                y.right.parent = y
            self.rb_transplant(z, y)
            y.left = z.left
            y.left.parent = y
            y.color = z.color

        if y_original_color == "black":
            self.fix_delete(x)

    def rb_transplant(self, u, v):
        if u.parent == None:
            self.root = v
        elif u == u.parent.left:
            u.parent.left = v
        else:
            u.parent.right = v
        v.parent = u.parent

    def fix_delete(self, x):
        while x != self.root and x.color == "black":
            if x == x.parent.left:
                s = x.parent.right
                if s.color == "red":
                    s.color = "black"
                    x.parent.color = "red"
                    self.left_rotate(x.parent)
                    s = x.parent.right
                if s.left.color == "black" and s.right.color == "black":
                    s.color = "red"
                    x = x.parent
                else:
                    if s.right.color == "black":
                        s.left.color = "black"
                        s.color = "red"
                        self.right_rotate(s)
                        s = x.parent.right
```

```
                s.color = x.parent.color
                x.parent.color = "black"
                s.right.color = "black"
                self.left_rotate(x.parent)
                x = self.root
        else: # Same as above, with left and right exchanged
            s = x.parent.left
            if s.color == "red":
                s.color = "black"
                x.parent.color = "red"
                self.right_rotate(x.parent)
                s = x.parent.left
            if s.left.color == "black" and s.right.color == "black":
                s.color = "red"
                x = x.parent
            else:
                if s.left.color == "black":
                    s.right.color = "black"
                    s.color = "red"
                    self.left_rotate(s)
                    s = x.parent.left
                s.color = x.parent.color
                x.parent.color = "black"
                s.left.color = "black"
                self.right_rotate(x.parent)
                x = self.root
    x.color = "black"
```

In the delete function, like the insert function, different cases handle the deletion to ensure the properties of the Red-Black Tree are restored. This may involve node replacements, recoloring, and rotations.

The combination of these rules and algorithms ensures that Red-Black Trees provide a robust and efficient data structure for insertion and deletion, maintaining their balance and performance guarantees.

10.6 Splay Trees

Splay trees are a type of self-adjusting binary search tree where recently accessed elements are moved to the root through a series of tree rotations. This property is beneficial in applications where certain elements are accessed more frequently than others, as it ensures that those elements have shorter access paths, thereby optimizing the average time complexity for operations. Splay trees were invented by Daniel Sleator and Robert Tarjan in 1985 and are known for their simplicity and efficiency in scenarios where access patterns exhibit temporal locality.

The primary operations in a splay tree are insert, delete, search, and splay. Each of these operations involves the splay operation, which adjusts the tree such that the most recently accessed node is moved to the root.

Splay Operation

The splay operation is the cornerstone of splay trees. When a node x is accessed, it is moved to the root through a series of rotations. There are three types of rotations used in the splay operation: Zig, Zig-Zig, and Zig-Zag.

1. **Zig**: This rotation is performed when x is the left or right child of the root. A single rotation is performed to move x to the root.
2. **Zig-Zig**: This rotation is performed when x is the left child of a left child or the right child of a right child. Two rotations are performed in the same direction to move x to the root.
3. **Zig-Zag**: This rotation is performed when x is the left child of a right child or the right child of a left child. Two rotations are performed in opposite directions to move x to the root.

```
class SplayTreeNode:
    def __init__(self, key):
        self.key = key
        self.left = None
        self.right = None

class SplayTree:
    def __init__(self):
        self.root = None

    def _rotate_right(self, x):
        y = x.left
        x.left = y.right
        y.right = x
        return y

    def _rotate_left(self, x):
        y = x.right
        x.right = y.left
        y.left = x
        return y

    def splay(self, root, key):
        if root is None or root.key == key:
            return root

        if root.key > key:
            if root.left is None:
                return root

            if root.left.key > key:
                root.left.left = self.splay(root.left.left, key)
                root = self._rotate_right(root)
            elif root.left.key < key:
```

```
            root.left.right = self.splay(root.left.right, key)
            if root.left.right is not None:
                root.left = self._rotate_left(root.left)

        return root if root.left is None else self._rotate_right(root)

    else:
        if root.right is None:
            return root

        if root.right.key > key:
            root.right.left = self.splay(root.right.left, key)
            if root.right.left is not None:
                root.right = self._rotate_right(root.right)
        elif root.right.key < key:
            root.right.right = self.splay(root.right.right, key)
            root = self._rotate_left(root)

        return root if root.right is None else self._rotate_left(root)
```

Insertion

Inserting a node into a splay tree involves first inserting the node using the standard binary search tree insertion algorithm and then splaying the newly inserted node to the root.

```
def insert(self, key):
    if self.root is None:
        self.root = SplayTreeNode(key)
        return

    self.root = self.splay(self.root, key)
    if self.root.key == key:
        return # Key already exists

    new_node = SplayTreeNode(key)
    if self.root.key > key:
        new_node.right = self.root
        new_node.left = self.root.left
        self.root.left = None
    else:
        new_node.left = self.root
        new_node.right = self.root.right
        self.root.right = None

    self.root = new_node
```

Deletion

Deleting a node from a splay tree involves splaying the node to be deleted to the root position and then deleting it in such a way that the remaining tree remains a valid splay tree.

```
def delete(self, key):
    if self.root is None:
        return

    self.root = self.splay(self.root, key)
```

```
    if self.root.key != key:
        return # Key not found

    if self.root.left is None:
        self.root = self.root.right
    elif self.root.right is None:
        self.root = self.root.left
    else:
        temp = self.root
        self.root = self.splay(temp.left, key)
        self.root.right = temp.right
```

Search

Searching for a node in a splay tree involves splaying the node to be searched to the root if it is found. If not found, the last accessed node (the closest value) is splayed to the root.

```
def search(self, key):
    self.root = self.splay(self.root, key)
    return self.root if self.root and self.root.key == key else None
```

The time complexity of the basic operations insert, delete, and search in a splay tree depends on the depth of the nodes. However, due to the splaying operation, the amortized time complexity of these operations is $O(\log n)$, making splay trees efficient for various applications, especially when certain elements are accessed more frequently than others.

Moreover, splay trees have the remarkable property of **amortized optimization**, adapting quickly to dynamic usage patterns without requiring explicit rebalancing, which is particularly beneficial in real-time systems and caches.

10.7 B+ Trees

B+ trees are a variation of B-trees, with enhanced characteristics making them particularly suitable for systems that perform extensive disk reads and writes, such as database and file systems. They are a self-balancing tree data structure that maintains sorted data and allows search, sequential access, insertions, and deletions in logarithmic time. The primary distinction between B+ trees and B-trees is that in B+ trees, all values are stored at the leaf level of the tree, and the internal nodes only store keys to guide the search process.

A B+ tree of order m is characterized by having the following properties:

- Each node contains at most $m - 1$ keys and m children.
- Each internal node (except the root) contains at least $\lceil \frac{m}{2} \rceil$ keys.
- All leaves are at the same level.
- Leaf nodes contain keys and pointers to the data records, or, if used as an index, contain pointers to the actual records.
- Leaf nodes are linked to form a singly linked list, providing efficient sequential access.

Node Structure and Invariants

The nodes in a B+ tree can be classified into two main types: internal nodes and leaf nodes.

Internal Nodes: Internal nodes serve as directories that guide the search process. Each internal node contains two types of elements: keys and pointers. The keys act as separators that determine the range of values stored in the child nodes. A typical structure for an internal node can be represented as:

```
InternalNode {
    keys[] // an array of keys
    children[] // an array of pointers to child nodes
}
```

To maintain balance, the internal nodes must adhere to these invariants:

- If an internal node has n pointers, it must have $n - 1$ keys.
- The keys within an internal node are ordered such that for any key k_i and child pointers C_i, the subtree pointed to by C_i contains values $\leq k_i$, and the subtree pointed by C_{i+1} contains values $> k_i$.

Leaf Nodes: Leaf nodes in a B+ tree store the actual data entries (or pointers to data entries). They are linked together to form a linked list, allowing efficient sequential access. The structure of a leaf node is typically:

```
LeafNode {
    keys[] // an array of keys
    dataPointers[] // an array of pointers or data entries
    nextLeaf // pointer to the next leaf node
}
```

Operations on B+ Trees

The primary operations on B+ trees are insertion, deletion, and search. These operations are implemented to maintain the B+ tree properties and ensure logarithmic time complexity.

Search: Searching in a B+ tree is efficient due to its balanced nature. The search starts from the root and progresses down the internal nodes, following the appropriate child pointers until a leaf node is reached. The process can be described as:

```
Search(Key k) {
    node = root
    while node is not a leaf {
        locate the child pointer for key k
        node = chosen child pointer
    }
    locate key k in the leaf node
    if key k is found
        return dataPointer associated with key k
    else
        return null // key not found
}
```

Insertion: Inserting a key into a B+ tree is a multi-step process that ensures the tree remains balanced and maintains its properties. The process involves:

- Finding the appropriate leaf node where the new key should be inserted by performing a search operation.
- Inserting the key into the leaf node. If the node has enough space, the key is simply added.
- If the leaf node is full, it needs to be split into two nodes, and the middle key is promoted to the parent node. If the parent node is also full, this process continues recursively up the tree.

The insertion algorithm can be outlined as:

```
Insert(Key k, Value v) {
    leaf = findLeafNode(k)
    if leaf is not full
        insert k and v into the leaf
    else
        split leaf node into two nodes
        promote the middle key to parent node
        recursively split and promote if necessary
}
```

Deletion: The deletion operation in a B+ tree involves locating the key to be deleted, removing it, and rebalancing the tree if necessary. The process can be summarized as:

- Searching for the key in the leaf node.
- Removing the key and associated data pointer from the leaf node.
- If the leaf node underflows (contains fewer than $\lceil \frac{m}{2} \rceil$ keys), it may need to borrow a key from a sibling node or merge with a sibling node.
- This rebalancing can propagate to the parent node, and the process may continue recursively up the tree.

The deletion algorithm can be described as:

```
Delete(Key k) {
    leaf = findLeafNode(k)
    if key k is in leaf node
        remove k from the leaf
        if leaf node underflows
            try to borrow a key from sibling
            if not possible, merge with sibling
            recursively balance the parent node
}
```

Advantages and Use Cases

B+ trees have several distinct advantages, particularly in applications requiring efficient storage and retrieval of large datasets:

- *High fan-out:* B+ trees have a high branching factor, which reduces the height of the tree and minimizes the number of disk I/O operations.
- *Efficient range queries:* Since leaf nodes are linked, B+ trees enable fast sequential access, making them ideal for range queries.
- *Balanced structure:* Self-balancing properties ensure that the tree remains balanced after insertions and deletions, maintaining consistent performance.
- *Persistence:* Due to their disk-friendly nature, B+ trees are extensively used in database systems and filesystems, where they provide efficient indexing mechanisms.

A concrete example demonstrating the use of B+ trees can be seen in the storage and indexing strategies of major database systems like MySQL and PostgreSQL. These systems rely on B+ trees to implement primary and secondary indexes, ensuring efficient data retrieval and management.

```
Example: Suppose we have a B+ tree of order 4
and we want to insert the keys 10, 20, 30, 40, and 50. The tree
should adjust by splitting nodes and promoting keys to maintain balance.
```

Implementing a B+ tree in Python would encapsulate these operations within class methods, ensuring efficient management and access of the data structure. Below is a simplified Python class for a B+ tree:

```
class BPlusTree:
    def __init__(self, order):
        self.order = order
        self.root = LeafNode()

    def search(self, key):
        current = self.root
        while not isinstance(current, LeafNode):
            current = current.find_child(key)
        return current.search(key)

    def insert(self, key, value):
        split = self.root.insert(key, value)
        if split:
            new_root = InternalNode()
            new_root.keys = [split.key]
            new_root.children = [self.root, split.new_node]
            self.root = new_root

    def delete(self, key):
        underflow = self.root.delete(key)
        if underflow and len(self.root.keys) == 0:
            self.root = self.root.children[0]

class LeafNode:
    # Implement the leaf node with necessary methods
    pass

class InternalNode:
    # Implement the internal node with necessary methods
    pass
```

Proper implementation of methods such as find_child, search, insert, and delete is necessary to complete the functionality of the B+ tree.

By integrating B+ trees into sophisticated software systems, developers can achieve efficient and reliable data management, crucial for performance-critical applications.

10.8 Suffix Trees

Suffix trees are a powerful data structure designed to enable quick and efficient substring searching within a given text. The concept of a suffix tree was first introduced by Weiner in 1973 and has since become an essential tool in various computational applications, particularly in string processing problems.

At its core, a suffix tree for a string S of length n is a compact representation of all the suffixes of S. It is a trie of the suffixes of S, but with internal nodes that may have a label, and edges that may represent substrings of S rather than single characters.

The key properties of a suffix tree are as follows:

- It represents all suffixes of a given text in $O(n)$ space.
- It enables substring search in $O(m + k)$ time, where m is the length of the substring being searched for, and k is the number of occurrences of the substring in the text.
- Construction of the suffix tree can be achieved in $O(n)$ time using advanced algorithms such as Ukkonen's algorithm.
- It supports other operations, such as finding the longest repeated substring, longest common substring, and the longest palindromic substring efficiently.

Structure Construction: To build a suffix tree, we consider each suffix of the string S. For a string $S = aabaa$, its suffixes are:

- $aabaa$
- $abaa$
- baa
- aa
- a

The suffix tree of $S = aabaa$ is constructed by progressively inserting each suffix into the tree. Below is a Python implementation to construct a suffix tree using Ukkonen's algorithm:

```
class SuffixTreeNode:
    def __init__(self, start, end):
        self.children = {}
        self.start = start
        self.end = end
        self.suffix_link = None

class SuffixTree:
    def __init__(self, text):
        self.text = text
        self.root = SuffixTreeNode(-1, -1)
        self.build_suffix_tree()

    def build_suffix_tree(self):
        # Insert code to construct a suffix tree using Ukkonen's algorithm
        pass
```

Applications: Suffix trees find applications in a variety of fields due to their efficiency in handling string operations. Some notable applications include:

- **Exact String Matching:** Querying if a pattern exists in a text can be done in $O(m)$ time.
- **Longest Repeated Substring:** By performing a depth-first search on the tree, we can identify the longest substring that appears more than once.
- **Longest Common Substring:** For strings S_1 and S_2, constructing a generalized suffix tree helps in finding the longest common substring.
- **Gene Sequence Analysis:** In bioinformatics, suffix trees are used to analyze DNA and protein sequences.

Efficient Operations: The efficiency of suffix trees in executing various operations lies in their construction and traversal mechanisms. Consider the operation of finding a substring in a large text:

```
def find_substring(self, pattern):
    current_node = self.root
    for char in pattern:
        if char in current_node.children:
            current_node = current_node.children[char]
        else:
            return False
    return True
```

The find_substring method traverses the tree based on the input pattern characters. If it successfully finds the path in the tree corresponding to the pattern, the substring exists in the text.

Overall, suffix trees offer a balance of complexity and efficiency, making them indispensable in fields requiring rapid string processing capabilities.

10.9 Disjoint Set Union (Union-Find)

Disjoint Set Union, commonly known as Union-Find, is a data structure that manages a partition of a set into disjoint subsets. This structure supports two primary operations: finding the representative (or leader) of the subset containing a particular element, and uniting two subsets into a single subset. These operations are essential in many applications such as network connectivity, image processing, and is an integral part of algorithms like Kruskal's minimum spanning tree algorithm.

The primary goal of the Union-Find data structure is to perform these operations efficiently. To achieve this, Union-Find uses two main techniques: Union by Rank and Path Compression.

Union by Rank: This technique ensures that the tree representing each subset remains shallow. Each node is assigned a rank, which approximates the height of the tree rooted at that node. When performing the union operation, the root of the tree with a lower rank is made a child of the root with a higher rank. This keeps the resulting tree balanced, preserving efficiency.

Path Compression: This technique flattens the structure of the tree whenever the find operation is used. After finding the root of the tree, the nodes visited during the find operation are directly connected to the root. This significantly improves the efficiency of subsequent operations by reducing the height of the trees.

Implementation

Below is the implementation of the Union-Find data structure with Union by Rank and Path Compression in Python.

```
class UnionFind:
    def __init__(self, size):
        self.parent = list(range(size))
        self.rank = [0] * size

    def find(self, node):
        if self.parent[node] != node:
            self.parent[node] = self.find(self.parent[node]) # Path compression
        return self.parent[node]

    def union(self, node1, node2):
        root1 = self.find(node1)
```

```
    root2 = self.find(node2)

    if root1 != root2:
        if self.rank[root1] > self.rank[root2]:
            self.parent[root2] = root1
        elif self.rank[root1] < self.rank[root2]:
            self.parent[root1] = root2
        else:
            self.parent[root2] = root1
            self.rank[root1] += 1
```

In this implementation:

- The __init__ function initializes two lists: parent, where each node is initially its own parent, and rank, which starts with all zeros.
- The find function uses path compression by recursively setting the parent of each node to the root of the tree.
- The union function connects two trees by comparing their ranks and attaching the shorter tree to the root of the taller tree. If both trees are of the same rank, one becomes the root and its rank is incremented.

Complexity Analysis

The time complexity of both the find and union operations can be analyzed using the inverse Ackermann function, denoted as $\alpha(n)$. This function grows extremely slowly, so for all practical purposes, it can be considered nearly constant. Therefore, both operations effectively run in amortized constant time, $\mathcal{O}(\alpha(n))$.

Applications

The Union-Find data structure is used in various applications, including:

- **Kruskal's Algorithm:** This algorithm for finding the minimum spanning tree (MST) of a graph heavily relies on Union-Find to detect cycles efficiently.
- **Connected Components:** In graph theory, Union-Find can determine if two vertices are in the same connected component.
- **Dynamic Connectivity:** This problem involves answering connectivity queries on a graph that changes over time, and Union-Find provides an efficient way to handle these updates.

Path Compression and Union by Rank Example

Consider a set with 7 elements: $\{0, 1, 2, 3, 4, 5, 6\}$. We perform the following operations:

1. Union(0, 1)
2. Union(1, 2)
3. Union(3, 4)
4. Union(4, 5)
5. Union(2, 5)
6. Find(5)
7. Find(6)

The sequence of operations and the effect of path compression can be visualized as:

```
uf = UnionFind(7)
uf.union(0, 1) # Union sets containing 0 and 1
uf.union(1, 2) # Union sets containing 1 and 2
uf.union(3, 4) # Union sets containing 3 and 4
uf.union(4, 5) # Union sets containing 4 and 5
uf.union(2, 5) # Union sets containing 2 and 5
print(uf.find(5)) # Finds the representative of the set containing 5
print(uf.find(6)) # Finds the representative of the set containing 6
```

This will result in:

```
0
6
```

Initially, each element is its own parent. After the unions, the internal structure with union by rank and path compression would be optimized, ensuring that subsequent operations are efficient. The element 5 is found under the representative element 0 after the $\text{find}(5)$ operation.

By ensuring an efficient, practical implementation and understanding of the Union-Find data structure, it is possible to apply it to numerous problems requiring disjoint set management, optimizing both performance and readability.

10.10 Bloom Filters

A Bloom filter is a probabilistic data structure designed to test whether an element is a member of a set. It is space-efficient and supports fast insert and query operations. However, Bloom filters do not store the elements themselves and can produce false positives but no false negatives. This trade-off makes Bloom filters particularly useful in applications where performance and space efficiency are prioritized over exactness.

Structure and Functionality

A Bloom filter consists of a bit array of size m and employs k independent hash functions. Each hash function maps an element to one of the positions in the bit array, uniformly and independently. When an element is added to the filter, each of the k hash functions processes the element and sets the corresponding bit to 1. The query operation checks if all positions corresponding to the k hash functions are set to 1. If any bit is 0, the element is definitely not in the set. If all bits are 1, the element is probably in the set, acknowledging the possibility of false positives.

```
class BloomFilter:
    def __init__(self, size, hash_count):
        self.size = size
        self.hash_count = hash_count
        self.bit_array = [0] * size

    def _hashes(self, item):
        return [hash_func(item) % self.size for hash_func in self.hash_funcs]

    def add(self, item):
        for hash_val in self._hashes(item):
            self.bit_array[hash_val] = 1

    def check(self, item):
        return all(self.bit_array[hash_val] for hash_val in self._hashes(item))

def hash_func1(item):
    return hash(item) * 17

def hash_func2(item):
    return hash(item) * 23

filter = BloomFilter(size=1000, hash_count=2)
filter.hash_funcs = [hash_func1, hash_func2]

filter.add("hello")
print(filter.check("hello")) # Output: True
print(filter.check("world")) # Output: False (probably)
```

False Positives and Parameters Optimization

The false positive probability p is a critical factor in designing Bloom filters. The probability depends on the size of the bit array m, the number of hash functions k, and the number of inserted elements n. The probability can be approximated by:

$$p = \left(1 - e^{-\frac{kn}{m}}\right)^k$$

To minimize p, the optimal number of hash functions k can be derived as:

$$k = \left(\frac{m}{n}\right) \ln 2$$

The optimal size of the bit array m for a given false positive rate p and number of elements n is:

$$m = -\frac{n \ln p}{(\ln 2)^2}$$

Applications

Bloom filters are widely used in various applications including:

- **Database Systems:** To quickly check if a key is present in a large database table before accessing it, thereby reducing the number of disk reads.
- **Network Applications:** In distributed systems, such as web caching systems, to avoid fetching an item that is not in cache.
- **Cybersecurity:** To check for malicious URLs or IP addresses against a blacklist.
- **Bioinformatics:** Used in sequencing data to reduce the storage and processing of false sequences.

Variations and Enhancements

Several variations and enhancements of Bloom filters exist to address specific limitations. For example:

- **Counting Bloom Filter:** Extends the Bloom filter by maintaining a counter for each bit instead of a single bit. This allows for deletions but requires more memory.
- **Compressed Bloom Filter:** Used to save space by compressing the bit array. This is particularly useful in scenarios like network protocols where space efficiency is paramount.

- **Scaled Bloom Filter:** Designed to handle dynamic datasets by creating additional Bloom filters when the number of elements exceeds the capacity.

Example Usage in Data Flow Systems

In large-scale data flow systems, Bloom filters are employed for routing and avoiding redundant data transmission. Suppose we have a streaming system where nodes must decide whether or not to forward a data packet. Bloom filters enable nodes to check quickly if a packet has been processed without the need for centralized control.

In general, Bloom filters provide an efficient mechanism for membership testing in large-scale and performance-critical applications. Their simplicity and effectiveness in various domains underscore their utility despite the inherent drawback of false positives.

10.11 Trie Trees Revisited

Trie trees, also known as prefix trees, represent a distinct and powerful form of data structure, particularly useful for storing associative arrays with string keys. Unlike binary search trees or hash tables, trie trees leverage the prefix commonality of the keys to enhance search efficiency. They are eminently applicable in scenarios such as autocomplete systems, spell checkers, and IP routing tables.

A trie is a tree where each node denotes a common prefix of strings. The root node corresponds to an empty string, and each edge represents a character from the strings stored in the trie. Nodes can store various meta-information like the weight of the prefix or a boolean flag indicating whether the node completes a word.

Let us explore the construction and operations on a trie tree in considerable depth:

```
class TrieNode:
    def __init__(self):
        self.children = {}
        self.is_end_of_word = False

    def __str__(self):
        return f"TrieNode(children={self.children.keys()}, is_end_of_word={self.
            is_end_of_word})"
```

The TrieNode class encapsulates the basic unit of a trie. Each node maintains a dictionary children to store references to its child nodes, making insertion and traversal operations straightforward. The is_end_of_word boolean flag denotes whether the node marks the conclusion of a complete string stored in the trie.

The Trie class encapsulates the higher-level operations, such as insertion and search.

```
class Trie:
    def __init__(self):
        self.root = TrieNode()

    def insert(self, word: str):
        node = self.root
        for char in word:
            if char not in node.children:
                node.children[char] = TrieNode()
            node = node.children[char]
        node.is_end_of_word = True

    def search(self, word: str) -> bool:
        node = self.root
        for char in word:
            if char not in node.children:
                return False
            node = node.children[char]
        return node.is_end_of_word

    def starts_with(self, prefix: str) -> bool:
        node = self.root
        for char in prefix:
            if char not in node.children:
                return False
            node = node.children[char]
        return True
```

The Trie class manages a trie with three core methods: insert, search, and starts_with. The insert method iteratively adds characters from the string to the trie, creating new nodes where necessary, and sets the is_end_of_word flag upon completion. The search method traverses through the trie for the given string, verifying the presence of each character, and finally checks the is_end_of_word flag. The starts_with method performs a similar traversal but does not check the is_end_of_word flag, supporting prefix searches.

Consider the following example of inserting and searching in a trie:

```
# Example usage
trie = Trie()
trie.insert("hello")
trie.insert("world")

print(trie.search("hello")) # Output: True
print(trie.search("hell")) # Output: False
print(trie.starts_with("hell")) # Output: True
print(trie.starts_with("wor")) # Output: True
print(trie.starts_with("xyz")) # Output: False
```

```
True
False
True
True
False
```

Here, the insert method adds two words, "hello" and "world," to the trie. Subsequently, the search method verifies the presence of complete words, while the starts_with method efficiently checks for specified prefixes.

Trie trees possess intriguing properties that make them suitable for certain types of problems. Their search time complexity, denoted as O(m), where m is the length of the string, proves advantageous over binary search trees and hash tables in several applications. However, the trie's space complexity can be substantial due to its requirement to store multiple node references.

A potential optimization involves compressing the trie into a structure known as a radix tree or compressed trie, where nodes with a single child are merged. This compression drastically reduces the number of nodes and edges, though at a slight cost to traversal time.

To illustrate, let us implement a basic version of a compressed trie:

```
class CompressedTrieNode:
    def __init__(self, prefix=""):
        self.prefix = prefix
        self.children = {}
        self.is_end_of_word = False

    def __str__(self):
        return f"CompressedTrieNode(prefix={self.prefix}, children={list(self.children.
            keys())}, is_end_of_word={self.is_end_of_word})"
```

```
class CompressedTrie:
    def __init__(self):
        self.root = CompressedTrieNode()

    def insert(self, word: str):
        node = self.root
        i = 0
        while i < len(word):
            found = False
            for char, child in node.children.items():
                if word[i:].startswith(char):
                    node = child
                    i += len(char)
                    found = True
                    break
            if not found:
                break
        while i < len(word):
            new_node = CompressedTrieNode(word[i:])
            node.children[word[i:]] = new_node
```

```
            node = new_node
            i = len(word)
        node.is_end_of_word = True

    def search(self, word: str) -> bool:
        node = self.root
        i = 0
        while i < len(word):
            matched = False
            for char, child in node.children.items():
                if word[i:].startswith(char):
                    node = child
                    i += len(char)
                    matched = True
                    break
            if not matched:
                return False
        return node.is_end_of_word

    def starts_with(self, prefix: str) -> bool:
        node = self.root
        i = 0
        while i < len(prefix):
            matched = False
            for char, child in node.children.items():
                if prefix[i:].startswith(char):
                    node = child
                    i += len(char)
                    matched = True
                    break
            if not matched:
                return False
        return True
```

Radix trees blend the benefits of tries and binary search trees, combining efficient search operations with optimal space usage. The implementation provided includes the insert, search, and starts_with methods, leveraging string prefixes to minimize node creation.

Trie structures serve essential purposes in modern computational tasks, finding applications across various domains. Their design, characterized by leveraging common prefixes, adds a layer of efficiency not present in other data structures. This revisitation underscores the versatility and efficacy of tries, ensuring their continued relevance in complex problem-solving endeavors.

10.12 Applications of Advanced Data Structures

Advanced data structures are essential tools in the implementation of efficient algorithms for a wide range of complex problems. Understanding their applications provides insights into how these structures are leveraged in real-world scenarios. This section covers the applications of various advanced data structures, including segment trees, Fenwick trees, K-D trees, red-black trees, splay trees, B+ trees, suffix trees, disjoint set unions, bloom filters, and trie trees.

Segment trees are particularly useful in scenarios where there is a need to perform multiple range queries and updates efficiently. Common applications include range sum queries, range minimum queries, and range maximum queries. For instance, in competitive programming, where the efficiency of algorithms can be the difference between success and failure, segment trees offer a robust solution for handling such tasks.

```
# Segment Tree Example: Range Minimum Query

class SegmentTree:
    def __init__(self, array):
        self.n = len(array)
        self.tree = [0] * (2 * self.n)
        self.build(array)

    def build(self, array):
        for i in range(self.n):
            self.tree[self.n + i] = array[i]
        for i in range(self.n - 1, 0, -1):
            self.tree[i] = min(self.tree[2 * i], self.tree[2 * i + 1])

    def update(self, index, value):
        pos = index + self.n
        self.tree[pos] = value
        while pos > 1:
            pos //= 2
            self.tree[pos] = min(self.tree[2 * pos], self.tree[2 * pos + 1])

    def range_query(self, left, right):
        res = float('inf')
        left += self.n
        right += self.n
        while left < right:
            if left % 2:
                res = min(res, self.tree[left])
                left += 1
            if right % 2:
                right -= 1
                res = min(res, self.tree[right])
            left //= 2
            right //= 2
        return res

# Sample usage
array = [1, 3, 2, 7, 9, 11]
seg_tree = SegmentTree(array)
print(seg_tree.range_query(1, 5)) # Output: 2
seg_tree.update(4, 0)
print(seg_tree.range_query(1, 5)) # Output: 0
```

Fenwick trees, also known as Binary Indexed Trees (BIT), are used in applications requiring fast prefix sum queries and updates. They are widely utilized in applications like voting systems, large-scale financial computations, and any other domain that requires cumulative frequency tables.

```
# Fenwick Tree Example: Prefix Sum Query

class FenwickTree:
    def __init__(self, size):
        self.size = size
        self.tree = [0] * (size + 1)

    def update(self, index, value):
        while index <= self.size:
            self.tree[index] += value
            index += index & -index

    def query(self, index):
        sum_ = 0
        while index > 0:
            sum_ += self.tree[index]
            index -= index & -index
        return sum_

# Sample usage
fenwick_tree = FenwickTree(6)
for i, v in enumerate([1, 2, 3, 4, 5, 6], 1):
    fenwick_tree.update(i, v)
print(fenwick_tree.query(3)) # Output: 6 (1+2+3)
fenwick_tree.update(3, 4) # Adding 4 to the 3rd position
print(fenwick_tree.query(3)) # Output: 10 (1+2+7)
```

K-D trees (k-dimensional trees) are employed in multidimensional search problems and machine learning, particularly in nearest neighbor searches and range queries in spatial databases.

Red-black trees and splay trees find their applications primarily in the design of balanced dynamic sets. They are frequently used in associative containers, such as maps and sets in the Standard Template Library (STL) of C++ and the Java Collections Framework. These structures ensure operations like insertion, deletion, and lookup are performed in logarithmic time, offering a balanced trade-off between complexity and performance.

B+ trees are used extensively in database systems and file systems. Their structure, which allows efficient disk reads and writes, makes them suitable for scenarios involving large amounts of data, enabling quick retrieval.

Suffix trees are particularly important in bioinformatics for tasks such as genome alignment, search, and analysis, as well as in text searching, where patterns within large texts need to be identified efficiently.

Disjoint set unions (or union-find data structures) are foundational in algorithms that deal with network connectivity, such as Kruskal's algorithm for finding Minimum Spanning Trees (MST) and in image processing for pixel connectivity analysis.

Bloom filters are employed in applications where space efficiency is critical and where occasional false positives are acceptable. They are widely used in network security for packet filtering, database systems for existence checking, and in distributed systems to reduce the need for full data transfers.

Trie trees are paramount in scenarios involving retrieval of strings or prefixes, such as auto-complete features in search engines, spell checkers, and IP routing in networking.

Each advanced data structure has been honed for specific tasks, answering the computational needs of modern applications. While they offer speed and efficiency, the choice of an appropriate data structure depends on the problem constraints and performance requirements.

10.13 Performance Considerations in Advanced Data Structures

When selecting an advanced data structure for a particular application, a detailed analysis of performance characteristics is indispensable. Understanding both theoretical and practical performance considerations will guide the choice based on the requirements and constraints of specific computational problems. This section will discuss the performance of advanced data structures introduced earlier, focusing on their time and space complexities as well as the trade-offs involved.

Segment Trees are primarily used for range query problems, where operations such as range sum and range minimum queries are frequent. The segment tree's construction time is $O(n \log n)$, and both query and update operations have $O(\log n)$ time complexity. However, the space complexity is $O(n)$, but can sometimes be $O(2n)$ due to the structure's need for a balanced binary tree representation. Segment trees are highly efficient for large datasets where frequent updates and queries are necessary, providing a balance between construction time and operational efficiency.

Fenwick Trees or Binary Indexed Trees provide another efficient way to handle frequency tables and cumulative frequency tables. They offer operations like prefix sums in $O(\log n)$ time. The space complexity remains $O(n)$. The construction time of a Fenwick tree is $O(n \log n)$ when constructed incrementally. Fenwick trees are notably simple and perform well for dynamic cumulative frequency table operations in competitive programming and real-time systems.

K-D Trees are crucial for multidimensional search problems, such as range searches and nearest neighbor searches. The expected time complexity for a balanced K-D tree for each query is $O(\sqrt{n})$, whereas the worst-case time complexity is $O(n)$. Insertions and deletions in a K-D tree have an average time complexity of $O(\log n)$. The space complexity is $O(n)$. The balance of a K-D tree can degrade after several insertions and deletions, negatively affecting query performance, which may demand periodic re-balancing.

Red-Black Trees provide a balanced binary search tree with efficient insert, delete, and lookup operations. Each operation has a time complexity of $O(\log n)$. Red-black trees ensure balancing after every modification to the tree structure, making them more robust for applications that require frequent insertions or deletions with the need to maintain a balanced tree. The space complexity is $O(n)$.

Splay Trees are self-adjusting binary search trees that offer amortized time complexity of $O(\log n)$ for all basic operations. Although individual operations might take $O(n)$ in the worst case, the average time complex over a sequence of operations remains $O(\log n)$ due to the splaying mechanism. Splay trees are particularly effective for applications with a non-uniform access pattern, where frequently accessed elements are quickly moved to the root.

B+ Trees are predominantly used in database and file systems to store large amounts of sorted data. B+ trees maintain a consistent $O(\log n)$ time complexity for insertions, deletions, and lookups. The structure of B+ trees, with all records at leaf level and internal nodes acting as indices, ensures excellent performance for range queries and sequential access patterns. The space complexity is $O(n)$, and due to their wide and shallow nature, B+ trees require fewer disk reads, making them highly efficient for storage systems.

Suffix Trees are integral for string processing tasks, such as substring queries, longest common substring, and pattern matching. Constructing a suffix tree requires $O(n)$ time and space using advanced algorithms like Ukkonen's algorithm. The query operations on a suffix tree are remarkably efficient, with $O(m)$ time complexity, where m is the length of the query string. While the construction overhead is substantial, suffix trees vastly improve the efficiency of fundamental string operations in biological data analysis, text processing, and information retrieval.

Disjoint Set Union (Union-Find) data structures are foundational for network connectivity and component analysis. Utilizing union by rank and path compression, both the union and find operations achieve nearly constant time complexity, specifically $O(\alpha(n))$, where α is the inverse Ackermann function. The space complexity is $O(n)$. Disjoint set union structures excel in dynamic connectivity problems where incremental updates and component queries are frequent.

Bloom Filters serve as probabilistic data structures for set membership queries, providing $\mathrm{O(k)}$ space complexity, where k is the number of hash functions. The insertion and query operations have $O(k)$ time complexity. Bloom filters can introduce false positives but never false negatives. They are remarkably space-efficient, suitable for applications like database query optimization and network security where memory usage is a constraint and occasional errors are tolerable.

Trie Trees are widely used for constructing retrieval structures. A standard trie has $O(l)$ time complexity for insertions, deletions, and lookups, where l is the string length. The space complexity can become $O(n \times \Sigma)$, where n is the number of keys and Σ is the alphabet size. Tries are exceptional for prefix matching problems, such as auto-completion, spell checkers, and IP routing tables.

The choice of an advanced data structure depends on a careful analysis of these performance characteristics relative to the specific computational problem at hand. Consider the operational constraints, such as the frequency and type of operations, memory limitations, and the need for data persistence when selecting the appropriate data structure.

Made in the USA
Monee, IL
05 November 2026

67845297R00184